ARMOUR AND WEAPONS

Volume 2

'The Furie of the Ordnance'

ARTILLERY IN
THE ENGLISH CIVIL WARS

The English Civil Wars have frequently been depicted as a struggle between Cavaliers and Roundheads in which technology played little part. The first-hand sources now tell us that this romantic picture is deeply flawed – revealing a reality of gunpowder, artillery, and a grinding struggle of siege and starvation.

As with naval warfare, developments in gun technology drastically changed land warfare in the years leading up to 1642. The Civil War was itself shaped largely by the availability of munitions. A failure to procure them in 1643 and 1644 – combined with abortive attempts on London – ultimately proved the downfall of the Royalists. Moreover a final move away from fortified local garrisons reshaped both the nature of warfare in England, and the country itself.

STEPHEN BULL is Curator of Military History and Archaeology, Lancashire Museums.

ARMOUR AND WEAPONS

ISSN 1746–9449

General Editor
Robert Douglas Smith

Throughout history armour and weapons have been not merely the preserve of the warrior in battles and warfare, but potent symbols in their own right (the sword of chivalry, the heraldic shield) representing the hunt and hall as well as the battlefield. This series aims to provide a forum for critical studies of all aspects of arms and armour and their technologies, from the end of the Roman Empire to the dawn of the modern world; both new research and works of synthesis are encouraged.

New proposals for the series are welcomed; they should be sent to the publisher at the address below.

Boydell & Brewer Ltd, PO Box 9, Woodbridge, Suffolk, IP12 3DF

'The Furie of the Ordnance'

ARTILLERY IN
THE ENGLISH CIVIL WARS

Stephen Bull

THE BOYDELL PRESS

First published 2008
The Boydell Press, Woodbridge

ISBN 978–1–84383–403–8

The Boydell Press is an imprint of Boydell & Brewer Ltd
PO Box 9, Woodbridge, Suffolk IP12 3DF, UK
and of Boydell & Brewer Inc.
668 Mt Hope Avenue, Rochester, NY 14620, USA
website: www.boydellandbrewer.com

The publisher has no responsibility for the continued existence or accuracy of URLs for
external or third-party internet websites referred to in this book, and does not guarantee
that any content on such websites is, or will remain, accurate or appropriate

A CIP catalogue record for this book is available
from the British Library

This publication is printed on acid-free paper

Contents

Illustrations

The author and publishers are grateful to all the institutions and individuals listed for permission to reproduce the materials in which they hold copyright. Every effort has been made to trace the copyright holders; apologies are offered for any omission, and the publishers will be pleased to add any necessary acknowledgement in subsequent editions.

Acknowledgements

Any project that takes almost thirty years to come to fruition must perforce accumulate considerable debts to those who have helped along the way – both amongst the living, and those who have already become part of that history which continues to fascinate us. The work that follows is no exception, building, as naturally it should, upon the shoulders of many that have gone before. Similarly without recourse to many different libraries, museums, archives, and archaeological sites it would have been illegitimate indeed.

At the head of the queue of contributing academic worthies stands Professor Sydney Anglo, my most indulgent supervisor during the rather too many years that it took to produce my University of Wales PhD thesis on this subject. Its examiners were Dr Hugh Dunthorne and the late Professor Sir John Hale, to whom similar thanks are due, though I now feel Sydney, in his guise of medieval combat authority, might well have 'run them through' had they the temerity to turn away the rambling offering presented to them in 1988. Professors R.A. Griffiths, Stuart Clark, and Richard Shannon – all of University College Swansea – encouraged me along the way. More recently Dr Colin Martin, formerly of the University of St Andrews Centre for Environmental History, has generously shared the fruits of his nautical archaeology work where land and sea artefacts quite frequently overlap.

In the world of museums and archives the Royal Artillery Institution played an important part in the research, particularly once the late Brigadier John Lewendon had satisfied himself that I was not a 'student agitator'. Brigadier Ken Timbers, his wife Bridget, and the staff of the Rotunda were all extremely helpful. The late Major General B.P. Hughes was also kind enough to offer encouragement at an early stage. At the Royal Armouries the then Master, Guy Wilson, and Head of Conservation, Bob Smith, were both extremely good facilitators – sometimes in quite unexpected ways. At the National Army Museum the Director, William Reid, and the then archivist, Dr Peter Boyden, offered both considerable encouragement and access to the papers of Brigadier Peter Young. The staffs of the British Library, National Archives, National Maritime Museum and the record offices for Gloucestershire, Kent, Devon, Cornwall and Essex all assisted wonderfully. More recently colleagues in Lancashire Museums, Libraries and Archives, the various branches of Lancashire's archaeology, and the national Portable Antiquities Scheme, have showered me with so many references, cannon balls, musket shot and other battlefield and range detritus that there is a distinct danger of further publications.

Outside these charmed professional circles I have found myself supported by a band of like minded enthusiasts who have ultimately made failure to complete the task in hand quite impossible, however much I have been inclined to shirk. Over the years these have included Jeremy Hodgkinson and members of the Wealden Iron Research Group; the members of the Fortress Study Group and Ordnance Society, also Mike Seed; Dave Ryan; John Tincey; Professor Charles Esdaile; Stuart Reid; Tim Slack and Roger Emmerson.

Abbreviations

BL	British Library, London
	Add. Ms Additional Manuscripts
	E Prefix for Thomason Tracts
CRO	Cheshire Record Office
CSPD	*Calendar of State Papers, Domestic*
DNB	*Dictionary of National Biography*
DRO	Devon Record Office
GRO	Gloucestershire Records Office
KAO	Kent Archives Office (now Kent Archive Service)
MD	Military Document
Ms	Manuscript
NA	National Archives (formerly PRO)
PRO	Public Records Office (now The National Archives but many records retain a PRO reference)
	SP State Papers
	WO War Office, or War Office series in The National Archives

A Selective Chronology of the Civil Wars

Royalist victories are denoted [R], Parliamentarian victories [P], outcome unclear or disputed [U])

1639

January	Covenanters begin to recruit; Charles I declares his intention to raise an army against Scotland.
May	Skirmishing around Aberdeen.
19 June	Pacification of Berwick concludes the abortive First 'Bishops' War' between England and Scotland.

1640

July	Opening of the Second 'Bishops' War'.
28 August	Battle of Newburn, Scottish victory.
26 October	England and Scotland sign the Treaty of Ripon.

1641

19 July	First proposal for a 'Militia Bill'.
October	Outbreak of Irish Rebellion.
December	Anti-Catholic riots in London,

1642

February	'Militia Bill' rejected by the King.
23 April	King Charles refused entry to Hull.
June	Royal 'Commissions of Array' issued.
22 August	King's standard raised at Nottingham: 'First' or 'Great Civil War' formally commenced.
September	Siege of Manchester; end of first Siege of Portsmouth.
23 October	Indecisive Battle of Edgehill [U].
13 November	Royalist army blocked from London at Turnham Green
December	Royalist headquarters established at Oxford.

1643

19 January	Sir Ralph Hopton's victory at Braddock Down [R].
19 March	Hopton Heath [R]; Earl of Northampton killed.

3 April	Sack of Birmingham.
18 June	Chalgrove Field [R]; John Hampden killed.
30 June	Adwalton Moor [R].
5 July	Lansdown [R].
13 July	Roundway Down [R].
22 July	First 'Excise Ordinance'.
26 July	Storm of Bristol [R].
September	Relief of Gloucester by Earl of Essex.
20 September	First Battle of Newbury [U].
25 September	The 'Solemn League and Covenant' secures alliance of Scots and Parliament.
11 October	Winceby [P].

1644

January	Scottish forces enter England.
25 January	Nantwich [P].
29 March	Cheriton [P].
11 April	Selby [P].
20 April	York besieged by Parliament; Lyme Regis besieged by Prince Maurice.
28 May	Prince Rupert sacks Bolton.
12 June	Liverpool stormed [R].
2 July	Marston Moor [P].
2 September	Lostwithiel [R].
27 October	Second Battle of Newbury [U].
23 November	Proposal to 'New Model' the army of Parliament.

1645

30 May	King's army storms Leicester. [R]
14 June	Naseby [P].
10 July	Langport [P].
23 July	Bridgwater falls to Parliament.
15 August	Montrose at Kilsyth [R].
11 September	Bristol retaken by Parliament.
13 September	Philiphaugh; Montrose defeated.
24 September	Rowton Heath [P].
14 October	Storm of Basing House. [P]
27 November	Newark besieged by Scots and Northern Association.
2 December	Final capitulation of Lathom House.

1646

21 March	Stow-on-the-Wold [P].
6 May	Newark surrenders [P].
5 June	Benburb [Irish victory over Ulster Scots].

24 June	Surrender of Oxford to Fairfax, King already in Scottish captivity. Effective end of 'First Civil War'.
19 August	Surrender of Raglan Castle.

1647

30 January	Charles I handed over to Parliament.
16 May	The 'Declaration of the Army'.
August	New Model Army enters London.
8 August	Dungan's Hill [P], Ireland.
28 October	First 'Agreement of the People'.
November	King escapes from Hampton Court and goes to Carisbrooke Castle.
14 December	The 'Four Bills' passed.
26 December	King signs secret 'Engagement' with Scots.

1648

March–April	Revolt in Pembrokeshire, widespread unrest. Commencement of 'Second Civil War'.
28–29 April	Berwick and Carlisle occupied by Royalists.
8 May	St Fagan's [P].
27 May	Revolt of the fleet.
1 June	Maidstone [P].
12 June	Royalists occupy Colchester.
11 July	Pembroke renders to Cromwell.
17 August	Preston [P]; Cromwell defeats Hamilton's Scottish army and Royalists.
27 August	Surrender of Colchester. Effective end of 'Second Civil War'.
4 October	Parliamentarian forces enter Edinburgh.

1649

30 January	Execution of Charles I
22 March	Final surrender of Royalist Pontefract.
May	Leveller 'Agreement' – mutiny suppressed at Burford.
August	Cromwell's Irish campaign commences.
11 September	Sack of Drogheda.
11 October	Sack of Wexford.

1650

27 April	Carbisdale; Montrose defeated in Scotland.
26 June	Resignation of Lord Fairfax; Cromwell 'Lord General'.
August	Start of Cromwell's Scottish campaign.
3 September	Dunbar [P].

1651

July	English forces enter Scotland. Commencement of 'Third Civil War'.
20 July	Inverkeithing [P].
3 September	Worcester [P].
October– November	Execution of the Earl of Derby; surrender of Limerick; escape of Charles II to France; Parliament takes Jersey. 'End of Third Civil War'.

O Sieges and stormings
mentioned in the text

The Wealden Iron
working area

Newcastle
Carlisle

Skipton
York
Hull
Bolton
Lathom
Liverpool
Sandal
Chester
Lincoln
Newark

Lichfield
Leicester

Worcester

Gloucester
Colchester
Pembroke
Raglan
Oxford
London
Bristol
Reading
Bridgewater
Basing
Arundel
Lyme Regis
Portsmouth
Exeter
Corfe Castle
Pendennis

0   miles   50
0   km   80

Notable Battles of the English Civil Wars

Marston Moor

Preston   Adwalton Moor

Winceby

Nantwich

Hopton Heath

Naseby

Worcester   Edgehill   Cropredy Bridge

Stow in the Wold

St Fagans   London

Lansdowne   Newbury

Roundway Down

Langport   Cheriton

Lostwithiel

0   miles   50

0   km   80

Introduction

The spark for this book was struck as early as 1974 when – as a very young enthusiast of all things to do with the English Civil War – I read the following remarks in Brigadier Peter Young's *Cavalier Army*:

> Cannon were most useful in siege work but counted little in battles. Their slow rate of fire, perhaps one round every three minutes if served by an expert crew, meant that there would have to be a great concentration to cause a decisive number of casualties. However, cannon did not exist in great numbers in the England of that time.

A few years later the same author's *Civil War England* added the further detail that guns could 'seldom if ever' be moved once a battle had begun, moreover the 'rate of fire was slow, for the loading drill was complicated, and the provision of ammunition was but small'. Young was then regarded as the doyen of Civil War military history, and most historians of the Stuart period, including the remarkable C.V. Wedgewood, took his advice very seriously when it came to producing their own general histories of the wars. Opinion had obviously moved on little in the century since 1870 when H.W.L. Hime had been moved to write that the subject of artillery in the Civil Wars had 'seldom attracted' attention, and been 'generally disposed of in a single sentence'.[1]

Turning back to Young's first major, and arguably best researched, book on an English Civil War battle to discover just how few and inefficient English guns were in 1642 furnished the interesting statistic that Young believed that the Earl of Essex had a least 30 guns on the field of Edgehill. Since there were about 15,000 Parliamentarians at the battle this implied a ratio of about one gun per 500 men. The great battle of Marston Moor saw the Allied armies with 100 guns in the field, and, though most of these were Scottish light pieces, this was still one gun for about 300 men. At Cropredy Bridge, Parliament had 24 guns with its 9,500 men, a ratio of 1:400, but the Royalists had ten pieces for their 8,500, a ratio of 1:850. At Naseby in 1645 the King's army numbered about 9,000, and was accompanied by 14 pieces of ordnance, including two mortars – the ratio of guns to men here being a little under 1:650. The New

1 P. Young and W. Emberton *The Cavalier Army*, London, 1974, p 27; P. Young *Civil War England*, London, 1981; H.W.L. Hime 'The Field Artillery of the Great Rebellion: its Nature and Use', in *Proceedings of the Royal Artillery Institution* 6, 1870, reprinted Godmanchester, 2006, p 1.

Model Army which faced this force fielded at least 16 pieces, though this produced a somewhat lower ratio.[2]

Since such ideas mean very little in isolation a brief comparison seemed in order. At Waterloo the Duke of Wellington had approximately 150 guns and 68,000 men. So the ratio here was approximately one artillery piece per 450 men. This was very much the same as might have been expected in a Civil War engagement. Perhaps then Wellington was very poorly provisioned compared to his enemies. Napoleon was known as an artillery general, arguably *the* artillery general – and a former artillery officer – whose predilection was the deployment of guns on the monumental scale, mounting 'grand batteries' that could pulverise the opposition before the employment of cavalry charges and the infantry columns. Obviously the key exponent of artillery warfare, operating a century and a half after the Earl of Essex and King Charles, would be much more lavishly equipped with ordnance. Actually in the brilliant Prussian campaign of 1806 Napoleon fielded 300 guns and 180,000 men: one gun per 600 men, or much the same as the Earl of Essex at Edgehill. At the Wagram 190,000 Frenchmen were accompanied by 488 guns, or about one per 400 men. In 1815 his Army of the North had approximately 124,000 men for 290 guns, being about one gun per 430 men. At Waterloo it was these guns that came closest to breaking the Allied armies with their much celebrated bombardment.[3]

Maybe the problem was one of quality. Perhaps artillery pieces of 1642 were so poor and technically inferior as to be easily dismissed when measured against those of the early nineteenth century, but consulting authorities of the latter era who had made such a comparison swiftly disabuses any such notion. Captain Stoney of the Royal Artillery, writing from the perspective of the Peninsular War period, observed that

> Anyone who examines old guns in the Tower of London, or in the Museum of Artillery at Woolwich may see that they are of the same genus as modern smoothbores, and even notice some specimens quite as soundly and artistically cast as any of the present century; nay more, he may infer that our modern cast guns can scarcely be superior to their prototypes in range, power, or susceptibility to rifling.

A century and a half later Major General B.P. Hughes, one of the most respected twentieth century commentators on artillery, broadly concurred with this opinion. The period from 1630 to the early nineteenth century, had,

---

2   P. Young *Edgehill*, Kineton, 1967, pp 103–106; G. Foard *Naseby*, Guildford, 1995, pp 53–90; J. Sprigge, *Anglia Rediviva*, London, 1646, pp 32–49, 334–335.
3   F.L. Petre, *Napoleon's Conquest of Prussia* (1907) new edn with an introduction by D.G. Chandler, London, 1972, pp 23–24, 46.

despite minor changes and improvements, been one of 'stability' in terms of basic weapons technology.[4]

Moreover even if Captain Stoney was slightly overstating the case, and there had been some modest betterment of artillery since the Civil Wars, there had also been similar, or greater improvement in small arms. Whichever way the question was approached it seemed that field artillery had been a significant weapon in the middle seventeenth century – and numerically at least equally important as in the days of Napoleon. The discovery that seventeenth century field guns were not loaded by a 'complicated drill' in battle as Young had assumed – but by means of bagged charges, very similar to those used in the time of Bonaparte, further undermined the notion that they were necessarily slow and inefficient.[5]

If this was true of guns on the field of battle it was even more true of artillery elsewhere – there was no dissonance between what happened on land and at sea. Gun decks with cannon firing through rows of ports had made their appearance on ships of war by the sixteenth century, and the power of navies was already measured in terms of the amount of ordnance that could be crammed upon ships. Western powers using ships that were effectively floating gun platforms were already beginning to clear their maritime rivals from the sea. Cogent argument from a range of military historians and archaeologists suggests that it was this very fetish for ever more, and heavier, guns that had sunk both the *Mary Rose* in 1545, and the Swedish *Wasa* in 1628. Similarly, speculation, scholarship, and nautical archaeology all conspired together to promote the notion that numbers and types of guns, and how they were handled in 1588, had a significant role in the tactics and ultimate fate of the Spanish Armada.[6]

In the arena of the siege the 'high thin walls of the middle ages' had been brought tumbling down during the late fifteenth century, by French guns in Normandy and northern Italy, and by wide mouthed Flemish 'bombards' in many other places. As a Florentine observer of the French style of warfare at the end of the Middle Ages would note, once a significant siege train of modern guns had reached the walls of a town its days were numbered. The guns were unhitched from their teams, then pushed forward, little by little. Once the time came,

---

4   B.P. Hughes *Firepower: Weapons Effectiveness on the Battlefield, 1630–1850*, London, 1974, p 8; Hime 'The Field Artillery', p 2.

5   S. Bull 'Evidence for the Use of Cartridges in Artillery, 1560–1660', in R.D. Smith (ed) *British Naval Armaments*, Royal Armouries conference proceedings, 1989, pp 3–8.

6   J.R. Hale, *War and Society in Renaissance Europe 1450–1600*, 2nd edn, Stroud, 1998, pp 46–50, 191–196; C. Duffy *Siege Warfare*, London, 1979, pp 8–140; B.S. Hall *Weapons and Warfare in Renaissance Europe*, Baltimore, 1997, p 7: C. Jorgensen (et al) *Fighting Techniques of the Early Modern World*, Staplehurst, 2005, pp 171–249; M. Baumber *General at Sea: Robert Blake and the Seventeenth Century Revolution in Naval Warfare*, London, 1989, pp 112–116, 136–138.

thirty of forty pieces are fired so that the wall is soon reduced to rubble. The French say that their artillery can make a breech in a wall eight feet thick. Although every hole is small, their number is large for from the moment they begin to fire they do not stop day or night.[7]

Panic about the new vulnerability of traditional castle defences had led to the advent of the angled bastion in Italy, Henry VIII's sunken drum shaped coastal forts, and ultimately to the great Dutch fortifications which played so great a part in the liberation of the Netherlands from Spain. When the Civil War engulfed England it would be the strongholds that bristled with artillery that withstood armies the best. Parliamentarian Gloucester was equipped with 20 guns for a garrison of about 2,000, or one gun for every hundred troops. Royalist Bridgwater had more than 40 guns, with less than 2,000 in its garrison, or a gun to troop ratio of about 1:50. The Parliamentarian garrison of Bristol comprised barely 2,000 men, but during the siege of 1643 they deployed almost 100 guns – a staggering ratio of 1 piece of artillery per 20 defenders. Exeter's garrison was no larger, but when the Royalist defenders gave up, they yielded 75 guns, so there was a piece of artillery for every 25 defenders. In terms of sheer bulk of artillery to equip a tiny garrison Dennis Fort, near Pendennis Castle, may well be something of a record holder, since Parliamentarian commentator Joshua Sprigge claimed that 200 of the King's troops inside possessed 22 guns – or a piece of ordnance for every nine defenders.[8]

There was, to say the least, something very wrong with the accepted idea that artillery in the English Civil War was few in number, puny, and pointless. Increasingly the work of historians like Roberts, Parker, Childs, Duffy and others was exposing just how much of the effort of the early modern state was devoted to war – and indeed it is now obvious that in the seventeenth century state expenditure was overwhelmingly directed to war, or the provision of military facilities. Moreover the shape, type, and final cost of ships and fortifications was governed largely by artillery, and what it might be expected to do. The notion that artillery was hopeless in 1642 does not sit well with contemporary eyewitness evidence either. The general tenor of the utterances of those seeing what 'great ordnance' could do was one of awe and respect. Leaders and generals were prepared to plan and to pay for guns – the 'Train of Artillery' being what Clarendon was famously moved to call 'a sponge that could never be filled'. The idea that, at the moment of crisis, both sides in a war that was to decide the political future of Britain could be spending their already inadequate resources on weapons and munitions of no utility beggars belief. The war was a rough and unforgiving master: persistently unsuccessful commanders were killed or sacked, towns not fortified or protected to the latest standards

---

7 Quoted in P. Contamine *War in the Middle Ages*, English translation, Oxford, 1984, p 201.
8 Joshua Sprigge *Anglia Rediviva*, London, 1646, pp 334–335; S.P. Oliver *Pendennis and St Mawes*, London, 1875, pp 37–42.

fell or were burned. If fielding artillery was such a pointless exercise, successful commanders should have ignored it: but they did not. This apparent contradiction of Young, and of widely held views on the Civil Wars, has left many outstanding problems.[9]

9 See for example: Parker *The Military Revolution: Military Innovation and the Rise of the West 1500–1800*, Cambridge, 1988; J. Childs *Warfare in the Seventeenth Century*, London, 2001; J.R. Hale *War and Society in Renaissance Europe*, London, 1985; M. Duffy *The Military Revolution and the State, 1500-1800*, Exeter Studies in History 1, Exeter, 1980.

1

Of Guns and Gunners

In its most basic form the technology of the early modern gun is not highly complex. It consists essentially of a tough, fracture resistant tube, or 'barrel', closed at one end, into which is inserted gunpowder. A wad may be pushed into the barrel to hold it in place, before a projectile is put in. This may itself be confined by further wadding. A very small aperture, otherwise known as the 'touch hole', or 'vent', near to the closed end of the barrel, provides access to the charge. By inserting a pricker into the vent the gunner clears the hole of any obstruction or residue and pierces the cartridge, and then 'primes' the hole with a little more powder. By applying fire to the hole – by means of a hot wire, or piece of smouldering match cord, for example – the piece is discharged. 'Black powder' which was the gunpowder of the period – a mixture of saltpetre, sulphur and charcoal – combusts very rapidly. The charcoal acts as a fuel, and the sulphur helps to produce a stable reaction, but without the presence of the saltpetre to provide plenty of oxygen the burning would achieve nothing. As the carbon from the charcoal combines rapidly with oxygen forming large quantities of carbon dioxide and energy, so pressure within the gun barrel increases very quickly, driving the projectile out of the tube at great velocity.

Gunpowder made significant advances between its first use on the European battlefield, about 1300, and the early Stuart age. What had once been a rough confection of approximately equal parts produced by methods best described as mid way between alchemy and cookery, had gradually been refined and improved in a number of ways. Perhaps most importantly the proportion of saltpetre in the mixture had gradually been increased until in 1635 powder for English government service was fixed at a ratio of six parts to one each of sulphur and charcoal. This is not so different to the formula accepted as optimum by the lights of modern science. Another significant advance was the introduction of 'corning', or sieving the powder, whilst damp, into granules of given sizes. This apparently simple process not only provided air gaps between the grains which aided rapid combustion and gave greater power, but made the powder safer due to easier handling and reduced dust, and also reduced separation and damp problems. In terms of energy production in the barrel of the gun an increase of as much as 60% over the two centuries prior to the Civil

Wars seems highly probable. The corollary was that less powder was needed for a given task – and this effectively made it lighter to transport – or, if the same amount was carried, more could be done with it. At the same time powder prices fell with greater demands being satisfied with the help of imported salt-petre, improved domestic production, and increased use of machinery.

Powder had long been tested by the subjective methods of tasting and lighting, but now its effect could also be quantified. One of the easiest methods was to load a pistol with a set quantity of powder and fire it into a bank of clay, measuring the depth of penetration against other samples. Another was to load a small mortar and measure the ranges attained by the projectile. The third – and most scientific by modern lights – was to set it off in a purpose made device or 'eprouvette'. Early examples were merely containers with hinged lids, which blew open against a marked arc. Later models, in use by the 1620s, were more sophisticated, incorporating a little chamber and separate scale – against which a numerical reading of power was obtained. The German author Furten-bach claimed to have invented this improved version of the device, publishing it in an illustration of 1626, but it was certainly replicated in England by John Babington within a decade. From the reign of King James barrels of approved powder were marked up according to type and purpose of the content. Three crowns denoted the best powder, most suitable for hand held firearms, and two crowns a powder suitable for heavy artillery, and small arms in case of need. A single crown with the letters 'O.W' signified 'old powder, new wrought, yet strong, good, and fit for great artillery, for one years service at the least'. Coun-terfeiting the official marks was an offence, and the proof master was allowed to charge the producer or owner of the powder up to 6 pence per barrel for testing and marking.[1]

Many of the earliest guns were made using the methods of the blacksmith and the forge – hoops, staves and bars of iron being worked together to create the barrel of the gun, often with a separate powder chamber at the rear. Some of these antiquated pieces survived right through to the Civil Wars. Yet the casting of gun barrels was not new technology in the 1640s, having come of age in the later fifteenth and early sixteenth centuries when cast bronze pieces were key to the trains of artillery which had battered the castles of Italy into submission. As Guiccardini explained the French developed many pieces that were 'more manoeuvrable, constructed only of bronze, and they used iron

[1]   N. Nye *Art of Gunnery*, London, 1647, pp 3–9; *CSPD* CCLXXXVI, 16 April 1635, p 29 and CCXCIX, 9 October, p 422; S. Bull 'Pearls from the Dungheap: English Saltpetre Production 1590–1640', in *Journal of the Ordnance Society*, 2, 1990, pp 5–10; B.S. Hall *Weapons and Warfare in Renaissance Europe*, Baltimore, 1997, pp 41–104; H.W.L. Hime *Gunpowder and Ammunition*, London, 1904, p 182; G.I. Brown *The Big Bang: A History of Explosives*, Stroud, 1998, pp 10–25; J. Furtenbach *Halintro-Pyrobolia*, Ulm, 1627, p 9 – the copy in the Royal Artillery collection belonged to Babington explaining how the device found its way into Babington's repertoire; Nye *Art of Gunnery*, pp 33–34; John Bate *Mysteries of Art and Nature*, London, 1634, p 56. See also W.D. Cocroft *Dangerous Energy: The Archaeology of Gunpowder and Military Explosives Manufacture*, Swindon, 2000, pp 1–16.

cannonballs instead of stone as before', and they were pulled into position on their carriages by horses, not dragged by oxen or mounted on immobile beds on the ground. Guns were also being cast in iron before the sixteenth century; but it was not a simple case of a 'better' technology quickly eclipsing the old. Bronze could be cast at lower temperatures, was easier to work with, and could be recycled through the melting and recasting of old guns, bells, and statues. Furthermore bronze was not particularly prone to corrosion, and initially at least could make more reliable castings using less metal. Bronze guns could therefore be made lighter to perform a given purpose. Conversely iron was relatively plentiful, much cheaper, and appeared to be the thing of the future. Iron and bronze guns would therefore coexist for several centuries – in just the same way that bronze and iron blades had overlapped in a previous era of military technology. Nevertheless following the gradual evolution of effective blast furnaces in the fifteenth and early sixteenth centuries, it was iron guns that would gradually gain ground in seventeenth century England.[2]

The key to a sound gun barrel was good quality metal, flowed evenly into a well formed mould. As the author of the Coates Manuscript observed, 'in former times the founders of guns cast in all manner of unclean and filthie metall … and this occassioned the frequent spoilinges and breaking of the peeces' – and a number of contemporary sources similarly refer to the improvement of metals during the period. The heat in the blast furnace was created using charcoal – the best woods being coppiced and gathered for the purpose, then smouldered with very little air. In the Weald of Kent and Sussex, where most of England's ordnance was produced, iron ore and suitable wood were found in close proximity, and there was water from streams and rivers to drive bellows and hammers, and to float boats which could transport some of the heavy loads.[3]

Moulds for ordnance could be used only once, having to be broken up as the new gun was extracted; and to create a good mould was a skilled and time consuming business. However a series production of similar pieces was possible for larger orders, and a group of guns could be made from one original mould template. As Henry Hexam explained, a 'perfect model' of the piece had to be made of timber and clay, with 'all the mouldures, ornaments, and compartiments, even as you want the piece to be, which you must annount with hogs-

2   J.R. Hale *War and Society in Renaissance Europe 1450–1620*, 2nd edn, 1998 pp 46–50, 94–95, 155–157; S. Bull *Encylopedia of Military Technology and Innovation*, Westport, 2004, pp 21–23; Hall *Weapons and Warfare*, pp 157–164. F.J. Lopez-Martin 'Historical and Technical Evolution of Artillery From its Earliest Widespread Use Until the Emergence of Mass Production Techniques', PhD thesis, London Metropolitan University, 2007, pp 176–184.

3   For advice on gun barrels and stresses I am grateful to Professor B. Crossland of Queen's University Belfast; see also E. Shannon and B.A. Austin 'The Application of Fracture Mechanics to Failure of Thick Walled Cylinders', in *Journal of the Institution of Mechanical Engineers, Proceedings of the Conference on Practical Application of Fracture Mechanics to Pressure Vessel Technology*, 1971, pp 109–118, and R. Plot *The Natural History of Staffordshire*, Oxford, 1686, pp 160–165.

grease, and then cover it over with a collume of ... tempered earth'. The life size maquette was usually begun from the inside, starting with a core around which ropes or bark fibres were wound. Around this was plastered the clay which would form the pattern, and relief or ornamentation could be added in wax – a separate board template being used to produce the reinforcing rings or special detail. The mould proper was then made around the pattern, tallow being used to prevent the two sticking together. The clay for the mould itself had to be well integrated, being, as the Coates manuscript advised, 'beaten with iron rods and at the beating well wet and thoroughlie wrought'. Red or yellow clays were ideal, if 'neither too fat or leane', and were mixed with hair or flock, and, after shaping, allowed to set and 'varnished with grease'.

This being completed the exterior of the mould could now be strengthened with iron bands and 'plates of yron' around the outside. The whole edifice was now gently heated. This melted the wax and grease which ran out, releasing the central core and other parts of the pattern which were no longer required, and the mould heated and dried. According to modern research this drying also had the desirable effect that oxides were reduced in the clay, and that micro-porosites were formed which would allow gas from molten metal to escape without catastrophic failure. Once the outer mould was finished a new and narrower core made of an iron rod plastered with clay was placed centrally within the cavity to form the bore of the gun. Iron fittings known as 'chaplets' were used to suspend the core in the correct position. This was a particularly ticklish operation requiring great skill, and, according to Norton, was rarely accomplished to absolute perfection. To prevent the mould from becoming damp prior to use it was not placed in the casting pit any longer than 24 hours before the metal was tapped from the furnace.

When the metal reached the ideal temperature and fineness the furnace was opened and its contents run down a short channel into the mould. As the Coates manuscript explained,

> The mettall must be melted so that it runne well, continuali and fine. It must not be cast in the mould too hot, for it might burne the mould, nor too cold, for that will make chinkes in the peece. There must be as much mettall in the furnace as will be sufficient to fill the mould otherwise the peece is destroyed, as wanting both forme and matter. The moulds should have spiralls made in them or vents for the aire to get out for when the hot mettall meets with the aire which fild the cilinder of the mould, it rarifies it makes it firie & therefore requires a great deal more room then formerlie it had which it cannot get within the mould, and therefore if it have not vent to get to another place, it will not faile to make room for itself, by breaking the mould.[4]

Having cooled, the finished piece, still encased within its mould, was hauled from the pit with block and tackle. Next the reinforcing bands were removed

---

4   Coates Ms, Royal Artillery Institution, reproduced in S. Bull 'Furie of the Ordnance', PhD thesis, University College Swansea, 1988, pp 512–551.

and the mould was hammered off, and any extra metal at the mouth of the gun – known as a 'riser' – would be sawn away. The riser actually formed a useful function, since it was likely to contain any bubbles or impurities which had risen during casting. Massive drills and buffers – usually water powered – could now be used to smooth out any irregularities in the bore of the piece. Drilling out the barrel from the solid was not however usual until the end of the seventeenth century. Finally the touch hole or vent would be drilled using hand drills, and any decorative work or inscription could be finished by hand. The trueness of the barrel could be tested in various ways, perhaps by means of a device mounting parallel staves. Nye preferred the simple expedient of thrusting a closely fitting rammer into the bore, and marking it by means of a sharp priming iron pushed in through the touch hole – then setting the rammer on a flat surface to see whether the mark appeared on the correct place to agree with a true bore.[5]

Before being used in the field a gun would be 'proved' – or test fired – usually by means of an abnormally large charge. Only then would the gun barrel be mounted in a carriage, and it was at this point that pieces designed for land or sea service became easily distinguishable. Sea carriages, for use on shipboard or in some fixed land batteries, consisted of a relatively small, stout wooden box, on small wheels or 'trucks'. These sea carriages had the advantage of compactness, and, as Bourne suggested, the small wheels were well adapted to reduce the distance travelled during recoil. By contrast the land carriage had large wheels, which allowed for relatively easy movement, less impeded by uneven ground, and towing by horse or oxen teams. The primary concern in making a gun carriage was to ensure that it was proportionate to the barrel, and many contemporary authorities spoke of the carriage dimensions in relation to the bore or length of the barrel. According to Thomas Smith the best method to work out the size of the carriage was to,

> Measure the just length of the cilinder of your peece, the planks of your carriage ought to be one ans a halfe that length. Also measure the diameter of the peece, and the said planks at the fore end should be in depth four times the diameter, and in the midst three and a half times the diameter, and at the end next the ground, two and a half the diameter and in thicknesse once the diameter.[6]

Modern authorities have tended to assume that generalisations about seventeenth century guns can be extrapolated from the tables of ordnance types

5   See also C. Lehuga *Discurso Del Capitan Cristoval Lehuga*, Milan, 1611, passim; C. Foulkes *The Gunfounders of England*, 2nd edn, London, 1969, pp 8–19; M.H. Jackson and C. de Beer *Eighteenth Century Gunfounding*, Newton Abbot, 1973, pp 35–143; Nye *Art of Gunnery*, pp 95–96.
6   Smith *Art of Gunnery* p 21; Coates Ms. ff 36–37; Eldred, Roberts and Coates agree on a barrel to carriage length ratio of 2:3; see also St. Julien *La Forge de Vulcain*, La Haye, 1606 pp 44–45.

drawn up in the late sixteenth century. Some have even gone so far as to take a number of tables from different decades of the sixteenth and seventeenth centuries and jumble them together, in the hope of creating a more complete list of types. At best the results are misleading.[7]

Far more can be made from contemporary tables of ordnance types by leaving them in their original state and comparing differences over time. Questions may then be asked as to when specific types of gun came into or went out of use, or whether certain guns improved in performance, or achieved dominance, at different times. With tables of ordnance drawn up at approximately the same time, comparison may also yield some notion of the degree to which a given class of ordnance varied within a general classification. This methodology similarly tends to show up cases of plagiarism between the authors of different documents. So it is when we see that when William Harrison gives a calibre of 5.5 inches for a culverin, and William Bourne quotes a smaller figure, the deduction is not that one is 'correct' and the other 'incorrect' – but that in 1587 a variation within the class of culverins is possible. In fact several clear messages do emerge if tables and inventories of ordnance produced between the mid sixteenth century and 1680 are compared in sequence. Firstly it is apparent that stone shooting pieces gradually become rarer. 'Pot guns', 'bombards', 'serpentines' and finally 'cannon perrier' steadily drop out of use, to be replaced almost universally by the reign of Charles I, by cast guns, firing cast iron shot. Spreading the comparative approach wider shows that this was a signal Western European achievement that had not percolated through to some older cultures even in the nineteenth century.[8]

For much of the period, and particularly from 1550 to the Civil War, 'Culverins' and 'demi Culverins' – long barrelled guns with a high powder to ball weight ratio – were particularly popular. Though dismissed by some recent writers as 'inefficient' because they were able to project less metal for a given powder expenditure this is hardly a fair assessment of their worth. The use of a high powder ratio increased both the velocity and the range of the projectile. Moreover if more damage could be done to fortifications or ships by a faster moving ball it might be possible to carry fewer, lighter, shot – itself a material saving when tons of iron round shot had to be transported around the countryside or loaded onto vessels. The Culverin indeed marked a temporary peak of

---

7   As for example O.F.G. Hogg *English Artillery*, Woolwich, 1963, p 29; C. Martin and G. Parker, *The Spanish Armada*, London, 1988, pp 197–226; and A. Caruana *History of English Sea Ordnance*, vol 1, Rotherfield, 1994, pp xv, 5–12.

8   The key tables and lists on which these observations are based are: Tower Inventory of 1559, PRO SP 12/ 6; James Sheriffe's Table of Ordnance, 1592, BL Harleian Ms. 304; Inventory of 1595, National Maritime Museum Ms CAD/C/2; Linewray's Survey, 1603, BL Royal Ms 17a XXXI; PRO WO 55/ 1680 comparing 1617 and 1620; Thomas Smith, in the *Complete Souldier*, 1628; PRO WO 55/1690 of 1635; Robert Norton in *The Gunner*, 1643; William Eldred in *The Gunner's Glasse*, 1646; and PRO WO 55/1699 of 1665. See also S.A. Walton 'The Art of Gunnery in Renaissance England', PhD thesis, University of Toronto, 1999, pp 216–222.

mechanical efficiency for, as Eldred observed, a 15 pound Culverin of the Civil War period could comfortably throw its shot a mile and a half. Such a distance was as much, or more than, most tactical circumstances would demand, and improvements after this achievement would focus on areas such as consistency, general accuracy, ease of loading and movement, supply, costs, and weight of metal required in the piece. Interestingly modern experiment suggests that long barrels in themselves did not add greatly to range, but the casting of a long barrel tended to increase the density and strength of the breech – creating a safer piece for a large loading of powder.[9]

Study of tables makes it obvious that nomenclature tended to become more specific with time. As Ufano correctly observed, early guns were given 'the names of cruel and dangerous beasts, such as dragons, basilisks, serpents and birds of prey – the most violent that can be imagined, like sakers, falcons and others similar'. These evocative names were bandied about between the European nations with remarkable ease. So it was for example that the artillery of King Henry VIII included not only 'serpents' but 'slings', which were themselves derived from German 'Schlange' or snakes, which were, in the language of the time 'serpents'. As the German Hulsius put it, writing in 1604, the many names of guns led to *grosse confusion*. Similarly, modern authorities have frequently criticised this state of affairs as 'confusion' or animated by some form of 'carnival' spirit. What it actually tells us is that diversity was the order of the day – and that guns were classified rather by what their makers hoped they might do, or might sell them, rather than describe in some mathematically quantifiable form what 'model' of gun was being identified. Gradually however attempts were made to define types of gun more closely, with the addition of prefixes such as 'demi' 'quarter' or 'whole' showing how large the calibre of a gun was in relation to the general average for that class. Variations in barrel thickness, weight, or length, might merit the addition of suffixes such as 'bastard' or 'reinforced'. Broad distinctions might also be drawn as to whether a particular piece was at is best on the battlefield or in a siege situation, and clearly gun manufacturers were now setting out with the intention of making ordnance as good as possible for a specific tactical purpose. Towards the end of the sixteenth century, we find definite terms of measurement being applied. A cannon in the government stores is no longer just a 'whole' or a 'half' cannon but a cannon of 'seven inches' or of 'eight inches'. That the uniformity of the ordnance was considered at the highest level, and not easy to achieve, cannot be doubted. As late as January 1640 in reference to action against Scotland a report to the King's Council of War, stated frankly that:

---

[9] J.F. Guilmartin *Gunpowder and Galleys*, Cambridge University, 1974, pp 156–175, 277–291; M. Lewis *Armada Guns*, 1961, passim; C. Trollope 'The Guns of the Queen's Ships During the Armada Campaign', in *Journal of the Ordnance Society*, 6, 1994, pp 23–38; C.J.M. Martin 'Guns of the Armada', in *British Archaeology*, 64, April 2002, also web site published at www.britarch.ac.uk.

> We are of the opinion that there is but one just and best length of all pieces
> which ought to be regulated by the calibre or bore of the piece a condition
> not observed in this kingdom. The pieces to be now cast must be governed by
> such lengths as have been formerly prescribed and observed according to the
> intention of the present service, or by particular direction.[10]

The next advance towards what might be termed 'scientific' exactitude is
the beginnings of thinking of guns in terms of their shot weights – as distinct
from a 'series' production by individual founders who attempted only to
match similar guns made by their own works. By the end of the sixteenth
century standard examples of shot were being kept by the Ordnance Office
– and against these the suitability of new guns to match standard categories
were judged. In a practical, if low key, fashion late Tudor England therefore
attempted what Charles IX had decreed in the Edict of Blois of 1592, when
he had ordered that there should only be six calibres of ordnance in France.
In England this was effectively the start of the 'sealed pattern' system, that has
continued to modern times. Identifying classes of guns by the weight of their
shot appears to start in earnest in the 1620s and 1630s when '3 pound' guns
began to be regarded as ideal for field use. Not long afterwards 'Sakers' and
'demi culverins' are being equated with guns of 6 and 12 pounds. Though
older types of gun are still to be found listed for some years afterwards by 1665
it is clear that artillerists were classifying all new guns by weight of shot. So it is
that artillery pieces firing balls of 3, 6, 8, 12, and 24 pounds become regarded
as standard for light and medium weight artillery, with 'cannon of seven' and
'cannon of eight' filling the really heavy duty roles.

Another interesting feature that emerges by studying lists of guns over time
is the way in which guns of a given class tended to converge in terms of overall
weight. As Eldred encouraged them to do, English gun founders marked their
wares with their hundred weights, quarters and pounds – and, doubtless as
much for payment purposes as other reasons, kept lists of weights of guns in
given batches. So it is that we can say with some confidence that smaller guns
were able to keep within a tight weight conformity: brass Sakers for example
rarely varied by more than half a hundred weight. Demi cannon could however
vary up to three hundred weight within the same batch. Interestingly we also
get a notion of the degree of accuracy in overall weight that might be expected.
Nathaniel Powell, for example, weighed his guns only to the nearest seven
pounds, whilst some other suppliers weighed down to two pounds. As early
as the nineteenth century Lieutenant Hime came to the conclusion that of
the legion of different types of guns in existence during the Civil War period
perhaps only eight or nine categories were of much significance, and when we

---

[10] Levinus Hulsius *Erster Tractat der Mechanischen Instrumenten*, Frankfurt, 1604, p 10; John
Seller, in *The Sea Gunner*, 1691 defines 'legitimate', 'reinforced', and 'bastard', as respectively
normal metal thickness, greater, and lesser metal thickness; *CSPD* CCCCXLI, 4 January
1640, p 301, CCCCXLII, 16 January 1640, p 340.

look at what was being produced – rather than what was left in stores – this general picture tends to be confirmed.[11]

By such evidence it is clear that we have to regard the Civil War as a significant era of transition in the way conventional guns were classified. However the period 1610 to 1650 was also a period of experiment with unconventional weapons. It has been cogently argued that Gustavus Adolphus of Sweden led the way with modern, light, battlefield artillery – yet the aspiration for a new and effective type of field gun was actually rooted in the previous century, and there were several precursors in England and elsewhere. As early as 1578 William Bourne had explained that 'Small Ordnance' was highly desirable, to be 'driven forwards' in battle towards the enemy muzzle first, 'as men commonly drive a wheelbarrow'. Using such guns, mounted on light carriages with four foot diameter wheels, fire 'six times' the force of ordinary hand held firearms could be vented upon the enemy from close range. Against such shot no armour would be of any avail.

In 1611 George Carew designed a demountable brass field piece for the difficult topographic conditions of Ireland. This was cast in several pieces, so as to be 'taken asunder' or 'sett together againe at the pleasure of the Commander', presumably by means of screw threaded sections. The claimed advantages were legion. It could be taken apart for transport over soft or mountainous ground, or taken up into otherwise inaccessible towers and battlements, and if any section failed a spare part could be refitted without having to replace the whole gun. Block carriages, pioneers, and many draught horses could be done away with over night as a few ordinary carts could carry the parts. Carew had in fact invented a species of 'mountain artillery' a couple of hundred years early – and in May 1612 a model 'falcon of copper' in nine pieces was indeed cast by Henry Pitt and proved in the presence of Ordnance Officers. One can only speculate that it was the difficulty and expense of making such a gun that prevented it becoming fully operational at this early period. Nevertheless some of the more forward thinking Lords Lieutenants of the English county militias did succeed in adding light field guns to their inventories. Just a few years later the Irish writer Gerat Barry credited Count Mansfield with the invention of a 'new kind' of light gun, drawn by just two horses, which he employed with success at the siege of Breda. The Swedes would also be credited with casting short, light, guns, or even with cutting long pieces down to more manageable lengths.[12]

The most celebrated of the new types of light artillery introduced in the first three decades of the seventeenth century was undoubtedly the so called 'leather

11 PRO WO 51/1, f 48, 9 May 1631; WO 51/2, f 9 and ff 16–17, 1656; WO 51/2, f 47, 1657; H.W.L. Hime *Gunpowder and Ammunition*, p 3.
12 William Bourne *Inventions and Devices*, London, 1578, p 87; Carew's 'New forme of Great Artillery', 1611, BL Royal Ms 17a LIII; G. Barry *The Siege of Breda*, Louvain, 1627, p 76; L. Boynton *The Elizabethan Militia*, London, 1967, pp 128–132.

gun'. This emerged soon after 1620 – but ascribing it to a single inventor is problematic. Its existence certainly pre-dates the most celebrated campaigns of Gustavus, and also the work of James Weymss, who is sometimes credited with this invention. In fact a more credible source for the leather gun is Weymss' own uncle, Robert Scott, who served with the Swedish army from about 1623 to 1628, and accounts suggest that both Scott and an Austrian, Melchior Wurm-brandt, were instrumental in producing 'leather' pieces for the Swedish King in 1627. Another version of events states that the original idea was actually copied from a Swiss, Philip Eberhard, whose first gun was made in 1622. Scott was apparently disappointed in his expectation of payment from Gustavus, and therefore moved to Denmark where further trials of leather guns took place in 1628 and 1629. Christian IV proved similarly ungenerous, and Scott was advised to 'tender his service to his own prince'. He accordingly moved to England, where, in February 1630, he and his family, including his nephew James, were granted residence by Charles I. Work on leather guns continued at Vauxhall, and after the death of Robert Scott in 1631 James Weymss took up the task himself. Another Scotsman associated with the development of leather guns was Alexander Hamilton, who had made cannon at Arboga for Gustavus Adolphus. In 1633 he carried out an experiment before the King, his kinsman the Marquis of Hamilton, and Master Gunner John Reynolds using 'two peeces of ordnance brought out of Germany'.[13]

The classic 'Swedish' leather gun, popularly identified by means of the monogram of Gustavus in its dolphins, has been examined at least twice with the aid of modern X-ray techniques. These have shown that leather was in fact the least important element of this innovative new gun's construction, the strength of the design being a central tube of copper wound with wire – a similar idea to the wire windings used in the nineteenth century. As we lack a contemporary description of how leather guns were constructed it is worth examining the report prepared for the Quality Assurance Directorate in 1984, according to which,

> The tube was fabricated from a sheet of copper approximately 2 mm thick which was hammered around a mandrel. The mandrel would presumably be shaped to enable the construction of the bore, corresponding to the trunnion, to be made. The taper at the chamber end would also be formed. Soldering the seam of the tube would take place after the mandrel had been removed. If the soldering did not contribute to the strength it would certainly prevent hot

[13] I am grateful to the late Brigadier J. Lewendon, Major F.J. Davidson and Mrs B. Timbers for bringing various sources on leather guns in the Royal Artillery collections to notice. See H.W.L. Hime 'Who Invented the Leather Guns?' in *Minutes of the Proceedings of the Royal Artillery Institution*, 25, 1897, p 121, and 1898, p 595; A. Dolleczek *Geschichte der Österreichischen Artillerie*, Vienna, 1887, p 168, and D. Stevenson and D.H. Caldwell, 'Leather Guns and Other Light Artillery in Mid Seventeenth Century Scotland', in *Proceedings of the Society of Antiquaries of Scotland*, 1976–1977, pp 300–317; PRO WO 54/13–14; *CSPD* CLXI, 15 February 1640, p 188.

gas from penetrating the barrel. The use of lead based solder is supported both visually and also on the radiographs.

It was also possible to demonstrate that the main tube was reinforced at either end with metal pieces, which were probably separate fabrications shrunk in place. The breech closure was formed by a conical insert. The tube was tightly bound with iron wire, and sealed with hemp and plaster, and wooden lathes and strips of metal formed connections to the trunnions. The Woolwich example of the Swedish type leather gun had no distortion within the bore of more than two millimetres in any direction – a remarkable degree of accuracy in fabrication considering that this could have been caused partly or entirely during its service life, or by subsequent damage.

It is interesting to note that the surviving continental museum examples of leather guns are of this general 'Swedish' type – and the pieces in Les Invalides in Paris and the Swedish Army Museum, Stockholm, are virtually identical. The leather gun at the Tøjhusmuseet in Copenhagen differs slightly in that it lacks the characteristic Gustavian dolphins. It is tempting to speculate that this was one of the guns constructed for Christian of Denmark in the 1620s, but its museum provenance states that it was brought to its location in the Danish Cannon Hall from Germany in the nineteenth century, and it is tentatively dated to 1630.[14]

Some 23 surviving Anglo-Scottish examples of leather guns have been described by Caldwell, and these differ from the Swedish type in several important respects. Most obviously the majority are double or quadruple barrelled, and more subtle examination demonstrates that the inner cores are of wrought iron, not copper. They are far heavier than the Swedish type but, as if to compensate for this shortcoming, they are relatively short in the barrel compared to their bore, measuring between eleven and fourteen times their calibre in length. Their fabrication appears less technically accurate, varying from geometric exactitude by several millimetres in their diameters. An interesting parallel to these Anglo-Scottish guns is a type patented by Dutchman Cornelius Schmit of Amsterdam in 1633, and it is believed that a piece from the Dutch East Indiaman *Batavia* is an example of this pattern. Somewhat unexpectedly it consists of wrought iron staves which have been in filled with lead to form the barrel inner, whilst the exterior has been covered with metal to create a smooth exterior. Despite the materials used it is perhaps only half the weight one might expect of a cast iron gun of its calibre. Innovative and useful as light leather guns were it is worth observing that they were used in small numbers compared to cast types by English forces, and that they were in

---

[14] G.M. Teare *Non Destructive Examination of a Leather Gun*, Quality Assurance Directorate Ordnance, Materials Branch Woolwich, 1984, pp 4–9; gun 173 in class II of the Royal Artillery collection; see also J.W. Wijn 'Military Forces and Warfare, 1610–1648', in J.P. Cooper *The Decline of Spain and the Thirty Years War*, Cambridge Modern History, 4, Cambridge, 1970, p 218.

at least relative decline by 1642. That they proved exceptionally popular with Scottish artillerymen is likely to have been due to two factors: the number of Scots who had experience with the Swedes, and that difficult terrain over which the Scottish army often had to operate was especially suited to light equipment.[15]

Another form of light artillery in use in the Civil Wars was the 'frame' – a light gun barrel mounted on what was usually a three legged platform. Not very much larger than a musket it occupied a position between full blown field artillery, 'wall' guns and small arms. The shot that they fired could be iron or lead, and varied from as little as a couple of ounces in weight up to a pound or two. The barrels of frame guns could be wrought or cast, with the larger examples tending to be cast. Again the main purpose of the frame was to give greater mobility to ordnance and to allow for rapid redeployment. Given that they had small, or no, wheels on their carriage it appears likely that they would usually have been dismounted for transport on horses or in carts. The frame was illustrated in several continental texts, and became a significant feature of Scottish artillery trains, forming, for example, a half of the complement of Scottish ordnance deployed in 1640. As with the leather guns their prominence in Scottish inventories is likely to be the result of continental influence and the need for guns which could be taken across rough terrain.[16]

From the 1620s 'Drakes' – guns of short length with tapered powder chambers – also came into use as light battlefield artillery. These could be of either bronze or iron, and were in widespread use during the Civil Wars. Many of the English examples were cast by John Browne, and these will be considered in greater detail along with the fortunes of their manufacturer.

The joker in the pack that was the artillery train was the mortar – technical, difficult to supply, and rarely used on the battlefield – but sometimes the trump card in sieges. It usually fell under the purview not of the gunner, but of the 'firemaster' or engineer. Two main features distinguished the mortar: it was designed to fire its projectile at high trajectory, and low velocity. It was therefore ideal to shoot into fortifications. Characteristically the mortar was much shorter than any other species of artillery, and was of considerably wider bore. Though its ammunition was heavy to handle the low velocity of its shots meant that it consumed less propellant powder. In Hexam's opinion the proportion of propellant to projectile weight might be as little as one seventh to one fifth. Given this factor the barrel of the weapon itself could be relatively thin, and the weapon might not be as heavy as its massive bulbous shape suggested. Mortar barrels were commonly of cast bronze, with short spigots or trunnions on either side. By means of the trunnions it was located in its carriage

---

[15] Stevenson and Caldwell 'Leather Guns', pp 308–316.

[16] *CSPD*, 1640 pp 219, 615; C.S. Terry *The Life and Campaigns of Alexander Leslie, First Earl of Leven*, London, 1899, p 121; and W.G. Ross in 'Paper iv', *Papers of the Corps of Engineers*, 13, 1887, pp 116–118.

– normally of a small, squat, box design with four wheels, or into a wheelless 'stock' set directly on the ground. Almost always the mortar was fired at an elevation of 45 degrees, or greater, throwing its shot in a great parabolic arc. As the elevation increased beyond 45 degrees, range shortened, and the projectile went even higher in the air – though obviously mortar crews were cautious of approaching the vertical too closely since it was theoretically possible for the mortar to land a bomb upon itself. Interestingly there are also one or two references to mortars being used for direct close range fire using stones, glass, or other scattering projectiles – a surviving sketch by Prince Rupert actually shows one mounted in this fashion in the bows of a boat.[17]

Despite its apparent modernity the mortar was not a new invention: late medieval bombards may well have been mounted to fire over obstacles on occasion, and mortars using explosive projectiles were certainly in use in the Low Countries in the early sixteenth century. Albrecht Dürer sketched mortars similar to those in use in seventeenth century England in 1520, and Fronsperger similarly illustrated some relatively up-to-date looking pieces around 1560. Little wonder then that the French theorist St. Julien was able to say that by the seventeenth century 'La bombe [explosive shell] est connue de tout le monde.'[18]

The primary type of mortar projectile was a large 'granadoe' also known as a 'bomb' or 'shell' – a hollow metal sphere packed with powder designed to explode into fragments, on or about, its time of arrival. The 'shell' of the projectile varied in thickness depending on size, but the biggest may have been two inches thick: a surviving 10.5 inch granadoe has a thickness about the fuse hole of 1.5 inches. Though the smallest mortar bombs could double as hand grenades, the largest were monsters 18.5 inches in diameter. Nathaniel Nye in his *Art of Gunnery* favoured mortars throwing a 9 inch projectile, presumably because this was big enough to cause significant damage, but not so massive as to cause serious transport and handling problems. Granadoes were fused by means of a wooden tube, filled with a train of powder, pushed into a socket in the casting. Large granadoes weighed in excess of 150 pounds and often had to be 'slung' into the mortar barrel by means of a team using ropes; for this reason the bombs commonly included integrally cast lugs or ears to facilitate lifting. Using granadoes required great skill, and, apart from expense, posed a number of technical problems. Firstly the metal sphere had to be strong enough to withstand discharge from the mortar. If it did not a premature explosion was the likely result leading to the 'spoiling' of both the mortar and its crew. Since castings might not be implicitly relied upon it was desirable that bombs should be tested, and where necessary reinforced with pitch and cording. As Nye observed,

---

[17] Rupert's sketch is reproduced in C. Wilkinson *Prince Rupert*, London, 1934, p 53; see also S. Bull *Granadoe!*, Leigh-on-Sea, 1985, passim.

[18] L. Fronsperger *Von Kaiserlichen Kriegsregiment*, Frankfurt, 1564, sig CLIV–CLV; LXXX v.; XVIII; F.J. Brechtel *Buchsenmeistery*, Nuremberg, 1591, sig JVIII v.

Wash every one of your shells before you coat or put the chord upon them, when you have made them clean, put a little powder into one of them, and give fire to it with a match, then suddenly clap a clot of clay upon the hole, then observe diligently whether any smoke come out on the sides, if it do then that must be carefully coated or not used.[19]

Another significant technical difficulty was to ensure that the fuse of the bomb was lit at the same time as the mortar itself was set off. There were two ways to overcome this problem, both of which were in use concurrently. The first method was to use a 'tampion' or circular bung of wood which fitted the bore of the mortar. The fuse of the granadoe was then placed so as to project backwards through a hole in the bung, and the complete assembly loaded into the mortar – fuse end first. All being well the fuse would then be lit as the propellant fired. The other method was more certain but required great coolness and co-ordination. For this the engineer would hold a means of ignition, such as a length of smouldering slow match, in each hand. Then he would reach into the barrel of the mortar and light the granadoe, which had been loaded fuse upwards, and, as he withdrew this arm, immediately light the mortar fuse with the other. A variation on this method was to employ an assistant to light one of the two fuses, but this required an even greater sense of timing. To prevent the bomb fuse from setting off the propellant charge prematurely, and to ensure a snug fit between bomb and charge, a thick bung or tampion was recommended.

Once the granadoe was safely airborne one last technical issue became apparent – fuse length. If the crew had misjudged the range, and made the fuse too short, the bomb would burst in the air, possibly far short of the target. Too long and the projectile would sit fizzing upon the ground, allowing alert persons in the target area to run for their lives, or even to extinguish it with water. The ideal fuse was one which burned well, and would ignite the explosive charge at the moment of impact, but such exactitude was rarely achieved in reality. In practice any crew that could make their missile explode just before hitting the ground, or within a few seconds of arrival, was pretty efficient. Extensive practice with live rounds would have been prohibitive, both on grounds of expense and in terms of lives lost. Nye's recommendation was that useful training could therefore be done by shooting grenades without the main charges, the correct weight being replicated by a fill of earth and an ounce or two of powder. These practice rounds would behave very much like their highly lethal cousins, and the firer would be able to tell whether the fusing was precise without actually bursting valuable granadoes. Ordnance papers from the Protectorate demonstrate that some mortar practice took place in Hyde

[19] N. Nye *Art of Gunnery*, London, 1647, pp 59–62, 68, 72; L. Zubler *Nuewe Geometrishe Buchsenmeisteren*, Zurich, 1614, p 52.

Park as part of the proof testing procedure – on the strict understanding that the turf was replaced afterwards.[20]

It has to be acknowledged that Civil War mortars were not greatly accurate: it was difficult to replicate the same circumstances with every shot, and granadoes were not as identical to each other as might have been desired. Shells which flew high into the air at relatively slow speeds were also subject to variable atmospheric conditions. Nevertheless the targets that were fired at, principally towns and castles, were usually huge, so this rarely mattered. Careful engineers might also take steps to assure best possible performance from their weapons. Perhaps most importantly they could judge distances as accurately as possible, and a mortar team that had practised in advance would be able to predict how far a projectile would travel at given barrel elevations. These elevations could be checked using a quadrant, and given that the mortar could be placed in a deep pit, partly or totally obscured from the enemy, some time could be taken over the measurements. Another useful precaution was to balance the missiles, under weight granadoes being brought up to specification by putting in lead shot. If a granadoe was to be used against personnel rather than buildings lead shot might be used as a matter of course.

Where wooden buildings were the target granadoes might be dispensed with altogether and incendiary rounds substituted. The simplest types were a pitched canvas cover containing sulphur and saltpetre. In his *Art of Gunnery* Thomas Smith also suggested balls of pitch and resin which would 'cleave to anything', whilst John Roberts, author of the *Complete Cannoniere*, preferred a 'hedgehogg' or ball with steel spikes, which must have been almost as difficult to remove. The methods of Thomas Binning were even more devious – recommending that enemy towns be set alight with incendiary rounds first, then bombarding the unfortunates who emerged from shelter to extinguish the blaze with stones. Another use for the mortar was to throw illuminating rounds, designed not to burn the enemy, but to expose his movements at night. These were usually shot at the steepest possible trajectory towards the target area, so as to give maximum burning time in the air. Nor was this all that the ever flexible mortar might achieve. Some engineering authorities were keen on the idea of 'stink balls' – intended by means of stench and smoke to discomfit or gas the opposition into surrender. Such missiles might include ingredients such as horses' hooves and excrement. Little wonder that the Polish author, Simienowicz, described them as causing 'extreme nauseousness'.[21]

---

[20] F. Malthus *Pratique de la Guerre*, Paris, 1646, pp 92–152; Nye *Art of Gunnery*, pp 68–71; PRO WO 47/4, 23 July 1658, f 321.
[21] T. Smith *Art of Gunnery*, London, 1600, p 97; J. Roberts *Complete Cannoniere*, London, 1639, p 56; C. Simienowicz, *Art of Artillery*, English translation J. Shelrocke, London, 1729, p 269.

FIRING: 'THE FURIE OF THE ORDNANCE'

Almost as critical as the material technology of gun and powder were the human elements. Men had to know how to load and shoot, and at least the rudiments of aim, if not every nuance of geometry, ballistics and tactics. Just as significantly they required organisation to get the right gun and crew, to the right place, at the right time, with enough ammunition to do the job that was required of them. To do all this also needed fiscal organisation and enough money, or credit, to arrange all of the other matters.

How the early seventeenth century gunner learned his craft was by no means the same in every case – and is open to some conjecture. Clearly there were some who obtained positions as 'matrosses' or assistant gunners, and labourers, on ships, in garrisons, or with 'trains' of marching artillery, and by desire or by default learned in the same way as did the apprentices of many other trades. As early as the Tudors there were attempts to form what amounted to a corporation of licensed gunners. About 1581, for example, a petition was put forward by the gunners of the Tower of London and the navy calling for testing and licensing. This would not only have made available a more skilled force of gunners for use by the Crown, but also have created a form of closed shop or guild, forcing the owners of larger vessels to carry two or more licensed gunners on their ships. Anybody not adhering to the rules could be fined, the proceeds of which would accrue to both the gunners' fraternity and the Crown.[22]

Though this was never carried into practice there was interest in regulation at the highest levels of government, Lord Burghley apparently deciding that an order should be made 'to have a register of gunners' for the explicit purpose of preventing them leaving the kingdom in time of war. If implemented this would hardly have been of advantage to the gunners themselves, for it would have limited their freedom of action without any of the compensations offered by making their calling a monopoly. In the event it appears that Burghley's idea was not systematically put into practice either. Nevertheless there was a tradition of formal instruction carried out by the Master Gunner of England in London which continued throughout the late sixteenth and early seventeenth centuries. The place used for training was the 'Artillery Garden' at Spitalfields, outside Bishops Gate, a location shared at various times with the 'Artillery Company' whose part time soldiers drilled with small arms and pikes on the open ground. This piece of land, also known as the 'Teasel Ground', had once been monastic property, but military men claimed use of it by virtue of a long lease granted by the last Prior at the time of the dissolution.

'Great Ordnance' was fired both within the relatively small enclosure of

---

22 PRO SP 12/157/40, f 75; see also S.A. Walton 'The Tower Gunners and the Artillery Company in the Artillery Garden Before 1630', in *Journal of the Ordnance Society*, 18, 2006, pp 53–66.

the Artillery Garden itself, and on adjoining open land. As one commentator, writing about 1630, explained,

> in time past it was a use with the Mr Gunner on & besides trayning his Schollars at the butt, sometimes to have apeece out of the garden into the field for exercise of the shollars at Randon and unknown marks which is now out of use. And againe where powder, shot, plancke etc was wont to be [taken] out of her majesties store for that purpose to the encouragement of Schollars but since his quarterly allowance doth not only pinch and spare of the wanted expense, that they shall make but 3 shott one day a weeke which they accompted well, but yet he would be paid of the schollars for the same: and being paid for so much as is expended whie should he have allowance of LXX a yeere of his majestie therefore out of Thordinary of the of Thoffice [the ordinary financial supply of the office] to the prejudice of his majesties store of so much provision.

This is interesting, not only in confirming regular training, but in that it suggests that the students made a financial contribution for being taught. Moreover it shows that shooting was demonstrated not only 'point blank' against a target but at 'randon', or with the piece elevated for long range. At the same time this is a complaint that the current Master Gunner, John Reynolds, had neglected training of late. That gun training was indeed carried out over a long period at the Artillery Ground is confirmed by the issue of powder from stores for this purpose, as for example a hundred weight delivered to Stephen Bull, master gunner, as early as 1589.

On one side of the Artillery Ground there was also a house belonging to the Ordnance Office, which eventually became the home of the Master Gunner of England. As the same manuscript notes,

> in the Artillery Garden against the waule next unto the preaching place in the spittle where a scaffold yeerely at Easter was wont to be erected and sett up for the sitting of officers artificers clerks pertaining to thoffice [of the Ordnance] to heare the sermons is since erected a fair howse. And in the daies of her late Majestye of famous memory under colour of that purpose to be continued, which after Stephen Bull, William Bull, William Hammond and now John Reinolds useth as a dwelling house, with benefit of all the fruit, grasse and great garden lett to his great benefitt and his man dwellinge in the gatehouse and selleth drinke, yet all the houses there [are] repaired by his majestie all the fruite trees digged up and made a place for the trayninge of Souldiers and a faire store house builte for keeping their furniture.[23]

---

23 BL Sloane Ms 871(5), f.150. Though titled a *Copy of Linewray's Book*, the manuscript refers to 'his' majesty, and thus post-dates Linewray's tenure of the post of Clerk of Deliveries which ended in 1603. Moreover since there is also reference to John Reynolds as the current Master Gunner it has to have been written some time between 1623 and 1638, and not earlier as is assumed by S.A. Walton in *Art of Renaissance Gunnery*, p 302.

Not all gunners read text books, some indeed were illiterate, but there is evidence that a significant number were aware of them – and at least a few studied avidly. The books of William Bourne, William Eldred, Henry Hexam, John Babbington, Nathaniel Nye, Thomas Smith and others, all make internal reference to other works – and in many instances draw on other authors to a degree that we might now consider plagiarism. There is also manuscript evidence that some gunners, who were not themselves writers of text books, read widely and digested what they learned. Instances include Edmund Parker who fought in Ireland and died in 1602, the unknown author of the *Secret of Gunmen* manuscript produced about 1620, and the author of the very substantial 'Coates Manuscript', or *Some Observations of Artillerie, or the Greater Guns*, which probably dates to the immediate post Civil War period. Interestingly all of these last three were less interested in mathematical abstraction, concentrating instead upon the practical detail of the art of gunnery, as for example: what constitutes a good gunpowder, how to determine whether a piece was properly cast, how types of ordnance are categorised, and problems of accuracy.[24]

A skilled gunner exercised caution with any gun with which he was not yet totally familiar, and took precautions against wear or 'honeycombing' of the barrel, perhaps by searching the bore with the aid of sunlight and a mirror. Checking that there was no obstruction, or unused charge, in the gun by means of his wadhook was also very sensible. Elaborate tests using water might help to show up any cracks in the metal, but experienced men could also observe the satisfying 'ring' from their pieces as the sponge was withdrawn briskly from the void of a sound barrel. Whether the bore lay true within the casting could also be tested, perhaps by means of a pair of parallel staves joined by right angled bars, or by a single staff adapted to the task by a series of discs along its length. Long limbed callipers or scissors could similarly be used to examine metal thickness at various points along the barrel. Where the 'metal' of the gun tapered towards the muzzle of the piece a gunner could improve his aim by setting up a 'dispart' on the end of the gun furthest from the breech. This post or straw served to bring the concavity of the barrel into line with the aiming eye as the firer sighted the target over the breech – thus improving general accuracy.[25]

For many years it was assumed that artillery of the Civil War period was loaded by means of a ladle. The ladle was very much like a grocer's scoop – constructed of sheet copper, or an alloy, first shaped by bending around a former, then fitted to a long stave. The use of non-ferrous metal minimised the

---

24 Lambeth Palace Library Ms 280; Bodlian Library, Ashmole 343, ff 128–139, and Coates Ms, Royal Artillery Institution.

25 W. Bourne *Art of Shooting in Great Ordnance*, London, 1587, p 9; Nye *Art of Gunnery*, pp 71, 95–96; H. Lorraine *La Pyrotechnie*, Pont à Mousson, 1630, p 14; Malthus *Pratique de la Guerre*, Paris, 1650, p 85.

possibility of a spark being struck whilst charging the gun. Ladle capacity was usually calculated in terms of volume, using the diameter of the round shot as a unit of measure. So that the ladle did not have to be uncomfortably large, the powder required could be divided into two, and the ladle used twice to charge the gun. Using a ladle meant that a powder supply had to be kept close at hand during firing, and 'budge' barrels with a leather cover and drawstring, or other means of closure to help prevent accident, are referred to in contemporary literature. Ladles feature frequently both in artillery manuals and in surviving inventories of gunners' stores. In the decades leading up to 1642 many were supplied via the Ordnance Office, which purchased materials for their manufacture through merchants, and then had them made up, either by Ordnance Office employees, contractors, or London pike makers.[26]

The difficulties of loading a gun with a ladle are apparent. In the heat of battle dipping a large scoop into a barrel was not likely to have achieved any more exact measurement than a 'heaped spoonful'. Henry Hexham was one practitioner all too aware of this drawback, and helpfully suggested 'a little jog' to the ladle so that excess would fall back into the barrel; Thomas Smith favoured a brisk tap with a ruler. Slowness was less easy to avoid. Most ladles had to be used twice, and it was a reckless gunner who left the powder barrel anywhere near the muzzle of a gun during firing – so it had to be pushed around every time the gun fired, or the ladle had to be filled in one place and walked to another. Lastly, and perhaps most significantly, the ladle could be highly dangerous. Loose powder could fall onto the boarded floor of a gun battery or ship's deck and be ignited by flash or embers, dust could rise from the powder, and the burning match which put fire to the gun might come into contact with open barrel or ladle. Walking back and forth with exposed powder was tantamount to suicide at the best of times; how it could have worked at all, on board ship, or whilst under fire, is difficult to imagine. Experienced gunners were well aware of these problems as early as the reign of Elizabeth. As William Bourne explained in his *Shooting in Great Ordnance*, 'The ladell shall have sometyme more pouder, and sometyme less, by a good quantitye, and especially if that hee doth it hastely as in time of service it always requireth.' Spilt powder could spell the 'spoyling of men', and in short there was 'no worse lading or charging of Ordnance than with a ladell'. Antiquated loading methods have therefore been postulated as a significant limiting factor to the effectiveness of seventeenth century artillery.[27]

Nevertheless it is obvious that there was a simple solution – the use of

26 R. Norton *The Gunner*, London, 1628, pp 42–43; H.W.L. Hime *Gunpowder and Artillery*, London, 1904, p 235; O.F.G. Hogg *English Artillery*, Woolwich, 1963, p 45; PRO WO 54/3, 6, 7, 8, 9, 11.

27 H. Hexham *Principles of the Art Militarie*, The Hague, 1640, part III, p 3; Thomas Smith *Art of Gunnery*, London, 1600, p 81; W. Bourne *The Art of Shooting in Great Ordnance*, London, 1587, pp 30–31.

bagged charges, or cartridges – sewn or glued containers of paper, linen, or canvas. Moreover contemporary manuals were remarkably consistent on this point. As early as 1573 Peter Whitehorne had pointed out,

> For the more speedie shooting of ordinance, the iuste charge in pouder of everye peece may aforhand be prepared in a readinesse and put in bagges of linnen or in great papers made for the same purpose, which in a sodaine may be chapt into the mouth of a peece with the bollet thereof thrust after, as farre as they will goe, and then thrusting a long wyer into the touchehole with some pouder so soone as it is leveled, it may incontinent be shot of: which maner of charging is done most quickly and a great deale sooner than any other waye, and when haste requires very needfull.[28]

Similar advice was repeated time and time again in the decades leading up to, and including, the Civil Wars. Many manuals gave instructions on the making of cartridges for artillery; significant examples included William Bourne's *Art of Shooting in Great Ordnance* in 1578, Cyprian Lucar's edition of Tartaglia, 1588, Thomas Smith's *Art of Gunnery* in 1600 and William Eldred's *Gunner's Glasse* of 1646. The next year Nathaniel Nye described the process as follows,

> take canvas, such as the powder will not creep thorow, and let it be in breadth … just three diameters of the peece … and for the length you will find it by the filling of them, these being sewed together upon a mould; which must be a very little lesse than the diameter of the bore, and about 4 diameters long.

Paper cartridges could be made in a similar fashion, but in this case the former was first smeared with tallow to prevent sticking, and the seams were glued.[29]

Parallel examples for cartridge manufacture can be found in every major European language of the period, a point perhaps best illustrated by Diego Ufano's *Trato de Artilleria*. The original edition of which, published in Spanish, in Brussels in 1613, notes how 'el cartoucho' could be made for the handy loading of ordnance. In 1621 the French version translates cartridges as 'patron' and 'sachets' – these becoming 'secklein oder patronen' in the German printing. In Norton's *The Gunner* the diagrams made by De Bry for continental editions of Ufano are pirated and dropped straight into an English text as handy illustrations of cartridges. Nor were the Italians left out, indeed Luigi Collado's *Practica Manuale* shows that knowledge of this method of loading guns was known in Italy by 1586, if not earlier.[30]

All of this serves to demonstrate that cartridges and cartridge making was common knowledge throughout Europe and England well before the Civil

---

28 P Whitehorne, *Certain Wayes for the Ordering of Souldiers in Battelray*, London, 1573, p 33 v.

29 Nye *Art of Gunnery*, London, 1647, p 42; J. Roberts *Compleate Cannoniere*, London, 1639, p 29.

30 D. Ufano *Trato de Artilleria*, Brussels, 1613, p 306; *Artillerie, C'est a Dire*, Zutphen, 1621; *Archeley*, Frankfurt, 1614; L. Collado *Practica Manuale Di Artegliera*, Venice, 1586.

Wars. Proof that they were used on a regular basis is more difficult to establish, given that they were not commonly a central 'issue' store prior to 1642. However that evidence does exist in sufficient quantity and quality to demonstrate that cartridges were made and used on a regular basis by individual gunners is beyond reasonable doubt. Perhaps the first suggestion that they were used in cannon on board English ships comes from the 1545 archaeology of the *Mary Rose*, where reamers for puncturing them have been recovered from the wreck. Later in the sixteenth century many inventories and 'remains' of stores show that cartridge making materials were supplied as a matter of routine to the Elizabethan navy. In 1572 we find that cartridge formers were allotted to the *Hoape* on fitting out, whilst not only formers but lengths of canvas 'for cartouches' and reams of 'Royal Paper' are mentioned in connection with the *Swallow*. In the *Book of the Remaynes* made up in 1595 and 1596 itemising stores returning aboard Royal Navy vessels we discover that every ship was provided with cartridge making materials – most of which had been expended whilst at sea. From 1597 we have a record of no less than 57 yards of canvas being delivered by Richard Ascue, purser of the *Warspite* to Master Gunner William Bull, at a total cost of 71s 3d.[31]

The closest we have to a combat report demonstrating the use of cartridges in action at sea comes from the *Observations* of Richard Hawkins in 1593. This implies that the loss of his ship the *Dainty* in action with the Spanish was in fact due mainly to the failures of his master gunner in his cartridge making duties,

> For bearing me ever in hand, that he had five hundred cartredges in a readinesse, within one hours fight we were forced to occupie three persons, only on making and filling cartreges, and of five hundreth Elles of canvas and other cloth given him for that purpose, at sundry times, not one yard was to be found.

Perhaps the most interesting point is that Hawkins did not even appear to have considered using ladles – it was deemed far more effective to detail men to fill cartridges, even in the midst of action.[32]

The Stuart naval records are even more explicit regarding the use of cartridges. The fleet which went to Cadiz in 1625 set out with formers, canvas, Paper Royal, glue and thread amongst its gunnery stores. When the ships returned the clerks of the Ordnance were able to see finished cartridges aboard. In the minutely detailed records of the fleet of 1639 cartridges were made up in the early part of the voyage, and much powder was wasted when they had to be emptied again later. However it is possible that a certain percentage of 'waste'

---

[31] National Maritime Museum Ms CAD C/1; ADL/H/14; PLA/P11; PRO WO 55/1627.

[32] *The Observations of Sir Richard Hawkins, in his Voiage to the South Sea Anno Dom 1593*, London, 1622, p 127. An 'ell' in English usage was a length of measure equalling 1.25 yards: a Scottish 'ell' was 37.2 inches, a Flemish 'ell' 27 inches.

or spillage was an accepted perk of the job. The picture of cartridge making materials being supplied centrally, but made up locally, also holds good for land garrison service prior to the Civil War. Records exist showing the supply of cartridge making equipment as do the petitions of gunners asking for more. One letter written from the gunners of Dover to Lord Zouch, Warden of the Cinque Ports, in 1629 explicitly mentions a need for 'Royall Paper to make carthridges withall'. Ordnance Office stock-taking in 1635 reveals the presence of not just materials but 600 formers on which cartridges are made. In the Civil War period itself Eldred states that it was the duty of gunners to make up their own cartridges 'at spare times ... in garrisons or other places'.[33]

Evidence relating to actual and planned field armies also reveals plenty of cartridge making materials. In 1620–1621 an expedition intended to go to the aid of the Elector Palatine was to be equipped with 'canvas for cartouches 1000 elles at 6d the ell' – an innocent little entry which entails a length of cartridge-making canvas three quarters of a mile long. The 1627 Isle de Rhe expedition took with it at least 500 yards of cartridge canvas, and two tons of cartridge paper. None of these stores were intended for any other purpose, for there were also separate supplies of writing paper, and canvas sand bags. By the time we reach the Civil War, cartridges are taken as a given, and were clearly carried in the artillery train along with the guns. The Scottish theorist Thomas Binning would later suggest that the universal scale of issue should be 24 per gun, half of which were to be kept filled and ready for use at all times; the same advice would be repeated by John Seller in 1691. Various of the Royalist Ordnance papers of the Civil War show that this was very much the sort of standard that the King's gunners wished to maintain – even if it was not always achieved in practice.[34]

In regards to artillery cartridges the instance of the New Model Army is particularly interesting, for not only was it provided with cartridge making equipment – but, unusually, with finished cartridges from central stores, and cloth cartridge cut outs which required only to be sewn up. Very probably the advent of the New Model Army gives us the approximate date from which cartridges came to be considered an issue store, rather than something which was primarily the duty of individual gunners to make up. Interestingly this also confirms that the guns of the of the New Model Army artillery trains had reached a reasonable degree of standardisation – for had their 3 pound and 6 pound guns varied very much in terms of bore, an issue cartridge would not have been guaranteed to fit. Similarly this gives us a retrospective clue as to why finished cartridges may not have been issued in earlier decades – non standard guns, could not take a 'one size fits all' cartridge. One of the largest contracts for finished cartridges for the New Model Army was placed with Nathaniel

---

[33] PRO WO 49/110; 55/1601; BL Egerton Ms 2584, f 362.
[34] BL Harleian Ms 5109; Royal Artillery Institution MD 979 *Inventory of the Equipment of the Artillery Embarked*, 1627; I. Roy.

Humphrey and Richard Bradley for 1,000, 'at ten pence a peece ... ready money'. Few things were paid for in 'ready money' by any English administration of the period, and this perhaps gives us a better idea than anything of how important artillery cartridges were deemed to be.[35]

Given that it is now proven that the cartridge, not the ladle, was the usual method of loading artillery during the Civil War period – and in many instances long before – it does beg the question why we encounter ladles, both in the manuals and in the archaeological record. Two possible explanations may reasonably be put forward. First is that the ladle may have been regarded as an added security. If cartridges proved insufficient in number, got damp, or lost, the gunner could have resorted to the use of the ladle as an emergency measure. In the case of smaller guns it may even have been possible to insert the cartridge using the ladle. Second, in ceremonial or practice firing, speed was not important – it was the quality of the show that mattered. In such circumstances few gunners would have bothered with the expense of a cartridge. So it is that we find the highly choreographed descriptions of the use of the ladle – handled, as Eldred put it like 'an artist'.

The manuscript *Short Military Treatise* gives us a good picture how guns were actually aimed and discharged. The gunner, 'steps into the carriage', and then:

> causes the peece to be drawne on this or the other hand, till it stand right with the loope holes, and one of his assistants standinge at the trayle of the carriage with a leaver in his hande, removes it according to the gunners commands, untill such time as it be as he would have it, then another assistant or labourer ought to be ready with his leaver to raise the breech of the piece, and the gunner fitteth the coines so that the piece may be in its true levell, this being done he makes the labourer signe to let fall the breech of the piece and then all being right he thrusts a priming iron into the touch hole up to the powder, primes the piece and causes one of his assistants to give fire, himselfe standing aside to marke where the shot will light, that he may afterwards guide himselfe accordingly[36]

In priming the weapon the gunner was to make sure that some of the priming powder was around the top of the hole, so that the man who gave fire to the gun did not have to place his linstock or portfire directly into the hole. Doing this ensured that the large flash from the touch hole did not 'blow up' the linstock, injuring the gunner's assistant in the process.

It is interesting to note that, ideally, aiming was carried out by three people: two assistants who performed the physical tasks of traverse and elevation, whilst the gunner himself sighted on the target. Though the gunner carefully primed

---

35 Museum of London MS 46–78/709; see also G.I. Mungeam 'Contracts for the Supply of Equipment in the New Model', in *Journal of the Arms and Armour Society*, 6, part 3, 1967.
36 BL Harleian Ms 6844, f 176; a full loading and firing cycle based on Eldred's instructions of 1646 forms Appendix X.

the piece the actual firing was the job of an assistant, the gunner observing what we might now call 'fall of shot' to aid subsequent aim corrections. Interestingly the New Model Army would allow a total of one master gunner, four 'mates', 40 gunners and 120 matrosses, for a train of 20 pieces of various sizes – suggesting that gun crews of five to ten were commonplace in 1644. This allowed one or more experienced gunners to command and aim each piece, and several matrosses to load, bring up ammunition, and move the gun. With the pieces deployed in small groups the master gunner's mates were available to act as battery commanders. Royalist lists of 1643 and 1644 suggest that a 12 pound gun could be crewed by about six men, whilst a mortar needed seven.

When shooting from an embrasure in a battery or open loophole in fortifications the gunner was to, 'have a care to keepe himselfe behind the breech of the piece and so take his right time to aim, and if he can do it well may save himself, for the enemies musketts will not faile to play roundly upon him'. Men who could learn such simple practicalities might well 'pass for gunners', even though they had 'noe skill for mathematicale instruments'. This being said some 'mathematical instruments' were undoubtedly used – at least some of the time. Perhaps the one most commonly seen in contemporary illustrations is the quadrant, which had been popularised, if not actually invented, by the Italian Niccollo Tartaglia in the sixteenth century. This was effectively a set square on which was superimposed a protractor and a plumb bob. The gunner inserted one limb of the quadrant into the barrel of the gun, and by means of the bob could show whether the barrel was level or elevated, and if so to how many degrees. Measurements could be compared to fire tables to determine how far the shot might fly, and how much adjustment was required to hit a given target. It would seem unlikely that quadrants were often used in battle, but could serve to improve first round accuracy in siege situations, and were probably used quite extensively by mortar crews for whom range and elevations were particularly difficult to judge by eye – and for whom there was usually little ammunition to waste. 'Gunners' rules', with lengths and conversion tables engraved on them, and shot gauges for checking the size of round shot were also used fairly widely.[37]

Contrary to popular belief firing a solid iron ball from a seventeenth century

[37] Ibid, f 176–176v. T. Smith *Art of Gunnery*, London, 1643, pp 57–60. There are a number of period gunnery instruments in the Royal Armouries collections, as for example a German gunner's quadrant dated 1585 (item XIV. 19); and a slightly later example that is described as a 'calibre compass' – combining a rule with callipers (item XIX. 222). The Royal Artillery collection contains a reproduction quadrant (XXIV. 32); an undated tangent scale (XXIV.50); undated quadrants (XXIV. 63, 64 and 74) and various gunner's rules (XXIV. 117–119, 200–201). One of the best continental collections of gunnery instruments is that of the Institute and Museum of the History of Science in Florence, where there are at least three seventeenth century quadrants (items 659, 1303 and 1485). See also J. Green 'Further Information on Gunner's Rules or Tally Sticks', in *Journal of the Ordnance Society*, 2, 1990, pp 25–32. A number of other examples of rules have been recovered from shipwreck sites.

cannon does not leave the piece immobile, emitting a gentle whiff of smoke. When fire is applied to the priming there is a first hiss or puff as it ignites, followed rapidly by a great gout of fast moving gas and flame straight upward in a narrow cone from the touch hole as the main charge is set off. A split second later, and before the fiery geyser from the breech subsides, the ball leaves the muzzle on a burning column of expanding gas – so quickly that it is hard to appreciate what is happening without the use of slow motion photography. Interestingly tests conducted since the seventeenth century suggest that almost all artillery of the period had muzzle velocities exceeding 1,000 feet per second, and some of those which used large charges of powder in relation to the mass of the ball may well have challenged the 1,500 feet per second barrier. Most Civil War period ordnance was thus firing projectiles at supersonic speeds and, perhaps surprisingly, seventeenth century round shot were therefore travelling at similar velocities to bullets from modern handguns. To take one example a bullet from a 9 mm parabellum cartridge leaves the barrel of a modern military semi automatic pistol at about 1,200 feet per second – fractionally slower than the average ball from a smooth bored 3 pounder. The bullet from an AK 47 assault rifle exits the barrel at about 2,400 feet per second. Interestingly the author of the Coates manuscript came close to explaining the noise of artillery discharge in terms of breaking a sound 'barrier' when he described how a shot 'breaks violentlie thruigh the aire and that makes the cracke and noyse'.

The sound of the discharge of ordnance can occasionally be identified as a double bang, the first issue of gas from the vent at the breech end being closer to the firer's ear than the discharge from the muzzle, and there may also be reflection of sound waves from nearby hard surfaces. If guns are close to windows, or particularly between the walls of adjacent houses, shock waves alone can break the glass. Curiously the first shot from a gun sounds loudest; later rounds fired may seem quieter, or even silent, as the ears have been so roughly assaulted by compression as to provoke temporary deafness. Nevertheless every shot is felt by the body as the internal organs are shaken or wobbled by the blast. However there is no time to appreciate the nuances, for the exit of the ball from the barrel exerts an equal and opposite force on the gun, and by extension to the carriage. Even heavy guns are thrown backwards by the recoil. Lighter pieces, having less mass to be moved, and often higher proportions of powder to ball, may jerk extremely violently. If not laid firmly on a flat surface they may even buck, or lift a wheel from the ground. Thomas Smith once observed a gunner 'slaine with the reverse of the wheele' of his culverin, which 'crushed his leg and thigh in pieces'. Those giving fire to the ordnance were therefore best advised to do so 'nimbly' from one side, so avoiding the flame from the vent, and retiring briskly 'three or four yards' as soon as the task was complete. Depending on wind speed and direction billows of smoke may cascade away from the gun, or be blown back, obscuring the view. Either way the sulphurous reek of burnt powder soon reaches the nose. Depending on the type of gun and its loading burning embers or soot may be thrown out near the gun position, worst case scenario being the actual ignition of dry grass and the starting of fires.[38]

Though seventeenth century guns were often used at relatively short distances – with their barrels levelled at 'point blank' against their target – they had surprisingly long extreme ranges. In a table produced by Thomas Smith in 1628 the maximum range of the culverin with its barrel mounted to optimum elevation is given as 2,100 yards, or well over a mile. At the other end of the scale the little falconet is listed as having a 1,000 yard extreme range – this being still a good deal more than half a mile. With the barrel horizontal to the ground the equivalent distances the shot would fly were 420 and 220 yards respectively, which may not sound like much until one considers that muskets had little accuracy over 100 yards, and that a round shot did not stop dead when it hit *terra firma*, but bounced and scudded with considerable momentum. According to one modern estimate a 6 pound ball fired from a light artillery piece, which struck its first 'graze' on firm ground at 300 yards from the gun, would be likely to rise again to a few feet above the ground, and fly on before executing a further bounce at about five or six hundred yards. This second bounce could itself be another hundred yards. Given that during the complete flight of the ball – out to seven hundred yards from the firing point – it scarcely, if ever, rose above six feet from the ground, it was potentially lethal along a remarkably long path.

Close to the gun the dense fast moving shot would simply punch through anything except the thickest earth and masonry, with columns of troops or horses presenting very little resistance as it sliced through the ranks. Empirical tests conducted at Woolwich in 1652 showed just how destructive iron shot could be. A 32 pound ball, fired with ten or twelve pounds of powder, was found to smash its way through 19 inches of solid oak, fly a further 14 yards, then smash through a further 19 inches of oak – before flying a further eight yards to embed itself in an earthen back stop. This performance equated to shooting right through a major warship, perforating it from side to side. An 18 pound shot, fired from a culverin with a somewhat greater proportion of powder, managed a very similar performance. A 9 pound shot from a demi culverin cleared the first 19 inch baulk of oak, but failed to penetrate the second. Yet on the battlefield it was less the immediate penetrating power, and more what happened along the entire length of the path of shot which really mattered. After bouncing a ball would move more slowly but we should consider that, since energy is a function of mass multiplied by velocity, even a 3 pound ball travelling at only a few feet per second could still kill or badly maim. Even when forward momentum was lost and the shot finally fell to earth its mass against its relatively small size made it much more damaging than being hit by an equivalent sized lump of masonry. According to John Vicars' account of

---

[38] T. Smith *Art of Gunnery*, p 81; Coates Ms transcribed in S. Bull 'Furie of the Ordnance', PhD thesis, Swansea, 1988, p 528.

the action at Southam in Warwickshire Lord Brooke's cannonier, a 'marksman' with the field gun, was able to cut down 'a whole file of the enemy horse' with one shot as well as break the wheel of a gun. Five horses were 'found slaine', together with 'the legges and armes of some of the riders'.[39]

Heavier iron shot were not more destructive simply because they were larger, or were projected further by bigger cannon. Heavier shot have smaller surface area relative to their mass, and so are proportionately less impeded by drag – or any other form of resistance. Retaining far more kinetic energy, heavy balls remained highly destructive at longer ranges, continuing to bounce hard and fast through infantry and cavalry; close to they could also smash masonry. Happily for those on the receiving end of gun fire the seventeenth century battlefield was seldom an isotropic plain, a green billiard table from which all life could easily be bowled. Hills were an excellent protection for troops; wet or uneven fields could produce unpredictable results. Boggy ground or marsh could stifle bounces, banks could absorb shot which hit at steep angles. Undulations might result in balls bouncing clean over lucky troops who had appeared to be sitting ducks in the path of shot. Guns that fired with their barrels elevated to extend range might find that the ball bounced relatively little. Thick forests were a good protection where they concealed troops, or masses of thick trunks could absorb small balls – but open woods at close range were a different matter, with trees shedding branches and shattering to vicious splinters. Authorities were agreed that flat, hard, stoney ground was the very worst place to stand under artillery fire. Iron shot skidded fast over the ground, little impeded by friction, and stones shot asunder moving fast enough to kill in their own right, with flints or rocks shattered into razor sharp shards.

What limited the destruction wrought by the heavy artillery was seldom its maximum range, but what the gunner could see and identify – and what he believed his piece might be accurate enough to hit. On flat ground, with a target consisting of a formed body of troops a couple of hundred yards away, it was enough simply to level the piece in the right direction and let rip. At six hundred yards a target six feet high and several ranks deep looked like a pencil line, drained of colour, with individual soldiers difficult to distinguish, and minor errors in the laying of the gun or accuracy of the piece were magnified by the distance from the barrel. Elevating the muzzle by means of wedges was perfectly possible, but added another factor to go wrong. Even so, a brigade of troops occupied ground several hundred yards wide and tens deep, so great accuracy was still not vital. Given a clear field of fire and a big target, an opening cannonade with 12 pound guns was perfectly feasible at seven or eight hundred yards.

---

[39] 'An Account of Some Experiments for Trying the Force of Great Guns by the Learned Mr Greaves', in *Philosophical Transactions*, 179, 1685, pp 1090–92; J. Vicars *England's Parliamentary Chronicle*, London, 1646, part II, p 142.

Much further away, however, even the practised gunner was into the realms of uncertainty, wondering whether the range table in his book could be relied upon, and whether he had enough ammunition to indulge in shooting at such a questionable target. Correcting fire would be virtually impossible since it would be unknown whether the rounds were hitting home. Nevertheless a vast and immobile mark like a castle or town could certainly be bombarded at very long ranges, and at least one – Elizabeth Castle, Jersey – was very successfully engaged by mortar fire at 1,000 yards. Such dazzling feats required both skill and reasonable weather and light conditions – but at such distances the fall of shot would be distributed fairly randomly.[40]

For close range targets 'case', later known as canister, rounds could be fired for maximum antipersonnel devastation. These were effectively cylindrical containers, of thin metal or wood, holding lead balls, or fragments of metal. One surviving 4 pound example, recovered archaeologically from a shipwreck, has been found to have been made of turned alder, split and hollowed out to contain a payload of 48 musket shot. By extrapolation it seems probable that a 6 pound case would hold at least 72 shot, and those for the larger species of gun a hundred or more. For added close range laceration and wounding the individual lead shot could be deformed or 'burred', or supplemented with small pieces of scrap metal.[41]

Fired from the gun in the same manner as a solid ball the case split open as it left the muzzle of the gun, creating a massive cone shaped blast, not unlike that of a huge shot gun. Whilst the range of case in this period was usually no more than about two hundred yards a well aimed round could cause appalling casualties. Near to the muzzle a man caught in the still focused cone might literally be dismembered by the impact of multiple shot – further away, with the individual balls more randomly separated over a larger area, the effect was rather more like that of a volley of musketry. Various accounts speak of anything from a couple of casualties up to as many as 80 being caused by a single round of case. At the defence of Alton Church a 'drake' discharged into densely packed troops was thought to have incapacitated 'about fourescore'. In an incident near Chester sixty casualties were said to have been inflicted on the Royalists by 'a case of Drakes'. In a particularly well documented skirmish at Abingdon a group of cavalry were hit by a close range discharge, bringing down half a dozen riders including the unfortunate John Denton, who suffered between seven and fourteen wounds depending on the particular account consulted. Whilst propaganda and exaggeration doubtless inflated some of the

---

[40] B.P. Hughes *Firepower*, London, 1974, pp 24–25; A.R. Hall *Ballistics in the Seventeenth Century*, Cambridge, 1952, pp 166–171.

[41] See C.J.M. Martin 'An Iron Bastard Minion Drake Extraordinary by John Browne from the Pinnace Swan (1641–1653)', in the *International Journal of Nautical Archaeology*, 33, number 1, 2004, pp 93–94.

claims, hits numbering in dozens were perfectly realistic when several pounds of musket balls were discharged at a time.[42]

All battle wounds are dreadful, and sword blades and musket shot produced huge gashes and large holes as well as splintered bone; as surgeon John Woodall recalled, gunshots in particular were usually 'compound' wounds – quickly attended by 'putrefaction'. Nevertheless the artillery trounced all in its ability to fragment the human form – sometimes into unrecognisable lumps. Heads and limbs taken clean off were by no means unusual. At Newburn in 1640 one Scottish 'poet' was moved to write the following description of the carnage wrought by the artillery upon the English foe,

> The Scots canons powder and balls did spew …
> Thundered so, as though they would have riven
> The burnisht vaults, and battlements of heaven …
> and through their bones did scud.
> The wisking bals made all their cheeks so smoth
> they sought no princers for to draw a tooth:
> Yea, legs and armes which in the air did flee
> were then cut of (like gibblets) fearfully:
> The Scottish bals so dash'd then with distain,
> That hips ou'r head, their skul did spew their brains.

In another poem about the Thirty Years War, penned in 1634, John Russell spoke of the artillery rending 'human bodies', like 'fields of corn'; so perhaps Cromwell's later simile of 'stubble' to 'swords' was not so original after all.[43]

There is similarly graphic description of the stand of the Red Regiment of the London trained bands, attempting to hold their position under bombardment at the First battle of Newbury. According to one Parliamentarian witness,

> They began their battery against us with their great guns, above one half hour before we could get any of our guns up to us; our Gunner dealt very ill with us, delaying to come up to us: our noble colonell Tucker fired one piece of ordnance against the enemy; and aiming to give fire a second time was hit in the head with a cannon bullet … The enemies canon did play most against the Red Regiment of Trained Bands, they did some execution against us the first, and were somewhat dreadful when mens bowels and brains flew in our faces. But blessed be God that he gave us the courage, so that we kept our ground, and after a while he feared them not, our Ordnance did very good

---

[42] BL E 114(25), passim; E 90(28) *Certaine Informations*, 20–27 February 1643, p 47; E 77 (4) *A True Relation of a Great Victory … Neere Chester*, 27 November 1643, sig A4. See also Hughes *Firepower*, pp 32–35, and H.L. Blackmore *The Armouries of the Tower of London*, vol I, *Ordnance*, London, 1976, pp 190–203.

[43] M.Z.B. 'The Battel of Newburn', 1643, in *Fugitive Scottish Poetry*, reprinted Edinburgh, 1853; J. Russell *The Two Famous Pitcht Battels of Lypsich and Lutzen*, Cambridge, 1634, pp 14–17.

executions upon them: for we stood at so near a distance upon a plain field, that we could not lightly misse one another.[44]

Though instant death was a very real possibility many remarked upon the often random catalogue of wounds inflicted by the ordnance. At Colchester in 1648 a Royalist Ensign struck down by a relatively slow moving five pound ball near the end of its trajectory discovered that he was able to hobble away supported by a comrade – but was horrified to see that the shot remained 'hanging in the skin of his side'. He was able to converse coherently, and made it as far as his quarters in the town, before 'he expired'. At the Second Newbury Parliamentarian units were caught in flanking fire from Royalist guns which sent their shot ploughing through the ranks, severely shaking Colonel Ludlow's regiment. One who fell was the Colonel's cousin Gabriel, who survived long enough to be examined by a surgeon who catalogued his massive compound injuries as including a 'broken belly', torn bowels, a hip bone 'broken all to shivers', and the shot still lodged in his abdomen. The doctor concluded that though the wounded man was still conscious treating him was a waste of time, 'looking upon him as a dead man.[45]

This was probably not uncommon. Medical practitioners of the period were often quite unable to do anything about the impact of roundshot, and relatively rarely did they get to treat a still breathing victim of artillery fire – but there were recorded instances. Richard Wiseman, surgeon to the Royalist regiment of Colonel Ballard in the West Country, encountered one unfortunate, 'at the siege of Melcomb-Regis'. A soldier who, 'by the grazing of a cannon shot', had 'the great part of his forehead carried off, and the scull fractured into many pieces, and some of it driven with the hairy scalp into the brain'. Naturally the man,

> fell down as though dead, but after a while moved; and an hour or two after, his fellow soldiers seeing him endeavour to rise, fetcht me to him. I pulled out pieces of bone and lacerated flesh from amongst the brain, in which they were entangled, and drest him up with soft folded linen dipt in Cephalick Balsam, and with emplaster and bandage bound him up, supposing I should never dress him more. Yet he lived 17 days; and the 15 day walkt from that great corner fort over against Portland to the bridge which separates Weymouth from Melcomb-Regis, only led by the hand of some one of his fellow soldiers. The second day after he fell into a spasmus, and died howling like a dog; as most do who have been so wounded.

Case shot wounds could be equally terrible. At the storm of Taunton, Wiseman had occasion to treat one of Colonel John Arundel's men who caught part of a blast of case in the face.

[44] *A True Relation of the Diurnal Marchings*, October 1643, BL E 69(15), sig B3.
[45] R. Mentent *History of the Troubles in Great Britain*, London, 1735, p 43; W. Money *The First and Second Battles of Newbury*, London, 1884, p 161.

He fell down, and in the retreat was carried off amongst the dead, and laid down in an empty house by the way until the next day: when in the morning early, the Colonel marching by that house heard a knocking against the door. Some of the officers desiring to know what it was, lookt in, and saw this man standing by the door without eye, face, nose or mouth. The Col. sent to me ... to dress the man. I went, but was somewhat troubled where to begin. The door consisted of two hatches; the uppermost was open and the man stood leaning on the other part of the door which was shut. His face, with his eyes, nose, mouth. and forepart of the jaws, with the chin, was shot away, and the remaining parts of them driven in. One part of the jaw hung down by his throat ... I saw the brain working under the lacerated scalp on both sides between his ears and brows. I could not see any advantage that he could have by my dressing. To have cut away the lacerated parts here had been to expose his brain to the air. But I helpt him to clear his throat, where was remaining the root of his tongue. He seemed to approve of my endeavours, and implored my help by the signs he made with his hands. I asked him if he would drink, making a sign by holding up a finger. He presently did the like, and immediately after held up both hands, expressing his thirst. A souldier fetcht some milk, and brought a little wooden dish to pour some of it down his throat: but part of it running on both sides, he reacht out his hands to take the dish. They gave it him full of milk. He held the root of his tongue down with one hand, and with the other poured it down his throat (carrying his head backward), and so got down more than a quart. After that I bound his wounds up.[46]

In sea fights wounds might be inflicted by whirling chain shot and secondary splinters of wood blown from the hulls of the ships. Wiseman treated a number of these noting that 'oftentimes' such missiles were apt to tear off 'a buttock, the brawn of a thigh', or, 'the calf of a leg'. Wherever possible his preference was to treat seriously wounded men straight away, amputating or operating as necessary, before the 'amazement' – or first shock wore off, and full sense of the pain set in – or infection had a chance to take hold causing fevers. In performing amputations he would recommend that the surgeon be led by the precise nature of the wound that the roundshot had inflicted. Where leg bones were shattered there was little option but to cut off just below the knee or at the thigh. If the patient were fortunate only to have suffered damage to hand or toes it might still be possible to save most of the limb, amputating only such fingers or toes as were beyond repair. Occasionally gunners were injured by accidents with their own pieces: powder explosions and guns which recoiled over limbs were probably not that uncommon in the heat of action, but there were other more obscure incidents. One such was an 'Irish mariner' treated by Wiseman, who, having discharged his gun, which was 'honeycombed' by flaws in the metal, 'loaded it suddenly again'.

---

[46] John Woodall *The Surgions Mate*, London, 1617, pp 125–146; Richard Wiseman *Several Chirurgical Treatises*, 2nd edn, London, 1686, pp 402–420.

> Whilst he was ramming in a cartridge, the powder took fire, and shot the rammer out of his hand, tearing the palm of his hand, also some of his thumb and fingers. The wound was not considerable, but the force of the blow extinguished both sense and motion of the member. I drest him … One night after he was cured of his wound, lying asleep in his hammock, he was wakened by the wet he felt upon his breast and belly; and getting up to a candle, he found the dressing on his hand all bloody, as also the place whereon it lay. I being called took off his greazy dressings, and found the palm of his hand and fingers gnawed by rats.[47]

Amongst those of deterministic religious persuasion, or people predisposed towards popular superstition, there was a persistent belief that the cannon might act as an agent, or at least a metaphor, for the almighty in striking down sinners. Preaching to the soldiers in the Artillery Garden in 1639 Obadiah Sedgewicke described his sermon as 'a field piece' for the men. In 1640 Archbishop Laud's 'canons' were parodied as 'cannons', being so wrongly charged, that they were like to explode in his face. Following a victory by the Parliamentarian commanders Brereton and Middleton over Lord Capel in Shropshire one devout commentator opined that the main reason for the triumph of the godly was that the 'Royalist cannon had no commission from heaven, to touch any of those who fought the Lord's battail'. One of the most elaborate tales which suggested that only the bad were hurt by artillery concerned a gunner who took a loaded cannon into Parliamentarian Norwich,

> which the cannonier through covetousnesse, it being his fees, thought to save and make money of, and thrusting his spoone [ladle] into the peece to unlode it, the handle of the spoone unloosed out of the socket, where at the cannonier being vexed, in a fury he violently strucke the halfe pike into the piece, supposing to have fastened it unto the socket of the spoone and so to have drawne it out, but the steele of the halfe pike striking upon the bullet, by force of the strong concussion betweene those two hard things struct fire … the bullet raked downe the whole streete.

Miraculously the only persons hurt in this incident were said to be those 'disaffected' to the cause. In some Parliamentarian propaganda the enemy were sometimes portrayed not merely as heathen, but as though their ordnance were in fact idols in some perverted world view. Thus it was that one particularly zealous tract referred to a demi cannon taken outside Hull as a 'forraign brazen stave' which in the event had proved a mere broken 'reed'. Another Royalist gun – popularly known as the 'Gog and Magog' – was noted in a witticism of General Meldrum as 'one of the Queen's Gods'.[48]

---

[47]   Wiseman *Several Chirurgical Treatises*, pp 437, 451.

[48]   O. Sedgewicke *Military Discipline for the Christian Soldier*, London, 1639, sigs A3v–A4, BL E 75(9); *Shropshire's Misery and Mercie*, 8 November 1643, p 5, and BL E 93(18) *Certain Informations*, 13–20 March 1643, p 69; BL E 71(22) *A True and Exact Relation of the Great Victories Obtained by the Earl of Manchester and the Lord Fairfax*, 1642, pp 5, 8, and E 71(12) *Fresh Intelligence*, 17 October 1643, passim.

How quickly the Civil War gunner could load and fire his piece is open to some discussion, and even an 'average' figure for rate of fire can be misleading. A gun that was already charged at the beginning of an action could be loosed off in the twinkling of an eye. Following the first discharge things rapidly became more complicated. The very smallest pieces, with a full crew of experts, fresh and rested, and plenty of cartridges and ball laid close to hand, could probably be fired almost as quickly as muskets – certainly twice by the end of the first minute if the gun commenced the action loaded. Thereafter many different things could happen – the target might be obscured by smoke, or move away, or become engaged with friendly troops. The gunner might require more radical corrections to aim, or discover that his piece had recoiled back into a position from which it could not conveniently be discharged and have to order it to be pushed back into place. In all these cases there would be enforced pauses. The gunner might direct the team to continue to blast away into the smoke or throng, but in an age when ammunition supplies were relatively slender this would only be likely in an emergency. Larger guns were obviously much slower than light field pieces, being heavier to realign on the target, and having weightier shot and charge, but in sieges speed was far less critical than focusing shot upon a vital point. Sir James Turner was of the opinion that a three pound field gun could be discharged 'safely fifteen times in one hour', a 12 pound gun 12 times an hour, a demi cannon ten times, and a full cannon just eight times an hour. Contemporary opinions certainly varied. In Eldred's view ten shots an hour was about right for a gun that was 'well fortyfyed and strong' – though the rate should be dropped to eight for any others, and a rest and cooling of the piece after 40 rounds was advisable.[49]

In an experiment by the crew of a modern reconstruction a 6 pound piece has been timed running through some of the most likely loading drills used on the seventeenth century battlefield. To complete the cycle, without the ball, took approximately one minute and six seconds. If a ball was included and the gun fired, one and a quarter minutes would seem a very fair estimate of the time required. It would therefore appear that neither the gun drill nor the equipment itself was the main factor of limitation in terms of speed. The condition of the gunners, the availability of ammunition, the ability to see the target, and what the enemy were doing are therefore likely to have been more important in determining how many rounds were shot in a given time.[50]

Just how accurate the Civil War cannon actually was is difficult to state with certainty – and this undoubtedly varied from piece to piece, and with the skill of the crew. There are reported instances of individuals being 'picked off', or even ropes severed with devastating accuracy; but these were feats of luck as well as judgement. A major part of the problem was that the ball fired by smooth bore ordnance was not a snug fit to the barrel, a degree of 'windage'

[49] J. Turner *Pallas Armata*, London, 1683, p 196.
[50] Experimental data compiled by Roger Emmerson.

being allowed to ensure that missiles were easy to get into the gun, and did not become stuck on their way out – the result of such an accident being catastrophic. The gap or windage was normally about a quarter of an inch: enough to allow for any lack of precision in the formation of the barrel or projectile, but also sufficient for some latitute in the manner in which the ball departed from the cylinder. Then there was the brief pause it took for a gun, loaded and layed, to actually fire. Nevertheless the ordnance was accurate enough for the job it had to do – at one or two hundred yards short sections of wall, or large bodies of troops, were hit more often than not, and case shot sprayed 'soft' targets more effectively than any other weapon known. Modern tests have shown that wooden panels ten feet square can usually be hit with ball at one or two hundred yards with little difficulty. As Hime observed in 1870,

> On the whole the vice of the guns of the seventeenth century, in regard to accuracy, seems to have been, not so much the inaccuracy of any individual gun, as the great difference of range that existed between any two guns of the same length, weight and calibre, fired under the same conditions.[51]

In short no two guns, and no two gunners, were absolutely identical. Nevertheless Hime's statement has been qualified somewhat by modern archaeological investigation: some individual founders were replicating castings with a fair degree of accuracy, and guns were produced in 'series' to fire balls of the same size. Nevertheless there was no 'mass production', and barrels could wear, and ill fitting shot could deviate considerably. A fraction of an inch in error at the muzzle might well translate to a miss of many yards at half a mile, which was one reason why close ranges were so desirable. The only real answer to improved accuracy was practice – effectively experiment – with each piece to determine its characteristics. Eldred certainly encouraged gunners to number each gun, and to draw up an individual table of 'randons' showing how far it shot at different elevations. This certainly worked up to a degree – and was indeed a method revived during World War I when guns were pushed beyond their normal normal service life and began to deviate substantially from each other in performance. Yet this assumed gunners would have the luxury of staying with the same pieces, and the powder and shot with which to experiment. During the Civil Wars this cannot always have been the case.[52]

It is difficult to exaggerate how stunning contemporaries found the spectacle of a gun battery in action. The seventeenth century was essentially quiet: the loudest noise a person might hear on a daily basis was a peal of bells, the black-

---

[51] H.W.L. Hime 'The Field Artillery of the Great Rebellion: Its Nature and Use', in *Proceedings of the Royal Artillery Institution*, 6, 1870, pp 10–11.

[52] Eldred *The Gunner's Glasse*, p 165; on the accuracy of castings see C.J.M. Martin, 'Departicularizing the Particular: Approaches to the Investigation of Well-Documented Post-Medieval Shipwrecks', in *World Archaeology*, 32, number 3, pp 384–389.

smith's hammer, or the clatter of hooves. The noise of guns was in a different category; the only thing that could be compared to it was thunder. The cannon was the ultimate agent of human destruction, potentially a weapon of terror, and only God or nature could wreak more impressive ruin upon the puny works of man. This was the 'furie' of the ordnance. Little wonder then that artillery, authority, and kingship were related in the popular mind.

One of the first acts of King James I on English soil was personally to fire a cannon from the battlements of Berwick, as one somewhat sycophantic observer noted, executing the task with 'such signe of experience, that most of the expert gunners there beheld it, not without admiration'. Likewise his first visit to the Tower of London was marked by a salute of 100 guns and 130 gun chambers, with fireworks organised by the Ordnance Office. Most people were delighted by the displays; a few were not, being 'spoiled, burned and hurt'. The arrival of Christian IV of Denmark in 1606 was similarly greeted with 'joy' from 'the cannon's mouth', with Danish ships and English blockhouses firing many cannonades. James also repeated his party trick of setting off a gun. At Woolwich dockyard two years later the young Prince Henry was similarly delighted when Phineas Pett arranged for Master Gunner William Bull to discharge 31 chambers at the sign of a 'secret signal'. The Prince also wanted to fire a volley – but Pett and Bull decided that allowing the heir to the throne to blow himself up was not a good career move, and respectfully persuaded his highness that giving them the signal to do the work was more fitting for a Prince. Further salvoes welcomed the martial youngster at Chatham and Gravesend in 1611, when he received 15 gun salutes. In 1613 the cause of national celebration was the marriage of Princess Elizabeth and Frederick, Elector Palatine, and the orgy of artillery fire was planned by gunners John Nodes and Thomas Butler. It was said that 2000 blasts were fired, to the great amusement of the King who took 'little delight' in any of the other activities.[53]

Charles I may not have been quite so enthusiastic about his ordnance; nevertheless salutes with gunpowder remained a key form of royal celebration during his reign. By 1627 celebratory gunfire had become so common that during the war with France the King actually issued a proclamation forbidding such 'excessive waste'. This was but a temporary suspension. On 16 March 1630 gunfire was used in a particularly complex way to mark the Christening of Prince Charles. The ceremony itself was held at St Paul's, but by means of a relay of visual signals five Ordnance Office staff were able to relay the firing order back to John Bevis who stood atop the White Tower. The same year demi culverins were mounted on the Tower for the coronation festivities. The passing of important people could also be marked with gunfire. In 1631 Master Gunner of England John Reynolds submitted a bill to the Ordnance Office of 31s 6d,

53 J. Nichols *The Progresses, Processions and Magnificent Festivities of King James the First*, 1828, vol 1, pp 65–66, 118.

for so much disbursed and laid out at the funerall of the right Hon. the Earle
of Totnes, late Master of of his Maties. Ordnance, for torches, lincks, candles,
lanthornes, and other disbursements hereafter mentioned, at the discharging
of a peal of ordnance at his Lordshipps going away into the country to be
interred.

Similar offices were performed for Lord Vere, another former Master of the
Ordnance.[54]

Interestingly, ceremonial shooting sometimes doubled as practice. On 27
May 1635 a saluting by the fleet was suspended due to the fact that a ball
had shot up the beach, towards Deal, and 'broke a woman's leg'. Sir John
Oglander and Sir Bevis Thelwell experienced a similar scare whilst observing
the fleet from a rowing boat when 'the shot fell thicke' about them. During an
official cannonade at Sandham Lord Cottington was distressed when his best
'Spanioll' took fright and ran away. Nevertheless when he visited Cowes the
guns here were still let off eight times in his honour. Events such as this had
once put Lord Carew in mind of his favourite story of ceremonial gunfire at
the French court, when the salvoes were so loud and unexpected that the King
and Queen had panicked believing that a revolt had broken out.

Farce turned to horror in December 1635 when the young Elector Palatine
arrived by sea to visit his uncle's court. Enthusiastic gunners firing a salute
from the shore using ball accidentally hit the Prince's vessel, and five people
were killed. Little wonder that the Venetian ambassador described the lad as
'careworn and sad'. In the summer of 1639 an English fleet destined for Scotland appears to have indulged in almost obsessive saluting: towns, other ships,
people and special events were all met with a battery of fire. News of the paci-
fication of Berwick was greeted by a general fire throughout the fleet. At the
other end of the scale the Dean of Canterbury got a mere five rounds when he
went ashore. The first sound that John Evelyn heard on returning to England
in 1641 was a 12 gun salute from a pinnace.[55]

Even after the outbreak of the Civil Wars there were still *feu de joie*. For
example a simple welcoming barrage was given to Sir Thomas Fairfax on his
arrival at Newport. A much more complex salute was fired as a mark of respect
during the state funeral of the Earl of Essex in October 1646. This began
with a large cannon being fired at Southwark Fort, which was followed by a
shot from Vauxhall, and so on all around the London 'Lines of Communication', the whole ritual being repeated three times. Some years after the wars

[54] *A Proclamation Against the Unnecessary Waste of Gunpowder*, 1627; PRO WO 51/1, p 89;
WO 54/14, April–June 1635; PRO WO 49/110, ff 47–48.

[55] J. Downes *Brief Journall*, 1635, BL Lansdowne Ms 213, ff 1–3; W.H. Long (ed) *The Oglander
Memoirs*, Newport, 1888, pp 59–60; J. McLean (ed) *Letters from Lord Carew to Sir Thomas
Rowe*, Camden Soc. 1860, p 58; Austin Dobson (ed) *The Diary of John Evelyn*, 1908, p 24.

Cromwell's funeral involved the expenditure of a ton of gunpowder and 230 cartridges. This was slightly topped by the Restoration itself, upon which the new King Charles II was received with a 250 gun salute. Yet the record for the most gun happy man of the age is held by the master gunner of the ship *Marmaduke*, who, on sighting Jamaica in 1657, is reported to have unleashed a 600 gun salute.[56]

[56] PRO WO 47/4, f 411; PRO WO 54/20, July to September 1660.

2

'England's Vulcan': Artillery Supply under
the Early Stuarts

Ordnance production at the end of the reign of Elizabeth I was characterised by diversity both in terms of manufacturers and commercial interests. In late 1594, for example, we find six active founders in the Ordnance Office registers: Henry Pitt, Peter Gyll, Thomas Johnson, George Elkyn, Richard Phillips and Samuel Owen. Of these Pitt, Phillips and Owen appear to have concentrated primarily on the production of 'brass' (bronze) ordnance. Other persons who were not actually founders, such as Robert Evelyn, sometimes provided guns for state service, both through sub contracting and providing foreign pieces, captured or otherwise, thus acting as middle men. At the same date six or possibly seven furnaces capable of supplying guns were working under different iron masters in the Weald of Kent and Sussex.[1]

This situation would change comparatively rapidly over the next few years with the birth of a major gun founding dynasty – perhaps best described as a cartel – which would integrate production vertically and horizontally, consolidating financial interests in a relatively few hands. It was built up not only through consummate craftsmanship, management, and product diversification, but by successive bargains with changing regimes – and single-minded exploitation of the methods of the period, judicious marriage and purchased monopoly. Perhaps unusually little resource was diverted to fund the traditional trappings of success such as titles or extensive estates, nor was the business put in hock to one creed or brand of politics which might have proved its undoing. The father of this concern was Thomas Browne of Brenchley (born 1559), a son of Thomas Browne of Yalding in Kent and his wife 'Cicely', a daughter of Jasper Iden. Young Thomas Browne's first industrial enterprise was the running of Thomas Willoughby's furnace at Bough Beech, near Chiddingstone. He actually purchased the ironworks, together with a parcel of land in 1589, paying £1,047, though whether capital to fund this purchase was gathered through

[1] PRO WO 54/1 October–December 1594; see also E.B. Teesdale *Gunfounding in the Weald in the Sixteenth Century*, London, 1991, p 40, and O.F.G. Hogg *Artillery: Its Origin, Heyday and Decline*, London, 1970, Appendix III.

other family interests or his work in the iron business during war with Spain is unknown. In the 1590s Browne was accredited as a supplier of shot to the Crown.[2]

At the accession of King James Browne's particular significance was recognised with the title of 'his majesties founder of yron shot'. With this post went a daily fee of 6d, though according to later complaints this nominal sum was seldom paid; what mattered was the formal status and commercial connections that the title bestowed. Within another three years Browne was working the Ashurst furnace, previously run by John Phillips. Though Browne was still behind the first rank of the 'King's gun founders' in the pecking order of patronage – their positions being worth 12d a day in 1603 – the fact that initially James ordered relatively few actual guns may paradoxically have worked to Browne's advantage. For whilst gun orders were limited demand for iron shot continued, and in 1604 he gained possession of the Horsmonden furnace that had once been run by Thomas Johnson. By his own testimony Browne had produced less than 500 tons of guns prior to the turn of the century, but in the reign of King James he virtually cornered the market, producing an estimated average total of 100 tons of ordnance per furnace per annum.

Geography formed part of the Browne strategy to capture the domestic market. Thomas Browne appears to have concentrated his efforts on the Kent side of the Weald; here at least part of the iron he required could be had from Tonbridge – William Bartlett being one of the suppliers of iron bars mentioned – and there was also access to charcoal. Both Tonbridge and Goudhurst were increasing in population, and already boasted cloth and iron works as prominent features. Similarly Horsmonden and Chiddingstone were relatively easy to reach from the Medway. The use of water transport to the mouth of the river enabled the delivery of heavy products to London via the Thames, or to the east coast ports and Low Countries. By good judgement or good fortune these would be the key markets for iron guns for several decades to come. For Browne's competitors on the Sussex side of the Ashdown Forest it was not so simple. Here the waterways were less convenient, and in any case ran south to the sea. Guns shipped from Meeching, near Newhaven, could be transported to France or Spain more directly – but in the seventeenth century these powers would become the enemy at different periods. Transport to London from the Sussex foundries was far more problematic, produce having to be carted long distance across country, perhaps via East Grinstead and Croydon, or alternatively carried all the way around the Channel coast, thereby adding to costs.

The Brownes further capitalised on their geographic advantage by use of their own wharf at Milhall on the Medway where the output of the furnaces could

---

2   Kent Archive Office, TR 1295/97 *The Pedigree of George Browne of Spelmonden*. PRO 54/1 January to March 1596 and October to December 1599; H. Cleere and D. Crossley *The Iron Industry of the Weald*, 2nd edn, Cardiff, 1995, pp 170–182.

conveniently be mustered on one site and the officers of the ordnance could examine and test the guns before accepting them for government service. Until the 1630s the guns were carted as far as Milhall, but thereafter the river was made navigable as far up stream as Yalding. Milhall however continued to be the most convenient place for testing as the narrow fourteenth century bridge across the river at Aylesford meant that large cargoes had to be transhipped in any case – carting and loading of the guns was therefore kept to the minimum. Doubtless most of the pieces were tested resting on beds or banks of earth, since at this stage they would not yet have been fitted with carriages. Guns that were accepted could be reloaded onto vessels for London, whilst failed guns and scrap metal were collected for return to the furnace. Thomas Browne may not actually have established the wharf at Milhall personally because proof testing had been going on here from at least the early 1590s. Since that time, over a period of half a century, successive proof masters, Stephen and William Bull, William Hammond, John Reynolds and John Dwarris, had ridden down from London to carry out this duty.

Another advantage of Milhall, which could not have been foreseen when ordnance work started here in the reign of Elizabeth, was its very close proximity to the old priory of Aylesford. 'The Friars', just a few yards from the wharf, had been sold into private ownership at the dissolution of the monasteries, and after the outbreak of the Civil War the substantial buildings here were sequestered for the use of Parliament. For some time the Kent County Committee met at the priory. It may be that the substantial 'Great Barn' and courtyard were then used as safe storage for ordnance, but even if this is not so the fact that the gentlemen of the Committee, and Browne and his employees, came into contact at this spot cannot but have made communication between customers and suppliers so much the easier.

Almost predictably the Browne clan would firmly cement its business relationships at Milhall, both with the local hierarchy, and with the Ordnance Office, by means of marriages. John Browne, who inherited the iron business, married Martha a daughter of the influential Tylden family in 1616, whilst one of his sisters married Henry Tylden. Perhaps most judiciously of all Thomas Browne's youngest daughter was matched with John Dwarris. Since Dwarris was the government proof master from 1623 until after the start of the Civil War, it becomes apparent that John Browne was having his wares tested by his own brother in law. This union may have been a love match between a young lady and a dashing visitor who had the glamourous job of dramatic detonations for a living; but if so it was still extremely convenient to all parties. Thomas and John Browne were wealthy men, not likely to have neglected the dowry of a daughter or sister, and Dwarris must have been acutely aware that any failure of the family business was not in his own interest either.

That the Weald was a hive of industry in the early seventeenth century, quite unlike its bucolic appearance today, is made clear by a description by William Camden, writing in his *Britannia*.

Full of iron mines it is in sundry places, where for the making and founding thereof, there be furnaces on every side, and a huge deal of wood is yearly burnt; to which purpose divers brooks in many places are brought to run in one channel, and sundry meadows turned into pools and waters, that they might be of power sufficient to drive hammer mills, which beating upon the iron, resound over the places adjoining.

Interestingly the village of Horsmonden, which became effectively the head-quarters of the Browne family business, came to be shaped by its industry. In the medieval era the population had not been nucleated, but dispersed widely over an area which extended almost five miles north to south. During the early modern era the settlement became centred on the Browne iron works, leaving the church standing a good distance off – as well it might, since even in those religious times God was entitled to only one full day of the week. Nevertheless founding in the Wealden iron works of the 1620s and 1630s was by no means continuous, but run as a series of 'campaigns', which it has been estimated occupied 30 to 35 weeks a year. By tradition it is the building which now serves as the 'Gun and Spitroast' public house at Horsmonden from which operations were now directed, though the family owned a number of other properties elsewhere. A few hundred yards away down a hill at the edge of the present village is the great furnace pond, though there is little surface evidence of the substantial buildings which must once have stood at the outlet nearest to the road. Wisely Browne did not only make cannon, but a range of domestic products including fire backs and pots and pans, which doubtless helped him through times of peace and other slack periods. He also ventured into bronze ordnance, so vying with competitors for their market share, hitherto safe from such domestic intrusion. A further squeeze was applied to the traditional bronze founders in 1611 with a rise in the price of their raw material, which left them petitioning Lord Carew for this increase to be recognised in the price they were given by the Crown for their wares.[3]

As early as the period from 1608 to 1615, when John began to take over the family business, the Brownes appear to have achieved a lasting market domi-nance. In 1609 there were only five furnaces reported as capable of casting guns, one in Kent, three in Sussex, and one in Glamorgan – the Brownes thus had the most significant interest in the part of the country which already had upwards of 80 per cent of production. That same year Sir Roger Dallison, Lieutenant of the Ordnance, was granted £1000 specifically for the purchase of ordnance from Brenchley and Horsmonden, and by 1613 it was claimed that 200 men were employed in casting ordnance at Brenchley. A formal monopoly was granted in 1614, and records of 1615 show the existence of debentures in favour of the business to the tune of £5000; John Browne was not slow to capi-

3 *CSPD* LXIV, 8 June 1611, p 24; PRO WO 49/25–35; BL Royal Ms 17A XXXI, *Survey of the Ordnance*, J. Linewraye, 1603.

talise on commercial opportunity. For the period from 1615 to the outbreak of the Thirty Years War the government appears not to have questioned the export of ordnance too closely, perhaps due to the funds which were incoming through export licences and customs payments. A market for ordnance was also found in the East India Company, and in 1616 Sir Noel Caron was given permission to transport 200 pieces of iron ordnance to the Dutch. In 1618 warrants were issued for the transport of a further 200 guns to Scotland, and it is probable that most of this was originally sourced from John Browne and his associates.

Rather more controversially a licence for the export of 100 brass pieces bound for Spain was granted to the Conde de Gondomar. This sounds like boom time, and there were also stories of unscrupulous sea captains who bought guns, ostensibly to outfit their vessels, then returned without ordnance at a later date only to require refitting. How large these 'invisible' exports became can only be guessed. Until the commencement of European hostilities in 1618 the government appears to have been largely unconcerned about these sales, but the following year John Browne was called to account for what was happening in the ordnance trade. He was also commanded to deliver existing stocks to the Tower. Perhaps understandably Browne pleaded ignorance of what was happening in the four Sussex furnaces which were then operating outside his direct business control, but stated openly that 'more than half' of the guns made by him and his 20 servants in recent years were bought for export to the Dutch. Orders were issued that 130 guns awaiting export were to be held, unless specific warrants could be shown that they were for the East India company, or other authorised outlets. At the end of 1619 government officials were also poking about the yard at Milhall, making inventories and checking that nothing was going 'by stealth beyond the seas'.[4]

Browne reacted badly to what he saw as hypocrisy on the part of the authorities. As they well knew, he made guns for the Crown and had paid for the privilege of doing so; he sought out relevant permissions, and also sold only to those of good reputation, no business being capable of surviving without a market. As he explained in 1620 regarding his sale of guns to Lord Caron,

> Having no employment either for his Majesty or the East India Company, I supposed that I might lawfully make my market where I might find it, especially to such as were never known to have shipped any ordnance, but had sufficient warrant for it. Four years ago my father and myself had special warrant to make for Mr Elias Tripp, Commissary for the States [of the Netherlands] 200 great pieces and less pieces in proportion, but more being cast than was needed, they yet remain at Milhall, in Kent. Lord Caron's merchant,

4   C. Foulkes *Gunfounders of England*, London, 1937, pp 75, 113; *CSPD* CXXVI, 4 February 1614; Kent Archives Office, TR 1295/48. The 20 persons referred to by Browne would appear to be subcontractors, foremen, founders and skilled craftsmen – but do not include temporary labourers, carters and the like; see also R.R. Brown 'Gunfounder to the Stuarts', part 1, in *Wealden Iron*, 2nd series, number 25, 2005, pp 38–61.

hoping to obtain another license from his majesty, bought more pieces of me, who never thought but that I might sell freely to one as his Lordship. The said ordnance was sold and delivered almost a year before the orders for the bringing of the same to Tower Hill. If I had not sold that ordnance to Lord Caron, I had not been able to keep my men at work.[5]

Not long afterwards came what Browne regarded as a cynical attempt to muscle in on his business by 'Master Crow' a kinsman of the solicitor general, attempting to profiteer on the war that was now raging in Central Europe. Browne's defiant response was at once robust and practical – stating his prior claim, but at the same time suggesting that if Sackville Crow wanted part of the action all he had to do was join with the Browne cartel.

my father has for the last 30 years cast ordnance for the late Queen, and the king, and for years maintained the trade alone. At request of the Ordnance Officers and the East India Company, I was put to the trade that I might continue if my father failed which I have done, and produced recently two such pieces as I would challenge others to do the like. If I may still cast for merchants, if the King wanted 200 pieces, I will cast them in 200 days. Mr Crow has got a patent for sole making of ordnance for merchants; this would confine me to the King's service, which takes only 10 days a year. You know how the patent was obtained, and that the Commissioners advised there should be two furnaces for King and merchants, intending me to have one.

You know what Parliament ordered: the knights to whom it was referred certified on my behalf. If anyone thinks he can perform the service without me, let him try. If I have to cease working and then should be ordered any sudden service, it would take a long time, for I must cut and coal the wood, draw the mine, and work it into ordnance, if it be but for 20 pieces. If Mr Crow will join me friendly, there will be work for both …

Browne would further point out that lack of experience on behalf of Sackville and his workmen made it highly unlikely that they would be able to produce large pieces of ordnance immediately – any new contractor would be better off practising making smaller guns. Nevertheless he was realistic, and accepting that powerful men had decided that Crow would share the trade, he later put forward various options as to the practical division of responsibilities. It is remarkable how similar John Browne's arguments were to those put forward regarding armaments industries in succeeding centuries. Home production of armaments was a major plank of national security, but maintaining the facility for production through times of peace was expensive – unless supported by exports. Unfettered export might however put modern arms into the hands of those very enemies against threat of whom the industry was being preserved. In the event the government, who wanted income from both monopolists buying their way into trade, and from taxes on trade, seem to have reached a some-what uneasy temporary compromise – maintaining Browne as supplier to the

5   *CSPD* XLII (Addenda) 1620, pp 629–630.

Crown whilst also allowing Sackville Crow to operate a furnace. Crow appears to have maintained some sort of interest in the market for supplying merchants until as late as 1632.[6]

Apart from what he viewed as unreasonable competition Browne was also faced with difficulties in receiving payment for the guns that he cast for the Crown. Commonly payment lagged months, or even years, behind delivery. Sometimes it was even worse. In a particularly well documented instance from 1625 Browne contracted with Francis Morice, Clerk of the Ordnance to provide 300 pieces for '30 Newcastle Ships'. It was agreed that he should receive £1,000 in advance from a Privy Seal allotment of £10,348 for the furnishing of the vessels, with the rest of the bill to be settled on delivery. Nothing was forthcoming. Browne was however a man of sterner mettle than many who dealt with government offices. Just before Christmas the officers of the ordnance were forced to write to Secretary Coke with unpleasant news: Browne, 'not finding any present satisfaction, and having spent five weeks in attending in hope to receive money they had not been able to persuade him to further patience'. Thus he had departed 'into the country with determination to employ himself in such works as would yield him ready money'. Though this was conduct which might have ruined a lesser man this dispute must have been resolved in some fashion, for within a couple of months Browne was again casting guns for government service.[7]

This time the object was to make light iron pieces, perhaps with the intention of supplanting more expensive 'brass' types. Elsewhere in Europe similar experiments were already afoot, and without adequate light guns of their own there was a significant danger that English forces, maritime and land, would be technologically eclipsed. Thomas Pitt the bronze founder already claimed to have reduced the weight of bronze cannon from 7,000 pounds to 4,100, demi cannon from 5,300 to 3,300 and culverins from 3,800 to 2,200 pounds. John Reynolds Master Gunner and Proofmaster tested six of Browne's new light iron guns at Milhall on 8 March 1626. Browne had fulfilled his contract but Reynolds observed that the lightness of the new design of gun had its drawbacks, lack of weight in the piece meaning that the shot was delivered 'uncertainly'. In his opinion therefore the best use of these 'drakes' would be on the upper decks of ships, for use when heavier guns could not be brought to bear upon the target. Nevertheless the new lightweight guns were useful at a range of 'eleven or twelve score yards' – or 220 to 240 yards – a distance which was perfectly adequate according to most mariners.

The Navy Commissioners who had been directed to conduct these lightweight experiments stated to the Privy Council that they had consulted 'divers

---

6 *CSPD* XLII, December 1621, p 639; E.W. Lloyd and A.G. Hadcock *Artillery: Its Progress and Present Position*, Portsmouth, 1893, p 4.
7 *CSPD* XI, 6 December 1625, p 171, and 8 December, p 173; IXX, 1625, pp 182, 184; warrant of 13 November 1625 in *CSPD* IX, 13 November 1625, p 149.

gunfounders' but had found only Browne willing to undertake the work. The guns had endured the 'King's Double Proof' – or double the normal charge of powder – and so they recommended that Browne should therefore be given £200 for his services. A report of November 1627 states that the key features of the new guns were short barrels, the use of better 'more refined metal' in their casting, and a chamber bore that tapered towards the touch hole – effectively creating a thicker walled breech. Interestingly it was also implied that there were already attempts afoot to make standard the 3 pound and 12 pound shot – the former approximating to the old 'falcon', the latter to the 'demi culverin'. Tragic illustration of the percipience of Reynolds and the Commissioners, and the very real value of researching light ordnance, was provided from Sweden less than a year later when the 64 gun Wasa fired a 'Svensk Losen', or gun salute, in Stockholm harbour – and promptly turned turtle. New 'Drakes' – already ordered from Browne – now began to be fitted to Royal Navy ships.[8]

About the time of these episodes, and probably as a result of renewed threat from France, Lord Carew received demands from the Privy Council that King's Lynn and Yarmouth should be supplied with 12 and 20 culverins respectively. The officers of the ordnance were forced to admit that 'his majesty has no such ordnance in his stores' – nor could these guns be taken off ships. The King's founder could supply them if the townsmen had funds, or the Crown could supply 'present money' to the tune of £1,109. Within three weeks Carew was able to furnish the weapons, but warned that such demands were likely to lead to requests from other towns to the detriment of the navy. In the four years between the accession of King Charles and August 1629 a total of 931 iron guns were brought into the government stores, and even allowing that some of these might have come from ships that were laid up, or moved to London from outlying fortifications, it is likely that the majority came from Browne and his confederates. This is made even more probable by the fact that by June 1628 he was owed £11,062 by the Crown, and that it was now thought that the various foundries, forges and other concerns under Browne direction were employing the better part of 1,000 workers.[9]

In the early 1630s another factor with which John Browne had to contend was the King's attempt to limit the use of the small 'Drakes', or lightweight taper chambered pieces, 'to his own particular service'. Strenuous efforts were also made to prevent knowledgeable workmen from going abroad, and to tie named founders and artisans to the trade – even making Browne responsible

8   *CSPD* XXII, 13 March 1626, p 279; XXV, 28 April 1626, p 320; PRO SP 16/25/79; see also R.M. Towes and P. McCree 'A Note on Drakes', in *Journal of the Ordnance Society*, 6, 1994, pp 39–47; L.A. Kvarning and B. Ohrelius *The Swedish Warship Wasa*, Stockholm, 1973, passim.
9   *CSPD* XXIV, 3 and 4 April 1626, p 301; XXV, 24 April, p 318; VII, 16 June 1626, p 165; CXLVIII, 5 August 1629, p 204.

for their conduct. This was a sure indicator that light field guns were perceived as the technology of the moment, but being unable to sell something which was in demand was anathema to Browne. He therefore argued that the spread of such ordnance amongst his majesty's subjects was no 'inconvenience', but on the contrary a protection of their lives and goods. Curiously whilst this attempt to limit the proliferation of technology was one facet of royal policy another was to export ordnance to the Netherlands in an effort to balance foreign debts. To this end Browne was granted new export licences, and the King agreed to take £11 on each ton. In the event however Browne claimed that the Dutch market was not sufficiently active, and requested permission to export to Italy. At the same time he complained that he was at a disadvantage against the Dutch who were able to bring their vessels to Upnor for loading whilst his own contractors were limited to Gillingham, though the ordnance officers denied that this was the case.[10]

Perhaps a more significant issue in the 1630s was competition from Sweden – and it was this, added to the perceived danger that the Crown might be reduced to sourcing guns from abroad that Browne stated as the motivation for applying for extensions to his monopoly. Actually the Swedes did have some advantages with which English manufacturers would have had trouble competing, and might be put forward as justification for a patriotic protectionist stance. In contrast to England Sweden was now fully committed to the Thirty Years War, leading to strong demand. Gustavus Adolphus and his ministers encouraged experiment, notably in the area of light battlefield artillery, and were themselves prepared to protect their home industry. Just as importantly Sweden had very significant reserves of copper and high grade iron, and by campaigning in central Europe could either extend their share of production, or at least deny like reserves to other powers.

In his lobbying Browne cleverly drew attention to musket makers, who, in the reign of James I, had moved themselves and their 'manufactory' to the Netherlands. To avoid the like occurring in the ordnance trade Browne proposed that his monopoly be extended to cast iron pots, kettles, fire backs, salt pans and soap pans – in short many of the staples of domestic life and cottage industry. Browne's pressure was also subtle and multifaceted as he noted that the Crown still owed him £10,250, and had himself paid £12, 000 over the period 1631 to 1634 for licences to export guns and shot – whilst Swedish competition had reduced the prices he could charge. In contrast to a situation where he had to pay dearly for materials and labour in England the Swedes actively encouraged Dutch entrepreneurs to relocate to Sweden by the grant of woods, mines and other privileges designed to boost Swedish production. Overall Browne estimated that he had engaged 'himself and his friends' to the tune of £26,000. If

---

10 *CSPD* CLXXV, 24 November 1630, p 389; CLXIII, 19 March 1630, p 214; CLXXIX, 1630, p 436; CCIV, 2 December 1631, p 195; *Acts of the Privy Council*, vol 45, p 135; R.R. Brown 'Gunfounder to the Stuarts', pp 56–57.

the King did not support Browne now he would sacrifice his ability to make war on a par with his European neighbours, lose revenue, and would increase the number of creditors at his door. Given the current situation of the eleven years without a Parliament, and the blow to the foundations of the monarchy that an inability to provide guns for ships or forts might strike, Browne, quite literally, had the authorities 'over a barrel'.[11]

In 1635 the noble lords of the admiralty came to consider Browne's proposals, and despite their very natural doubts were moved by the obvious 'great importance' of the manufacture of ordnance. Browne's request to be granted sole manufacture of industrial and domestic ironware, though it carried,

> the show of monopoly, yet considering the Swedish ordnance has so beaten down the market beyond the seas, that the petitioner makes no ordnance for exportation and only a small quantity to supply the market in England, and unless there may be some other employment to keep the petitioner and his servants at work, they will be compelled to seek employment beyond the seas, and the trade of making iron ordnance, first invented in England, will be lost.

They therefore recommended that the extension of the iron monopoly be granted, and though they suggested that there should be a proviso that it could be ended at a later date it was also advised that it continue long enough that Browne could be compensated for what he was owed.

Intriguingly Browne now argued that export licences were liabilities: he paid £11,000 to export 1,000 tons of ordnance to the Dutch, but found that Tripp's company, with their Swedish monopoly were able to sell at eight guilders per hundred weight against a normal price of twelve. A further reduction was expected with the specific intention of excluding the English from the market. Browne attempted, in his usual way, by 'sending a friend' to 'settle a contract' either to prevent the practices of the Dutch entrepreneur – or to make an agreement with him, thus forming an international cartel. Tripp had realised there was no advantage for him in such an arrangement, and had spun out negotiations in the hope of making Browne 'weary' and 'force him to forbear transporting'. Browne therefore requested permission to take his goods elsewhere, or, unlikely as it seemed, to be reimbursed. Whatever the detail Browne got his monopoly on both iron guns and domestic wares, and Sackville Crow – a long term annoyance – appears to have decamped his business to the Forest of Dean.[12]

This illustration of dealings with the Dutch in the 1630s is an apt reminder that though Browne vigourously pursued monopoly it is clear that we should regard him more as the head of a cartel – rather than a sole trader or simply

11 *CSPD* CCLXXIX, 1634, p 385. It is interesting to note the beginning of the Krupp family armaments industry in Germany at the same period: see W. Manchester *The Arms of Krupp*, London, 1969, pp 38–44.
12 *CSPD* CCXCIV, 22 July 1635, p 288; CCCVI, 1635, p 18.

head of one business. Indeed, when we consider that small pieces of ironwork such as nails, hinges, horse shoes and other products of the smithy were made all over the country, total control of all iron was never a practical proposition. There is certainly evidence in what remains of the family papers that his position of strength was achieved as much through efforts to control production, joint marketing, and price fixing, as much as attempts to take possession of furnaces. His relationship with his 'servants' and 'suppliers' varied, but some at least were essentially subcontractors, and others acquired significant wealth in the course of their association with the Browne family. Amongst these associates were Henry Quintayne, William Bassaige, Thomas Hawkins, and Richard and Thomas Foley.

William Bassaige of Horsmonden, described in a contemporary document as a 'gunfounder', had already amassed considerable funds as early as 1632, when he spent £300 on 72 acres of land purchased from John Tylden. According to Hasted's chronicle Bassaige eventually came to live at 'Catts Place' – though even in the 1630s he was described as living in a 'Mansion House'. Interestingly Bassaige was just one of at least 28 Wealden 'founders and fillers' working for John Browne and named by acts of the Privy Council as vital to the ordnance trade about this time. Whether Bassaige's level of wealth was usual in this group is unknown, but if it was anything like typical it gives a good reason for the way that the towns and villages of the Weald were growing at this time – and indeed attracting migrant workers and vagabonds from elsewhere. Some time during the Civil War Parliamentarian negotiators recognised that in the absence of Browne himself, some 'fitt person' might deputise to sign papers on John Browne's behalf. Henry Quintayne did indeed act as a proxy in exactly this way from time to time – and Browne gave surety that should he himself die during the 'terme of the contract' it would nevertheless be made good by others. Thomas Hawkins was perhaps only a servant or employee of Browne, but still appeared to have earned a very comfortable living. When he died in 1652 his will mentioned not only £100 in gold but £100 in silver – and he was still owed £33 6s 8d in unpaid wages. Loose change in his closet and desk amounted to a further £8 12s, and his horse was worth £10. A sum of £3 10s was owed to him 'by accompt of tobacco', and the whole estate totalled about £566 – a massive amount when many were supporting families on less than a shilling a day, and had little or no savings. His funeral and other charges at his death amounted to over £59.[13]

Whilst the Browne monopoly appeared secure for the time being, and at least some of the contractors were earning very good livings, new financial squeezes were never far away under a cash strapped King Charles. In 1636 the latest ruse to raise extra cash was the seventeenth century equivalent of a 'green issue'. This was financial penalties to be applied to iron masters, 'occupiers of

---

[13] H. Hasted *The History and Topographical Survey of the County of Kent*, Canterbury, 1778–1799, vol II, p 369. The indenture referring to Bassaige is in the possession of the author.

iron works, forges, furnaces or hammers' and the like, who had expanded their works beyond their pre-existing bounds, or had cut down trees, traditionally used for timber, for the making of charcoal. The commission granted to Sir David Cuningham tasked him and his agents to take the opportunity to 'treat and compound' with offenders, the bulk of the money raised from fines being returned to the Crown. John Cupper and Grimbald Pauncefoot were granted the title of 'Surveyors' of the iron works, and employed to mark iron production.

The Browne cartel diversified into the production of bronze ordnance for the Crown in 1634, partly, it is thought, to find a way around some of the financial problems that were manifesting themselves with the production of iron. It was certainly an opportune moment since the Royal Navy was now being modernised and expanded, and much bronze ordnance was required. The fact that bronze guns achieved much higher prices may also have been an attraction. Initially it was proposed that the old foundry of the recently deceased Richard Phillips, at Hounsditch, on the outskirts of London would be used, but Browne balked at the idea of using the old works. Instead he chose the familiar surroundings of Brenchley in the Weald. The reasons for this decision are unclear, and transporting the raw materials – including obsolete guns for recasting – a considerable distance, does not at first sight make much commercial sense. It has to be suspected however that Browne did have good reasons. He may have wished to keep his activity in one general locality so as to transfer labour and charcoal from one task to another; he may have been suspicious of the motives of those who wanted his furnace so close to London; or he may have seen ways to ensure that the transport that went up to London fully laden also came back full. Equally he may have seen an opportunity to have one of his sites refurbished at Crown expense, and indeed a few years later he does appear to have extracted £1,000 for this purpose. Whatever the reason from this time onward bronze as well as iron guns were cast in Kent, and a succession of navy vessels were equipped by Browne and his associates. These included the *James, Unicorn, Leopard, Swallow, Expedition* and *Antelope*. Despite a fire which caused considerable damage to the furnace the decision to reengineer the business in this way proved to be an extremely good one. Few iron guns appear to have been made by any competitor in the Forest of Dean, and rival manufacture in bronze was limited to the Pitt concern in London, which was apparently unable to contract for more than a dozen guns a year. Complaints by concerns who failed to compete effectively with John Browne suggest that he also managed to attract skilled workers from failing businesses.

It was arguably 1638 that marked the pinnacle of John Browne's achievement under the early Stuart monarchy. For that year he was engaged on the prestigious, and highly lucrative, contract to cast the bronze ordnance for the mighty new Royal Navy ship *Sovereign of the Seas*. The raw materials were copper sourced from the Society of the Mines Royal, smelted at Keswick, and tin from Cornwall. Delivered in bars to the works at Brenchley the metal was melted again and cast into eight different types of guns of the latest design, adorned with a rose, crown, anchor and trident. The biggest pieces were seven inch cannon, and 'demi cannon drakes', weighing anything up to 57 hundredweight, the smallest abbreviated 'demi culverin drake cutts'. In all 145 tons of bronze was used in the 102 pieces manufactured for the *Sovereign* and the total cost was £23, 525 – though the bills were not completely settled for about two years. Of this big order six guns were made by Pitt, and 96 by Browne. Somewhat unusually the Browne guns were proofed on site at Brenchley – and the heavy cannon balls ploughing through adjoining land 'spoiled' the ground so much that the owner was compensated to the tune of £6, being £3 for the use of the land and a further £3 for the damage. To this day the site is marked by 'Flightshott Farm'. Nor was this the only order at the time – some guns were made for forts, and 3 pounder Drakes were also made for a train of guns for land service. The crowning glory of 1638 was a visit to Brenchley by the King, who watched a 4 pound bronze gun being made, and upon the breech of which was incised the legend, 'Cast in presence of his Majesty October the Fifth. Mountjoy Earle of Newport Mr Generall of the Ordnance, John Browne Made this Peece'.[14]

Though fully comprehensive data on gun testing is lacking, Thomas Smith had laid out an ideal scheme in 1600 to determine whether a gun would 'hold or no' on firing. In his proof test plan guns firing ball of less than ten pounds weight and 'duly fortified with metal' were to be fired three times, once with a charge of powder equal to the weight of shot; once with a charge twenty per cent heavier than the shot; and finally with powder weighing fifty per cent more than the projectile. Any piece so tested would, he said, 'hold for any service, being charged with her ordinary charge, albeit the said peece were discharged 100 times in one day'. For larger ordnance Smith's recommendations were slightly less demanding, being three charges of two thirds projectile weight, five sixths, and finally a loading equal to the projectile in weight. The actual setting off of each charge was probably executed in exactly the same way as had been set out by Cyprian Lucar in the reign of Elizabeth, by means of a 'trayne of gunpowder', with the proof master safely hidden behind a sturdy bank of earth in case the gun split during trial.[15]

By the Civil War we do know that proof firing was rather less elaborate, being reduced to a single shot. This is made clear by five surviving examples of tests made by the Ordnance Office between May 1644 and July 1645 in which

---

[14] PRO WO 49/75; 49/78; R. Towes 'The Casting of Bronze Guns in the Weald in the Seventeenth Century', in *Wealden Iron*, 1st series, 11, 1977, pp 15–20; A.B. Caruana *The History of English Sea Ordnance: The Age of Evolution*, vol 1, Rotherfield, 1994, pp 47–74; the gun cast in the presence of the King is item XIX. 182 in the Royal Armouries collection.

[15] Thomas Smith *Art of Gunnery*, London, 1600 edn, p 53; PRO WO 54/2 April–June 1597 and 54/6 January–March 1609; Milhall, probably meaning 'mill corner' had existed since at least the fourteenth century, see J. Glover *Place Names of Kent*, Chatham, 1976, p 128.

only sufficient powder was allocated to allow for one discharge per gun. The only exception to this general rule were mortars, which usually appear to have been tested with three discharges. A table prepared by the Ordnance Office in 1657 specified exactly how much powder, in pounds, was to be used for each class of gun as follows,

Gun Type	'Fortified'	'Drake'	'Cutts'
Demi Cannon	22	12–15	—
Culverin	14	9	7
Demi Culverin	9	6–7	4.5
Saker [6 lb?]	5.25	4.25	2.75
Minion	4	2.5	1.75
Falcon	2.5	—	—
3 Pounder	3.75	1.25	—

This is particularly informative for it provides a list of the ordnance most likely to need testing at this time, and because it demonstrates that light 'drakes' were indeed regarded as a lower power type of weapon, and that short guns or 'cuts' were not expected to be as resilient as full length pieces. Moreover if we compare the weights of powder mentioned with those suggested by Smith earlier on, and with the weight of shot for each type, we discover that the tests used at this later period were actually somewhat less demanding. They do however continue to reflect the fact that smaller guns were proportionately stronger than larger ones. This reflected the basic mathematics of balls and hollow cylinders, as the mass of a sphere increases more rapidly with size than does the cylinder when both are increased in proportion. Interestingly Parliamentarian ordnance papers also refer to proof testing of guns at Snodland, a mile or two downstream from Milhall, and to some tests at the 'Gunfield' in London. Snodland would have allowed for greater space in which to carry out this dangerous work, whilst the trials in London are likely to have related to pieces which were delivered from other sources, or to guns which required retesting after long service. Another sign of the much expanded production at this later period was the work of James Rothwell at Snodland, who was hired by the State specifically 'to weigh old brasse at Snodland' – presumably being the debris from the non ferrous guns which had failed their test.[16]

By the eve of the Civil War the Browne achievements had been remarkable. In two generations, over a period of barely fifty years, the family business had risen from a small fragment of the artillery market in England to total dominance. Any competition from the West Country or the old London founders was modest at best – in domestic iron work Browne clearly had the whip hand, complaining about minor infringements from Gloucestershire, for example, as they came to notice. Browne himself began to take interests in the Forest of

---

[16] PRO WO 47/ ff 41, 53, 130–133, 316 – recording a total of 48 gun proof tests; PRO WO 47/2 ff 80, 164–165, 254, 325.

Dean – these being granted against outstanding debts that remained unpaid. The King was now clearly counted as a serious patron, and in September 1639 the Browne monopoly was extended for a remarkable 21 years. When some of the employees were conscripted for service in Scotland Browne was able to get them released – because they worked for him in what was effectively a 'reserved occupation'. The Weald was clearly the vital place for the government to source its guns. Orders for guns for field service and forts in Ireland were made from 1639 to 1641, and it was some of these, still undelivered in 1642, which were still on hand at the outbreak of Civil War. As with troops and other types of munitions, gathered for Ireland but as yet unused, these would be significant to the way in which events unfolded with the descent into conflict.

Technical expertise in manufacture, and entrepreneurial success in salesmanship and protection of rights, would not have been enough to maintain the industry in the absence of markets and customers. On both counts the strategic policy of Charles I and the management of the procurement system – in the shape of the Ordnance Office and its personnel – were crucial. The central figure in the London Ordnance Office of this period was undoubtedly Sir John Heydon (1588–1653), Lieutenant of the Ordnance. For whilst the title of 'Master' of the Ordnance was granted as a royal favour to noble non-specialists, the day to day work of planning, procurement, and preparation of ordnance stores fell to the Lieutenant and his immediate subordinates, the Surveyor, the Clerk of the Ordnance, the Keeper of the Store, and the Clerk of Deliveries. Sir John Heydon was a younger son of Sir Christopher Heydon of Baconsthorpe in Norfolk, and his early military experience was as Captain of Sandown Castle. His older brother William served as Lieutenant until his career was cut short by his death on the Isle de Rhe expedition of 1627 – 'carried by a rabble of flying soldiers into the sea and there drowned'. By the end of that year John had stepped into his brother's shoes, but was facing a monumental task.[17]

In May 1628 the Office was estimated to be underfunded to the tune of £227,000; Parliament was voting money that was undelivered; the Surveyor was dead; and the firemaster, Deacons Bull, had suffered 18 wounds including the loss of an arm in action. Sir Thomas Strafford acted as Deputy Master, receiving warrants direct from the Privy Council from which he was able to extract personal benefit. At this highly inopportune moment the Duke of Buckingham had now suggested that Sir John go and fight in France. Wisely Heydon had refused, he had many other problems, and was determined to tackle the key issue of to separation between the finances of the Heydon dynasty and those of the Office. The disgrace and fall of Sir Roger Dallison whose personal funds had become inextricably tangled with the Crown and

17 *CSPD* LXXXI, 20 July 1627, CXLV, 28 June 1629; Clarendon *History of the Great Rebellion*, ed Lockyer, Oxford, 1967, p 27; M. Toynbee (ed) *The Papers of Captain Henry Stevens*, Oxfordshire Record Society, 42, 1961, pp 57–59.

public whilst Lieutenant was a chilling example that Sir John had no wish to emulate.[18]

Fortunately the new Lieutenant appears to have had the benefit of royal favour and the ear of Secretary Nicholas, and in July 1629 the King ordered that Sir John was to have the authority to 'supply the place of Master of the Ordnance' whilst this post was vacant. Intriguingly Charles also put the Office under pressure to part with some of its stock of guns, which were to be sold off to replenish the royal coffers. Given that Sir John's position was due entirely to the King the response of the Office was robust: it listed all the 344 pieces of iron ordnance on hand, declaring that it was unknown how many of them his majesty might require in future. At the same time Heydon staunchly resisted the pressure to accept that the debt of the Office was the debt of the Heydon family. Sir John's position could have misfired badly; as it was he appears to have gained the respect of the King – and went on to serve him with great professionalism. In 1639 and 1640 he battled against huge financial odds in attempting to assemble the train of artillery without ready money – and accompanied many of his staff into the field during the campaign. Little wonder that Clarendon should later refer to him as 'his majesties faithful Lieutenant General of the Ordnance'. Another character in the office important to our story was the Sir Edward Sherburne (1616–1702), who only took up his post as Clerk of the Ordnance early in 1642, following the death of his father who had himself held the position for almost a decade until his death just before Christmas 1641. The young Edward, later better known as a translator and poet, was called back from a tour of the Continent only to be plunged into the midst of crisis. Despite the fact that the Crown owed his late father more than £900 Sherburne would also prove one of Charles' most loyal supporters, and it is mainly Sherburne's success in preserving the records of the Royalist Ordnance that makes it possible to study the King's logistics during the Civil War.[19]

---

18 E.M. Tomlinson *A History of the Minories*, London, 1907, pp 394–400; M.B. Young 'Illusions of Grandeur and Reform at the Jacobean Court: Cranfield at the Ordnance', *Historical Journal*, 22, number 1, pp 53–73; *DNB*, 'Monson'

19 *DNB*, 'Sherburne'; G.E. Aylmer 'Studies in the Institutions and Personnel of English Central Administration', DPhil thesis, Oxford, 1954, pp 49–68.

3

A Scramble for Arms:
The War of Ordnance Logistics

The causes of the Civil Wars were diverse and arguably included a complex web of conflicting political, religious, and financial motivations. They almost certainly happened when they did because of unrest in Scotland – which had started the 'Bishops Wars' of 1639 and 1640 – and the ugly Irish Rebellion of 1641. Yet a very good case can be made that the Great, or First, Civil War in England actually began over who controlled military forces and supplies. The shape of the opening campaigns was almost entirely dictated by the need to secure munitions of all descriptions – and not least artillery. Moreover the apparent hesitancy of both sides, and lack of boldness in their opening moves, can be explained as much in terms of the mechanics of war, as through politics. Since it was the seat of control of artillery and ordnance supplies, as well as the centre of government, London was unquestionably the most important place in the kingdom. The King's abandonment of London was probably his greatest mistake of the entire war – yet this was, to a large degree, forced by his opponents. Seizure of the Ordnance Office and the Tower would put Parliament in possession of both the biggest stock of guns, and the heart of the system of supply. Next in importance were the provincial stores of ordnance – the ports, notably Hull and Portsmouth, and the militia stores of the counties. The gradually unfolding process of capture and denial of these important strategic objectives, becoming increasingly violent with time, is in essence the history of the opening phase of war itself, up to the Edgehill campaign.

The argument that the 'English' war actually began over who was entitled to take charge of the machinery of war, and to make war, is very completely supported by the events of the winter of 1641 to 1642. As early as 7 December 1641 Sir Arthur Haselrig put forward a bill which would have put Parliament in control of the Militia. Though this ultimately failed to proceed beyond a second reading, it was soon succeeded by the famous Militia Ordinance which was introduced to the House of Commons in January 1642. This was the instrument by which Parliament would finally claim the power to raise troops a few months later. An abortive Royalist bill on the subject was thrown out in April. Coherent argument has been made suggesting that the very first efforts by Parliament to control a body of troops were no great leap of political theory, but a simple formalisation of the attempt to get a permanent guard, under its own commander, to protect Parliament itself against coup or riot. The need for a guard for Parliament was born partly out of fear of what the King might attempt, but also of suspicion regarding plots – especially those of papists and disbanded soldiers.

It would appear that the first guard to be mounted was actually in September 1641, led, prophetically enough, by Robert Devereux, Earl of Essex. A month later orders were also issued to the Justices of London, Middlesex and Surrey to procure their own guards, and Pym demanded that the Parliament guard should be continued, properly armed with live ammunition. These measures were accompanied by an apparently fawning and loyal address to the King which protested that a guard was necessary due to fear of 'mischievous Designs and Practices' which were afoot to 'ruin and destroy' the Parliament.[1]

On 31 December 1641 the Parliament began a formal review of 'how this Kingdom may be furnished with powder and arms', appointing a twelve man committee for the purpose. Key figures amongst these were Sir John Colepepper, Sir John Hotham, Sir John Evelyn, Sir Ralph Hopton and Sir Walter Erle – so even at this stage the enquiry team included both Parliamentarian characters significant to the story of the artillery, alongside a future Royalist. There is also evidence to show that the Tower was under observation by Christmas; in January the London Trained Bands took unilateral action to secure their own guns, much to the disquiet of the King. In response Charles wrote to the Lord Mayor, half pleading, half directing, that,

> whereas we are informed that 6 pieces of ordnance usually belonging to the artillery yard have lately been brought into the City, and are placed in Lead-enhall, but with what intentions we are not yet well satisfied. Considering the distempers and troubles of these times, our will and command therefore is that you take special care to see those pieces so safely disposed of that they only serve for the guard and preservation of the City, if cause should require.[2]

Whilst the King tried to ensure that guns and ammunition already at large did not get used against him, he also sought to preserve potential stocks from capture, or to place them out of harms way. Thus it was that on 7 January he ordered Lord Newport to move a ship laden with ordnance and ammunition, at present near the Tower, 'to fall down the river as far as Woolwich or Gravesend', in order so he said 'to take away all occasions of fright and jealousies from our good people'. When the King fled north in February it was still unclear where the allegiances of the Ordnance Officers lay. At the most liberal interpretation they still could not believe in a divided kingdom, nor perhaps did they wish

---

[1] *House of Commons Journal*, 2, 30 December 164, pp 362–366.
[2] See L.G. Schwoerer 'The Fittest Subject for a King's Quarrel', Journal of British Studies 1971, pp 45–76; *CSPD* CCCCLXXXVIII, 4 January 1642, pp 237, 265; and CCCLXXXIX, 8 February 1642, p 277.

to offend either of the potential warring parties. At this early stage 'neutralism' may be said to have extended even to the offices of state designed for the very purpose of war. Thus it was that on 10 February 1642 the Ordnance Officers reported a curiously mixed picture to the Munitions Committee of Parliament. They sought to underline the importance of the office to the King's military requirements, in supplying castles, ships and armies; but conversely they presented a list of defects. Stocks of match and muskets were low. Worse, the Parliamentary suppression of the saltpetre monopoly had caused powder supply to dry up to such an extent that whilst under normal conditions 20 lasts per month were delivered, there would now remain in store just four lasts and nine hundredweight once current commitments had been met.[3]

Perhaps the most surprising aspect of the Ordnance Officers' report to Parliament was that the navy and merchantmen were short of ordnance to the tune of 900 guns. To rectify this staggeringly large shortfall, they suggested consulting with the gun founders to ascertain when such pieces might become available. The picture painted by the Ordnance Officers report is interesting for a number of reasons. Perhaps its underlying purpose was actually to point out to Members the essential impracticality of attempting to undertake a war in the near future. More importantly the report strongly suggests that neither side had, as late as the beginning of 1642, laid any concrete or realistic plans to fight a domestic campaign – or any serious campaign for that matter. The military evidence is thus quite clear: the Civil War of 1642 was not orchestrated to a pre prepared plan, but wandered into by parties that had no real conception of what might be required to fight. The official conversations between the Ordnance Officers and Parliament provide fascinating insight into the way in which the machinery of war would be divided between the protagonists. They were also a measure of the moderate disposition of many on both sides of the divide that winter.

Even at this late stage there were hopes of a constitutional solution, or perhaps of a limitation of violence to some other part of the kingdom. Whether the Ordnance Officers were regarded as foot draggers or obstructionist by the most active Members of Parliament is entirely possible. Certainly there is evidence that the bureaucrats at the Tower were moving far more slowly than many would have wished. In mid May the officers were summoned to the House of Commons, and attended 'at the door', being then called in to explain why arms ordered to be sent to Chester by the Commissioners 'were not sent away accordingly'. The Ordnance Officers quickly laid blame for this apparent oversight elsewhere, though the precise nature of their excuses does not seem to have survived.[4]

In April 1642 Hull was an issue of greater significance than its simple value as a sea port might suggest. The ordnance stored there in case of trouble with

3   *CSPD* CCCCLXXX, 7 January 1642, p 244.
4   *House of Commons Journal*, 2, 18 May 1642.

the Scots was an important factor, as was the facility with which supplies could be unloaded there from the Continent. The store of ordnance there is believed to have totalled '49 brass pieces' and a mortar, together with over 900 barrels of powder, 2000 roundshot and 100 granadoes. Hull was also a test case, in that national opinion was likely to be effected by the outcome of this apparently marginal constituency. Paradoxically taking Hull was now virtually impossible for Charles unless he could succeed in winning the hearts and minds of its local leadership and people, because it was one of the few places in the kingdom which boasted modern defences. Charles needed artillery and stores, but without these very same supplies a proper siege was out of the question. So it was that the young Duke of York was sent to the town accompanied by Lord Newport in the hope that it would be rendered without a fight. The mission came close to success, but once Sir John Hotham had closed the gates of Hull against the King's party, who were few in number and ill prepared, they were forced to withdraw.

Predictably London viewed these events as a major escalation, and thereafter more than 90 Members of both houses of Parliament quit the city to make themselves available to the service of the King. Moreover the King's failure to secure Hull not only lost him a storehouse, guns and a port, but gave Parliament 'occasion to charge him as aggressor'. Parliament was therefore given justification in issuing orders to the Earl of Warwick to secure the passage of the Humber from the seaward side, so ensuring that it could not be properly invested or cut off from resupply. For the first time, but certainly not the last, Parliament would use its control of the navy to influence the outcome of events on land which might otherwise have resulted in a victory for the King.[5]

It is remarkable that all the key officers of the Ordnance, remaining loyal to the King, were still in place at the Tower as late as June 1642; but in the first week of that month it was Hull that put their pose of studious indifference to the test. On 4 June Parliament demanded that nothing should go in or out of the magazine 'without the King's authority' as 'signified by both houses of Parliament', and furthermore called upon the officers of the Ordnance to hand over everything that had come down from Hull. On 6 June the officers gave a carefully worded response using the absence of Lord Newport, Master of the Ordnance to play for time,

> In answer to your demand, requiring us positively to declare whether, after the receipt of provisons from Hull … we would deliver them out again according to the said order, we have conferred together and held fit to return you this answer … That all provisions of magazine within the Tower of London having hitherto been committed in the charge of the Master and other the respective Officers of the Ordnance jointly; and the earl of Newport, the present Master

5   F. Guizot *History of the English Revolution*, London, 1846, p 162; Powell and Timmings *Documents*, 105, 1963, pp 2, 10, 11, 19. *House of Lords Journal*, 32, p 70; M.C. Fissel *English Warfare 1511–1642*, London, 2001, p 298.

of the Ordnance, being now at York, to whom the said order in the first place is likewise directed; it will not become us to determine of any answer to the said demand, or any other business of the like importance concerning the duties of that office, until his lordship … shall signify unto us his pleasure and direction therein.[6]

Charles inadvertently made the position worse for his supporters within the Ordnance Office when he was issued a warrant from York on 20 June, ordering that as

We having present occasion for the use of ordnance and munition for the defence of our person, we require you to send by sea hither or to Newcastle, inasmuch as it will not be safe to do so by land, such cannon, arms, powder, shot, and munition as you can get out of our stores, ships or otherwise, in such secret and close manner that the same may not be intercepted by those who wish not well to our safety and person.

This message was intercepted by the King's enemies, and what exactly Heydon was able to dispatch north is unclear. However carts and other paraphernalia found at Heydon's house in the Minories suggest that he did make attempts to answer the King's call, and if Vicars' *Parliamentary Chronicle* is to be believed his hoard included three guns. The fact that Heydon's London house lay a mere 200 yards from the Tower, and that the Lieutenant's authority might well have proved sufficient to get the stores shifted outside its precincts also adds credibility to this tale, as do Parliament's orders for the searching of other properties. That very same week, for example, it was directed that the Constables examine two public houses, the Bell and the Queen's Head. The reason for singling out these two places was that information had been received that carts were being prepared for the journey to York, and that the Queen's Head in particular held a stockpile of granadoes.[7]

At any event with Parliament's officers vigilant against anything leaving London – and Heydon himself very much under suspicion – his usefulness in the capital was an at end. With the *Providence* landing seven or eight guns and two hundred barrels of powder from the Continent at Bridlington on 2 July the wherewithal for an embryonic 'train of artillery' was at hand. So Heydon slipped away, and soon afterwards he was at York laying the foundations for the King's new ordnance in the north. Surprisingly, and despite the extreme risk to the messenger, Heydon would continue to communicate with the families of various confederates in the Tower until at least the beginning of 1643. At this

---

6   *House of Lords Journal*, 5, 7 June 1642, pp 113–116.
7   *CSPD* CCCCXCI, June 1642, p 343; see also 'Haydon Street' in *A Dictionary of London*, 1918, web site published at www.british-history.ac.uk, and G.E. Aylmer *The King's Servants*, revised edn, London, 1974, pp 289–291; *House of Commons Journal*, 2, 27 June 1642.

time William Kempe was apprehended with 'letters from Oxforde', but though captured he managed to tear Heydon's letter into such small pieces that 'not one word ... could be read'. Another familiar figure from the Ordnance Office who joined the King's forces at an early stage was John Lanyon, currently the Proofmaster, but previously employed as 'Comptroller of the Train' of artillery in the Scottish war. Already implicated in Royalist plots hatched at the Dog Tavern in Westminster and the Dolphin at Gray's Inn Lane, Parliamentarian pamphleteers soon identified him as 'a Captain at Yorke', an engineer, 'now practising to cast Brasse Mortar pieces, wherein to shoot granadoes, which when they are finished are to be sent to Beverly and are intended for firing the toune'. In fact Lanyon did take part in the siege of Hull, though his efforts appear to have been frustrated by the explosion of the magazine at Cottingham in which precious stores were destroyed.[8]

Amazingly, even after these episodes, Francis Conningsby, the Surveyor; Edward Sherburne, the Clerk; and Richard Marsh, the Keeper of the Store, remained at their posts in the London Ordnance Office. Only six weeks later did Parliament finally lose patience with these closet Royalists. On the 17 August 1642 an order was issued that they be taken into custody, and not be 'suffered' to go into the office. Three days later the remaining staff at the Tower were given an ultimatum that

> the Office of the Ordnance in the Tower of London shall forthwith upon sight of this order deliver the keyes of the Office ... to such as the Committee for the defence of this Kingdome shall appoynt to receive them or else that the Dores of the said office shalbe forthwith broken upp. And the charge and keepinge of the said armes shalbe committed into the hands of [those] the said Committee shall think fitt.

Two days later Parliament nominated George Payler, former paymaster of Berwick, as the new Surveyor – and with this appointment he was granted the authority to take all the store keys into his own possession. Any employee refusing to hand over keys was to be instantly dismissed. Most of the remaining staff, being relatively junior men with few interests outside the capital, decided that discretion was the better part of valour and now went back to work for new masters. The Ordnance Office had effectively split top from bottom, with the officers and a few other senior figures departing to fight for the King – and the remainder staying in place for Parliament.[9]

---

8   BL E 108 (5) *Strange News from Yorke, Hull, Beverly and Manchester*, London, 1642, p 66, and E 108 (33) *Some Special Passages from Hull*, 1642, passim; A. Cooper *A Speedy Post With More News from Hull*, 30 July 1642, pp 5–6; *House of Commons Journal*, 2, 30 January 1643, pp 947–949.
9   PRO 55/1754, 'Warrants' August 1642; I. Roy 'The Royalist Army in the First Civil War', DPhil thesis, Oxford, 1964, pp 275–276.

This painfully slow cleansing of the Augean stables being complete Parliament could finally commence forming its own train of artillery. Philibert Emmanuel du Boyes had been nominated by the Guildhall Committee as Parliament's 'controller' of artillery as early as 16 June, and along with him had been chosen a 'Principal Conductor', a Commissary for draught horses, master gunner and a battery master – but so far they had but little to organise. Now they seized control of supplies at the Tower, and on 27 of August the Earl of Essex ordered that they should also take into charge Heydon's stockpile, the 'divers waggons, carts, tumbrells and other necessary habillments of war' that had been secreted in the Minories. Within three days the basic scheme was laid for an impressive train of artillery totalling 29 guns: 11 light field guns, 'short drakes of 3 lb bullet'; four 'brass ordnance of 6 lb bullet'; six brass 12 pound guns (two long barrelled and four short); a 'demi culverin drake'; a 'whole culverin', and six mortars – the latter under the control of the fireworker Joachim Haine. The allotment of ammunition was liberal by the standards of the day, being 200 round shot for each piece, plus a total stock of 300 case shot and 600 granadoes. 'Blynders' for covering the gunners from enemy observation were also included with the supplies. From early September further stockpiles were on hand including 1,000 tents and 850 pairs of pistols from Hull, and on 10 September final planning had reached the stage of specifying what hand tools and other small items would accompany the guns and stocks of munitions. The gunnery equipment was based on a provision of two ladles and two sponges per gun, plus a stock of 20 wadhooks, 36 beds, 100 quoins, 100 commanders, 200 levers, 30 budge barrels, 40 hand barrows, 30 crow bars, and a mass of ropes. At about the same time the Ordnance Office was called upon to begin an even bigger project, the supply of a further 50 guns to support the as yet largely non existent fortifications of London.

Two interesting points emerge from the mass of detail. The first is that Parliament's marching artillery, as planned in August and September 1642, was intended mainly to fight battles in the field. Only eight of its 29 pieces were of a size to be of much use in a siege, and these eight guns, together with the mortars, would only have been enough to besiege a relatively small town. The second point worthy of note is that du Boyes had constructed a large and comprehensive artillery arm in just two weeks – in direct contradiction of Young's suggestion that he had been dilatory in his preparations. In fact there had been delays during June and July – but these were none of du Boyes doing – being the period that it had taken Parliament to screw up its courage to demand access to the Tower, and to dismiss those loyal to the King. The Royalist Ordnance Officers Conningsby, March, and Sherburne did not stay long in prison, and their rapid release may have been assisted by the compliant attitude of the colleagues who remained at work under the new regime. On 8 September John White was appointed as Clerk of the Ordnance, and the very next day the prisoners were released. Two of the three left shortly afterwards to join the King, as a result of which their houses were searched and their families expelled.[10]

A major success of Parliament in these crucial early months was that its supporters at strategic points in the localities acted more speedily than the slow start in London might have suggested. The significance, not just of the navy, but of its coastal bases, was explained to Parliament by the Earl of Warwick early in August 1642, when he warned the House of Lords about the fate of Portsmouth. He pleaded that 'like inconveniency' should not be allowed to befall the three castles around Deal, nor the forts at Dover, or Upnor Castle, since if these were in enemy hands the navy would lack places to get water and ballast, and Chatham would be in danger. In seizing many of the key strongholds Parliamentarian supporters were materially aided by neglect, or the lack of commitment of their garrisons. At Dover where a Scottish commentator claimed to have seen dismounted ordnance lying around propped up on logs or in the long grass, it was the dashing Captain Richard Dawks who took the initiative. With a mere ten men he scaled the wall at night, and successfully disarmed the garrison – the only resistance being from the porter who shut himself in his room and refused to hand over the keys until Dawks threatened to batter down the door. Having gained control Dawks was bemused to discover an almost total lack of ammunition for the guns – fresh supplies of shot, sponges and ladles were ordered in from London, and in the meantime some powder was lent by the navy.[11]

At Woolwich it was the timely intervention of Captain Willoughby and his company that intercepted no less than 75 guns, stored in a wood yard on their way to be transported to the King's forces at Newcastle by Royalist William Barnes. Willoughby achieved double satisfaction when he searched Barnes' house and discovered 'Popish' vestments hidden in the garden. Chatham and Upnor fell soon afterwards, Parliamentarian sources claiming that stocks of over 300 guns were taken. There was less momentum outside the south and east, but even in the north there were a few crucial points seized for Parliament. Hull was the most obvious, but even in a predominantly Royalist Lancashire the magazine at Manchester was denied to the King's supporters, and the town would prove a continuing nuisance long afterwards.[12]

---

10 PRO WO 55/387 ff 1–8; P. Young *Edgehill*, Kineton, 1967, p 103; N.G. Brett-James 'The Fortifications of London 1642–1643', in *London Topographical Record*, 14, 1928, pp 2–33.
11 BL E 153 (22) *The Scots Scouts Discoveries by Their London Intelligencer*, 1642, pp 1–2; E 115 (8) Nicholas Payne *A True Relation of a Brave Exploit Performed by Captain Richard Dawks*, London, 1642, pp 3–7; E 115 (10) *A True Relation of the Late Expedition into Kent*, 2 September 1642 p 4; E 137 (20) *England's Safety in the Navie and Fortifications*, 1642, pp 1–6; S.P.H. Stathem *The History of the Castle, Town and Port of Dover*, London, 1899, pp 286–290.
12 BL E 115 (13) *A True and Perfect Relation of the Seizing of the House of One Master William Barnes a Cavalier*, 22 August 1642, passim; E 116 (33) *A Perfect Diurnall of the Severall Passages in Our Late Journey into Kent*, September 1642, pp 2–3; H.F. Abell *Kent and the Great Civil War*, Ashford, 1901, pp 48–87.

When the King finally called out his army Edward Hyde made no bones about the fact that for all the efforts of his loyal servants his artillery and supply system was still ill formed – if not in complete disarray. As his *History of the Great Rebellion*, so often a tale of woe, remarked percipiently,

> When the King set up his standard at Nottingham, which was on the 22nd of August, he found the place much emptier than he thought the fame of his standard would have suffered it to be. He recieved intelligence the next day that the rebel's army – for such he now declared them – was horse, foot, and cannon, at Northampton, besides that great party we left at Coventry. His [the King's] few cannon and ammunition were, however, still at York, being not yet equipped to march, though Sir John Heydon, his majesty's faithful Lieutenant General of Ordnance, used all possible diligence to form and prepare it; nor were there foot enough levied to guard it.[13]

The Royalist failure to seize the kingdom's main stocks of ordnance – or the manufacturing facilities and raw materials to make more – or the navy – early in the war, created a legacy which was very difficult, if not impossible, to overcome.

From this low point the King's artillery had effectively to be started from scratch. The Earl of Newport remained titular Master of the Ordnance, but it was a new body of 'Ordnance' or 'Artillery' Commissioners which was set up to deal with the actual equipping of the train. In addition to Heydon this body comprised Sir John Pennington, Sir Bryan Palmes, Sir George Strode, and John Wandesford. The Commisioners would have responsibility for everything south of the Trent, but north of this the Earl of Newcastle had a separate operation with Sir William Davenant acting as his General of Ordnance. At York there was much to do in a short time, gun carriages were made, and the personnel brought up to strength. Captain Henry Younger was named 'Comptroller of the Train', and effective second in command to Heydon, and it is probable that William Betts was nominated Master Gunner. The core of the train was thus able to join the main army before it departed Nottingham on 13 September.

Initially it would appear that there were just 12 guns, seven from the *Providence*, and a further five which had been captured by the Earl of Northampton at Banbury on 8 August. If Parliamentarian sources are reliable the five captured guns were light field pieces 'being mounted on running carriages' – these had been used by Lord Brooke as mobile reinforcement to his infantry. Deployed in the midst of his force they had been intended to 'offend the enemy, and yet indure no hazard'. When the Royalist artillery reached Shrewsbury some of the deficiencies in waggons and horses were corrected by bringing in from Chester teams that had been intended for shipment to Ireland, and some ready money was also raised for the payment of immediate wants. It was probably about this time that Prince Rupert visited the home of Richard Foley to order supplies of

---

[13] Clarendon *History of the Great Rebellion*, ed Lockyer, Oxford, 1967, p 27.

round shot. The number of pieces of ordnance was also increased from 12 to 20. The most likely sources of these additional pieces were Earl Rivers or Lord Strange – the former had landed five guns at Frodsham, and the latter was believed to have up to 11 to contribute.[14]

The Royalist field train of the autumn of 1642 was smaller than that of Parliament but had attained a respectable size. It comprised two demi cannon, two cluverins, two demi culverins, six fawcons and six fawconettes, and two rabonettes. The total weight of shot that could be fired from this battery was about 130 pounds with each discharge – much the same as could be fired by the enemy. Yet this apparent similarity masked a significant difference. The Royalist guns had been gathered on a distinctly ad hoc basis from diverse sources – Parliament's advantage was that its train had been carefully planned, and its small field guns were all of the same type, using the same 3 pound shot.

SUPPLYING THE LONG WAR

Contrary to the expectations of many the war was not decided in the autumn of 1642, and nobody had planned for a long war – financially or logistically. The result was that both sides needed more ordnance, but the potential to supply guns was far from evenly distributed. Though it cannot be claimed that the surviving data is comprehensive, the extensive documentation that we have shows that the ordnance and shot production of the Weald during the Civil War proved extremely significant. All of what was made in the Weald went to Parliament, or its friends, or was sold to others – such as the Dutch – in London and only as Parliament would allow. Though John Browne's name appeared on just some of the contracts it would appear likely that he and his collaborators saw the lions share of both turnover and profits. As one disgruntled Royalist seeking Browne's defection put it, 'the rebels have no guns or bullet, but from him'. In fact a minority of Parliament's guns were sourced elsewhere, notably some brass ordnance and 'leather' guns, which were made at Vauxhall. Similarly a few guns were brought into store by others, as for example by William Burrows and Richard Broome who supplied 14 small guns in September 1643. Exactly how many guns Parliament had on hand is difficult to state with certainly, and the number certainly fluctuated – usually upwards. The figures that we have for 1643 are suggestive of a relatively slow start, John Browne's main contribution to the stocks of the Ordnance Office that year being 36 brass guns and 17,000 cannon balls. Thereafter matters would improve considerably. According to statistics gathered by D.E. Lewis from the Ordnance Office ledgers no less than 263 guns were issued by Parliament to

---

[14] R.E. Sherwood *Civil Strife in the Midlands*, London, 1974, pp 29–30; R. Hutton *Royalist War Effort*, pp 76, 200; Worcestershire Record Office 1714/899/192; BL Add. Ms 5752.

local forces and garrisons and at least a further 79 pieces to field armies during the first two Civil Wars, with an additional ten or more guns from the stores of the navy. In excess of 47,000 round shot went to local forces, and about another 30,000 to the major marching armies. Gunpowder issues for land use exceeded 8,000 barrels from London stores alone.

These statistics are but part of the picture since many of the Ordnance Office papers for 1642 are missing. Also lacking are the 'minute books' for the period up until early 1644, and some of the books of receipts. To whatever ordnance is recorded in these lost documents should also be added numbers of guns taken off Parliamentarian ships and used in land defences, and any guns which were imported but did not pass through the Ordnance Office. Similarly the 77,000 iron round shot that have been counted do not include those that were already in garrisons, nor are cross bar or case shot taken into account. The number of pieces made by John Browne for ships has yet to be fully assessed. Nevertheless the navy certainly became one of Parliament's key assets, and as early as 1633 the 'List of the King's Ships' noted 50 vessels mounting 1430 guns. The number of ships in commission shrank to 42 shortly before the outbreak of war – though some of the vessels now afloat were bigger, and individually had more guns on their decks. Similarly, given that places like Hull, Dover and some of the south coast forts and castles had started the war with large amounts of ordnance in their fortifications it seems very unlikely that the King's enemies were equipped with less than 2000 pieces by Christmas 1642. Though there were many set backs and guns were captured by the enemy during 1643, the trend in stocks was ever upwards.

By mid 1644 not only were Royalist garrisons being taken in, but manufacture for Parliament was catching up with deficits in both guns and powder. It is significant to note that not only did Parliament have a preponderance in artillery, but that the guns it had were, on average, more modern than those of the opposition. This was because most of the new guns purchased under the first two Stuart monarchs went to the navy, and more new guns were cast in the Weald during the war than anywhere else. The Browne works also benefited from the fact that Parliament had access to obsolete ordnance in its stores – four tons of old brass chambers were delivered to him in early 1644, and there is at least circumstantial evidence of the reuse of metal from East India Company ships armament. It is therefore very probable that more than half of the guns under Parliamentary control were made after 1620 – whilst the Royalist artillery, from noblemen's castles, and more remote parts of the kingdom was often older. Very clearly Parliament's access to guns and their attendant munitions far outclassed that of the King – and made this aspect of the war pretty one sided.[15]

15 D.E. Lewis 'The Office of Ordnance and Parliamentarian Land Forces', unpublished PhD thesis, Loughborough, 1976, pp 152–153, 321–342; P. Edwards *Dealing in Death: The Arms Trade and the British Civil Wars*, Stroud, 2000, pp 93–97.

Huge as the figures are, and as significant as the potential appeared, Parliament still suffered many local shortages and delays, occasioned by financial and military pressures and quirks of bureaucracy. At the end of July 1644 the Committee of Safety asked for 500 round shot and 100 granadoes to be dispatched for active service, but realised that stocks were low. If the right types were not to hand, permission was given to 'contract with Mr Browne's agent' accordingly. At about the same time orders were repeated for 50 barrels of powder to go to Portsmouth, in case a previous request had not been satisfied. In August 50 barrels of powder, ordered from the contractor in February, finally turned up at the magazine. In September it was directed that General Fairfax's powder should be replenished because he had taken the initiative and supplied his own to the Scots in lieu of non existent central stores. Early in 1645 Parliament was forced to put its financial house in order so far as munitions was concerned and mortgage its future revenue for eight per cent interest – effectively creating war loans for this specific purpose. In July 1645 the Hampshire Committee wrote to the Committee of Both Kingdoms requesting a variety of supplies including two demi cannon, two culverins, three demi culverins, three sakers and a mortar. As this request related to land service it was passed on to the Ordnance Office. The reply from the Tower was that there was still 'noe ordnance of these natures but what belongeth to the Navy'. In June 1645 the Tower ordnance store houses themselves were showing wear and tear, and one 'great shed' fell 'flat to the ground', the Ordnance Officers again appealing for the £500 required for full repairs.[16]

Vexatious as such hiccups and delays in supply undoubtedly were, most were eventually overcome, and it appears that by 1644 to 1645 ordnance and other supplies were flowing in a much more satisfactory manner than they had been in the first two years of war. Critically Parliament was able to start with an effective blank sheet when it came to furnishing a complete new train of field artillery for the New Model Army in September 1644, and laid out a plan for two demi culverins, four sakers and 14 of the latest 3 pound drakes. The Lord General's new train was costed at £9,000, of which a third was to be supplied 'now', the remainder over the next six months. The drakes in particular were ordered 'with all speed' from 'Mr Browne in Kent', and it appears that at least part of the makings came from Dutch copper from which Browne was ordered to make as many 3 pound guns as possible. From November 1644 guns for the navy were again top of the agenda, and that month alone there are accounts covering 52 guns – the majority of them iron. An order for a further 60 guns for the fleet survives from the following February. Orders also survive for at least 172 guns to be made for the navy in late 1645.[17]

16 PRO WO 47/1, ff 92–93, 107–109, 327; *CSPD* DVI, 1 March 1645, p 330.

17 PRO WO 47/1, ff 107–118; R.R. Brown 'John Browne, Gunfounder to the Stuarts', part 2, in *Wealden Iron*, number 26, 2006, pp 31–50.

It is interesting to note how John Browne senior organised operations during the war. Commonly he appears to have stayed at an address in Martin's Lane, off Thames Street near the Tower of London. This would have been very convenient, both to converse with the Ordnance Officers, and to survey his wares at time of delivery. In any case he would have had less reason to remain in Kent after the death of his wife Martha in July 1644 – and fittingly enough she was laid to rest under an iron slab in the village church of St. Margaret's. Horsmonden. At least two agents, Richard Pierson of Philpot Lane and Samuel Ferriers at the Half Moon in Thames Street, helped to conduct business in the capital. Down in Kent the young John Browne was in charge, with the faithful factotum Henry Quintayne on hand acting as a deputy and providing accounts. Robert Cheek served as a clerk.

We used to have frustratingly little idea how the iron furnaces of 'England's Vulcan' appeared during the Civil War, but there are a number of depictions, archaeological clues, and at least one first hand account to give us some visualisation. Evidence from Dutch artworks, such as the painting by Henri Blès 'Landscape with Ironworks and Mines', concurs with the conclusion of modern excavations that it is probable that a central furnace stack would have been surrounded by other buildings and structures, such as a workshop, moulding shop, the water wheel and perhaps a store for charcoal that needed to be kept dry. The furnace itself might take the form of a reinforced box, or squat tower, made of two skins of sandstone blocks with an infill of rubble. A platform or bridge was often provided to feed the furnace from the top. An illustration from a fire back, dated 1636, shows a furnace bound externally with a framework of stout timber baulks, held together at the corners with tusk tenon joints. The bellows were attached to the furnace via a 'blowing arch' in the structure to supply the rush of air. On another side of the furnace was the 'casting arch' through an aperture in which the molten metal was channelled for casting. The gun moulds were positioned in a casting pit, and packed around with sand – an arrangement that provided sufficient strength and heat resistance to support the mass of hot metal as it flowed, and later began to cool.[18]

Investigation of the gun pit at Maynard's Gate has revealed a void, about five feet wide by ten deep, to contain the mould and sand, around which was constructed a cylindrical timber structure – not unlike a huge straight sided oak barrel – this itself being tightly packed within an outer container of rammed clay. The scale of the pit suggested that it might be large enough to cast a saker of about a ton in weight. The furnace itself appeared to have been constructed of sandstone, and water power for the bellows came from the Crowborough Ghyll, across which had been constructed a bay or dam. The layout, and debris found, suggested that the bellows were substantial and may have been covered by a tiled roof. Excavations uncovered the base of the pit for the water wheel, and a drain and vent for the furnace base, which was about

[18]   H.R. Schubert *History of the British Iron and Steel Industry*, London, 1957, pp 122–271.

20 feet square. In the downstream side of the wheel race was found a large 'bear' – or dense mass of solidified material typical of a smelting that had gone wrong, and might perhaps have spelt the end of the working life of the furnace. There was also evidence of a 'charging ramp' up which raw materials could be barrowed or heaved to the top of the furnace. Examination of the charcoal found around the site determined that beech, lime, birch, willow, hazel and dogwood had all been used in its production. The particular significance of the excavations at Maynard's Gate is that it is highly probable that the remains discovered there are of, or just pre, Civil War date. Documentary references show that the furnace here was operational by 1562, and was working in the early seventeenth century, but that it was ruined by 1653. Thereafter the works were not reused and became overgrown, though much of the building material was subsequently robbed out. Diagnostic finds from the site, such as coins, clay pipes and pottery, are in agreement with the furnace being operational in the late sixteenth and early seventeenth centuries, with demolition occurring about 1680 to 1700.[19]

Scotsman Sir James Hope visited the Browne mine and furnace at Barden in Kent in March 1646, in the company of his brother, and a man servant 'Robin'. His journal records that as they approached they apprehended heaps 'of yron stonne' along the track, the ores and wastes being of several different colours, reddish, black, grey, and even bluish in hue. Some of the heaps were actually being treated on the ground, being heated with charcoal as they lay. The furnace itself was about 20 feet in height, and about three feet thick in its walls, the overseer observing the 'temper of the furnace' by means of a small 'open hole'. It was also equipped with twin bellows about 14 feet in length that were powered by the water wheel by means of a counterweight system with cams and rods. Ore and charcoal were fed into the top of the furnace using baskets, perhaps 15 or 16 times in 24 hours, and every ten minutes or so the workmen would examine the furnace to see if slag needed to be raked clear.

According to what the workmen told Sir James the furnace was capable of casting a gun weighing 2100 pounds once a day. The furnace chief and the founder were paid £1 a week each, whilst the eight other hands received 8 to 10 shillings apiece. They guessed that the whole furnace operation would cost about £2000 a year to run in total, and the particular campaign that was being run would last a surprisingly long 45 weeks – during which time the furnace would not be allowed to go cold. As the strangers had asked so many sensitive questions, Browne's master founder appears to have grown suspicious that the Scotsmen were in fact intending to set up their own works, and were engaged in little less than industrial espionage. Sir James, by his own account, was beginning to come to the conclusion that his interlocutors were drunk

19 O. Bedwin 'The Excavation of a Late Sixteenth / Early Seventeenth Century Gun Casting Furnace at Maynard's Gate, Crowborough, East Sussex, 1975–1976', in *Sussex Archaeological Collections*, 116, 1978, pp 163–178.

about their work, fearing that they were about to 'take on with him', he made his excuses and left. On their way they saw the products of the furnace along the road, ordnance standing in four wheeled block carriages, ready to be transported. Apparently each carriage was capable of holding two barrels, and could be pulled by six horses – making anything up to 24 miles a day in summer and 16 in winter when the roads were in poor condition.[20]

How many Wealden furnaces actually cast cannon during the period of the three Civil Wars is difficult to state with absolute confidence. However, in addition to Barden the list includes Bedgebury, Cowden, Hawkhurst, Horsmonden, and very probably Maynard's Gate on the Sussex side of the Weald. A number of others may have contributed – some as subcontractors or makers of shot. Amongst those possibly involved are Ashurst, Brede, Cansiron, Hamsell, Imbhams, Maresfield, Mayfield, Marshall's 'New' Furnace, Pounsley, Robertsbridge, Scarlets, and the Stream Furnace, Chiddingly. Ashurst was a Browne site where ordnance was sold about 1600, but whether it produced guns later is unclear. Brede furnace was in existence throughout the period, and certainly produced guns later, whilst Cansiron was associated with the Courthope gunfounding family as early as 1627. The Hamsell furnace at Rotherfield cast ordnance in the reign of Elizabeth, was leased to the Browne family in the post Civil War period, and definitely made shot. Imbhams is thought to have been in operation by 1600, and was a significant producer of ordnance in the reign of Charles II. A furnace at Maresfield was re-equipped about 1615, and made guns under Sackville Crowe's patent; moreover archaeological investigation here has produced pieces of cannon mould. Mayfield was another place producing guns well before the reign of Charles I, and continued to work throughout the period. Pounsley furnace was certainly producing guns in the 1620s – continued to exist – and was probably still making ordnance as late as the 1670s. The Robertsbridge furnace operated from the sixteenth century right through to the eighteenth century, and the site has yielded pieces of cannon mould. The Scarlets facility was definitely operational in 1646, and was a significant munitions producer under Charles II, though its history is difficult to disentangle from the rest of the Cowden site. The Stream Furnace at Chiddingly is thought to have been set up alongside an older forge about 1600, and there is also mention of a water powered hammer. Ordnance was made here in the post Civil War era.[21]

20 'A Contemporary Description of John Brown's Gun Founding Furnace at Barden in Kent, 1646', reprinted in *Wealden Iron*, number 4, Summer 1972, pp 15–20.
21 E. Straker *Wealden Iron*, London, 1931, passim; H. Cleere and D. Crossley, *The Iron Industry of the Weald*, 2nd edn, Cardiff, 1995, pp 309–367; A.N. Kennard *Gunfounding and Gunfounders*, London, 1986, pp 50–51; C. Foulkes *The Gun-Founders of England*, 2nd edn, London, 1969, pp 71–81; *Wealden Iron*, 1st series, number 9, Spring 1976, pp 5–21; P. Edwards, *Dealing in Death*, Stroud, 2000, pp 94–95.

Some idea of how successful the Wealden industry ultimately was in satisfying the demand for ordnance is given by an inventory of Browne stocks on hand at Horsmonden and surrounding areas drawn up at about 1650. The 130 large guns there ranged from demi culverin to demi cannon and were valued at £6,200; a mass of smaller guns were assessed at £4,200 – also present were 170 tons of round shot, and charcoal, metal and tools valued at £2,360. This alone would have been enough to equip the largest battleship afloat and replace the ordnance defending London – with probably enough materials left over to refurbish the artillery of the field army.[22]

It is interesting to note that recent authorities tend to view the Wealden Iron industry as in decline from the seventeenth century, and in the absolute terms of numbers of production facilities this may be true. It is thought that in 1574 there were 52 furnaces and 58 forges in the Weald, these figures being reduced to 36 and 45 respectively by 1653. Yet this masks a far more complex picture, for whilst the production of Wealden pig iron declined against increases in other parts of the country – the output of specialist castings, most importantly ordnance, rose significantly. Over the long term the growing importance of the gun in Wealden Iron is even more obvious than the loss of other types of production. The four Wealden ordnance furnaces of 1606 had in fact grown to 24 by 1667, and as we might expect prosperity was linked to war. Moreover specialised high quality products attracted a significant premium. Whilst a ton of pig iron had fetched little more than £1 in 1549, rising to perhaps £6 at the time of the Civil Wars, well cast Drakes of fine metal were fetching up to £30 a ton by 1650. The bulk of raw materials handled in the Wealden works may not have grown greatly in the seventeenth century, but value added certainly did. Similarly whilst the Ashdown forest was very seriously denuded of trees by as early as 1632, careful coppicing of woods in the eastern Weald continued to ensure the supply of charcoal. Indeed, there were contemporary observers who viewed the iron trade as tending to preserve rather than destroy woodland, because to continue the industry renewable woodlands had to be conserved.[23]

The problems that Parliament did have regarding the supply of guns clearly had little to do with the capacity of John Browne and his compatriots to make ordnance, and depended much on cash flows, the course of the campaigns, and political allegiances. That Parliament failed to capitalise immediately on the advantages that it had was at least in part due to an early inability to organise the means to pay for the war. Some rather hand to mouth expedients were finally replaced by more reliable fund raising methods during the course of 1643. The first of these was the 'weekly assessment' tax in February – this did not raise as much as might have been expected but it marked the start of a far more draconian financial climate than that which pertained hitherto. Official

---

22 KAO TR 1295/23 and 54; for an inventory of 1655 see Herefordshire Records Office E 12/VI/2/4967.

23 Cleere and Crossley *Iron Industry of the Weald*, pp 166–169, 191, 284–287.

sequestration of Royalist property, which was similarly put on a formal footing in 1643, proved rather more successful – and had the significant advantage that it was really only unpopular with those hit by it. Sequestration could also be enforced in such a way as not to break those at whom it was targeted, by allowing those who chose to co-operate to 'compound', or to pay large fines, rather than be ruined. The real turning point however was the imposition of the 'excise' – a commodity tax first proposed as early as May 1643, and actually enacted after the war turned further against Parliament later in the year. The excise covered such items as alcoholic drink, currants, tobacco, sugar, thread, playing cards and silk, and became increasingly more irksome to those being taxed as time passed. Yet the surety of the excise allowed loans to be raised against its future income, and its proceeds could be directed to the Ordnance Office. On 3 August 1644 the position was formally settled so that a third was hypothecated for the reimbursement of merchants and artificers who had already supplied Parliament, and two thirds went to the Ordnance Office to be divided equally between land and sea service. Some suppliers would never be paid, and John Browne would later complain that he was short to the tune of £1,843 in fees alone – but the new system maintained sufficient confidence for contractors to keep working for Parliament.[24]

Though Kent, and thus the main gunfounding area of the country, was in the ambit of Parliament from 1642, this was no cut and dried situation unaffected by the ebb and flow of war, and again it was 1643 that marked a crisis. In July that year Kent Royalists rose and met Parliamentarian troops in a skirmish at Tonbridge, and though this insurrection was quickly suppressed it proved indicative that the county would not be supine in the face of what it perceived to be any 'new tyranny'. Kentish troops were often reluctant to be sent outside the county at the bidding of Parliament, and the County Committee was apprehensive of plots by 'the Malignants to blow up their county into a high discontent', and overthrow the existing regime. How realistic this actually was by 1644 and 1645 is difficult to judge, but the Committee's apprehension was clearly far more than mere paranoia. In April 1645 Kentish men pressed for the New Model Army actively resisted the draft, and again it took the intervention of troops and the imposition of martial law to regain control of Maidstone.[25]

Many of these events occurred uncomfortably close to Milhall, and strategically were a very real threat to bringing Wealden products of to London. As natives of Kent, and arms manufacturers, it was hardly surprising that the political position of the Browne family was regarded as ambiguous. Indeed in terms of simple self interest there was little point tying themselves ineluctably to one party. With neighbours who were closet Royalists, paymasters who were Parliamentarian, and lip service to the concept of monarchy still the order of

---

[24] See J.S. Wheeler *The Making of a World Power*, Stroud, 1999, pp 94–196; KAO TR 1295/52.
[25] H.F. Abell *Kent and the Great Civil War*, Ashford, 1901, pp 88–166.

the day, declaring definitively for what might ultimately be the losing side would have been poor policy indeed. In truth we shall probably never know what went on in John Browne's conscience, but the evidence we have is that he kept his options as open as the situation would allow – and so succeeded in serving as supplier to whoever was the government in the long term. It was in the aftermath of Naseby fought on 15 June 1645 that this pragmatic commercial professionalism was put most forcefully to the test, due to the capture of documents that suggested that he was integral to the Royalist plots to seize Kent for the King.

Less than a week after the Royalist defeat at Naseby a House of Commons Committee was established to look into the potential treachery suggested by the King's correspondence, and orders were given that John Browne senior, and junior, should be seized and held incommunicado, and any papers they possessed be examined. The prime evidence for holding them appears to have been a letter by Thomas Walsingham to Lord Digby that recommended that King Charles should give Browne ten days notice of his entering Kent. This would give the gunfounder opportunity to return from London and provide the King with the munitions that he required. The Brownes denied everything, and John Browne senior explained an order for 300 guns as made through Samuel Ferriers, who needed them not to supply the King – but to sell on the market, as permitted by Parliamentary order. Nevertheless on 27 June the Committee interviewed several other people, one of whom stated that Browne had attended the King when he came to Parliament to arrest the 'five members' before the war, and another who suggested that Browne had sent workmen to assist the King in making guns.

The truth of the matter was never very clear, but a further examination of Browne in July 1645 did establish that several of the Browne workforce had defected to the Royalists. These were Hugh Richardson, who had worked as an engraver and clerk at the brass foundry, gunfounders James Edberry and Jasper Diamond, and a man called Larking who had assisted in boring. Browne admitted that he had helped Richardson's wife with money, but this could be construed as simply humanitarian – rather than a political act. As we can see from corresponding Royalist documents, three of these few who left the Weald did indeed provide the nucleus of the Royalist ability to make guns. What exactly Browne was guilty of was more difficult to prove, and on 28 August Parliament ordered that he be released 'upon good security'. At the end of the year he was allowed to go back to work, taking up the reins from Ferriers and his son in law Thomas Foley who had worked the business during his enforced absence.[26]

Royalist artillery production, contrary to much of what has been previously published, was pretty feeble. By virtue of geography, monopoly, and political

---

[26] R.R. Brown 'John Browne, Gunfounder to the Stuarts', part 2, in *Wealden Iron*, number 26, 2006, pp 44–50.

chicanery, industry and experience had been concentrated in Kent, Sussex and London before 1642 – and those working on artillery outside this area had virtually to start afresh. It was one thing to make a decent wrought iron pike head weighing ounces – something very different to cast a 7000 pound cannon, with accuracy, and without flaws. The evidence we have is incomplete, but does suggest that the Royalist furnaces in the Forest of Dean, Oxford, and the Midlands cast some dozens of guns, but even with these the learning curve was steep.

The ordnance manufactory at the Royalist hub of Oxford made military, but little geographic or strategic sense. The Christ Church foundry was run by John Lanyon, a former artificer of the Ordnance Office, and at least a few who had been enticed from the Weald, including gun founder Hugh Richardson. The broadsheet *Speciall Passages and Certain Informations* suggests that their work had begun by December 1642. Papers of mid 1643 refer to nine 'gunfounders', being retained at 2s a day, though only eight are listed at the beginning of 1644, being Jasper Diamond, Thomas Wicken, James Edberry, Edward Laine, Richard Gower, Edward Dispert, and Andrew and George Petoe. Initially it does not appear there was ready access to large supplies of iron, which would have been a more technically difficult medium to work with in any case, and so at first activity was focused on the much more modest target of attempting to produce small bronze guns. However there was not very much brass or bronze to be had either, and so in early 1643 Anthony Carter organised collections of scrap. Old cannon were also recast, and metal in general came to be regarded as a spoil of war and was seized wherever possible. Though a Council of War now recommended that a train of 40 guns should be put together, this ambitious project was an uphill struggle. Apparently a high proportion of what ordnance was made went to Oxford's own defences, but it is likely that quite a lot of shot was cast for all purposes.[27]

Though both bronze and iron guns were eventually made at Oxford it does not appear that many targets were met. Interestingly there were Parliamentarian spies on hand to confirm the very real difficulties experienced by the Oxford Royalist Ordnance Commissioners in 1643. In January John Jennings reported want of both powder and shot. A month later Samuel Brayne reported on the gunfounding operation, noting that there were '4 newe peeces of ordnance made', but that 'upon tryal of them yesterday one of them broke in pieces and the other were unusefull'. Nevertheless the Oxford founders persisted in their enterprises – at least on a small scale. In July 1643 about 14 hundred weight of bronze, in the shape of eight very small obsolete or damaged pieces, was delivered to the founders for recasting. Useful as recasting probably was as a

27 BL Rawlinson Ms D. 395, ff 208–209; BL E 130(10) *Special Passages and Certain Informations*, London, December 1642, p 147.

form of repair or cannibalisation it does not seem to have added very much to the absolute number of field guns.[28]

Magdalen College grove was the King's main artillery park, but the guns that it housed were frequently not the product of Oxford's foundry – and more than a few of the pieces that crossed the threshold were of a distinctly motley description. Two 'brass' guns turned out under Lanyon's supervision in May 1643 were in some way unsatisfactory, and were put back in the furnace again that summer. Three iron sakers entering the stores from Cirencester in April 1643 did so on ships carriages, whilst the seven pieces returned to the magazines from Lichfield included two sakers of different calibres, and a couple of minions previously belonging to the Marquis of Hartford. The next month Robert Freeman brought in two guns, one of which was described as a 3 pound 'Spanish' piece, which, somewhat bizarrely, came accompanied by nine case shot and five lead balls. July's crop of misfits did include two mortars, and of six 'Dutch' pieces one had broken trunions. The mortar of 'Captain Fawcett's making' was broken by 1643 when it came back to Oxford. A full inventory of the King's artillery in the magazine at Oxford and in other Oxfordshire garrisons, as of 8 May 1643, revealed a total stock of 52 pieces. Of these, four were mortars and the others appear to have been of 12 different calibres and a variety of lengths; one gun was listed as 'newly taken' from the enemy, and the total included the two Lanyon guns soon to be scrapped.[29]

More quality items, mainly from the field armies, came in, and went out, during 1644 – but there were still some remarkable novelties, such as the two sakers 'mounted upon one carriage' returned from the army at Woodstock in June. When 'Spanish' and 'Dutch' 3 pound guns were sent out with a 'marching train' the same month it was obvious that someone was alert enough to realise that the shot for the two types of ordnance were not interchangeable, So it was that 60 projectiles went with the Spanish, but only 30 with the Dutch. It had been hoped that the campaign by the main Royalist army of the new year might be executed with a large train of 40 guns. By February 1645 it had however been realised that this was wildly over optimistic; the new train for the army was therefore scaled down to a far more realistic 20 pieces. A total of 14 guns actually attended the King's army on the Naseby campaign.

For Bartholomew La Roche, the King's Master Fireworker at Oxford who plied his trade in some houses beside Magdalen College, things were arguably even worse. Production of filled granadoes, incendiaries, and other engineering supplies was an expensive business – and it was calculated that he required about £70 per week to do his job. He rarely received all that he needed, and by 1644 was seriously at odds with Lord Percy – and with no money, as one of Prince Rupert's correspondents observed, La Roche had 'no more motion

---

[28]   I.G. Phillip (ed) *The Journal of Sir Samuel Luke*, Oxford Record Society, 29, 1950, pp 10–17; PRO WO 55/1661, f 9.
[29]   *Royalist Ordnance Papers*, pp 26–30, 55, 77, 95, 99, 107, 404.

than a stone'. This was a double blow to the King's cause, for it was very often La Roche himself who had to direct engineering in siege and battle. He was knighted and encouraged, but without enough money or materials there was bound to be a deleterious impact on Royalist operations – particularly sieges.[30]

There was probably greater success in munitions production in the Forest of Dean, as might be expected since a Royal ironworks had existed here before the war. At the time of a lease to Sir Bainham Throckmorton and his partners in 1635, this works comprised four furnaces and five forges. An inventory reveals quite a number of substantial buildings and suggests that most of the facilities had been built, or refurbished, since 1630, though not everything was in working order. The utility of the Forest of Dean for producing iron and smaller items is immediately apparent, and Gloucestershire iron was certainly sent along the Severn to workshops in the Midland counties; but the 1635 inventory makes no mention of any cannon, nor of any specific ordnance related equipment. Orders for munitions were issued soon after the start of the war, and by 1643 the Forest of Dean was producing significant amounts of round shot, much of which was used locally rather than being routed via Oxford. Other products from Gloucestershire – or from the Midlands using iron from the Forest of Dean – included pike heads, swords, and muskets.

Though it has been speculated that the Forest of Dean was capable of producing cannon prior to the Civil War, and iron works at Lydbrook and Cannop were leased to John Browne, hard evidence that it did so is as yet unforthcoming. In fact it is unlikely that any guns were produced here. As we have seen John Browne preferred to centralise his production of both iron and bronze guns in the Weald at this period – and extension of his interests into other areas could well be construed as an effort to protect and capitalise upon his 1635 monopoly on other types of iron work. Moreover whilst pre war orders had to be delivered to London, for supply to the Tower or the naval dockyards of the south east, manufacture in geographically distant parts was questionable. Some guns certainly were produced in the Forest of Dean during the war, but the numbers were very modest compared to the hundreds that came from Kent and Sussex to Parliament. In the spring of 1643 large convoys of shot were sent to Oxford along with 20 guns. From what was effectively a standing start this was a splendid effort, but closer examination suggests that all was not as well as many commentators would have us believe. There is no reason to suppose that the total supply of pieces ordnance from the Forest of Dean ever reached three figures, nor does it seem possible that much of the production was suitable for use as field artillery – it was iron, and unlikely to have been of the latest design. Even if some good field pieces we do not yet know about were manufactured this never did translate into an Oxford train

30 Ibid, pp 32–33.

of guns that matched each other – and Royalist artillery stocks for the field remained modest and ill assorted.[31]

Shropshire, a cradle of the Industrial Revolution in the eighteenth century, was a place with some potential for the production of Royalist armaments. As early as 1619 there was a works at Bringewood leased to iron master Edward Vaughan. There are more frequent references to iron production in north west Shropshire in the 1630s, and in 1635 Sir Richard Newport of Ercall Magna constructed a blast furnace. At that time, or not long afterwards, there was also a forge operating at Sheinton. In 1638 the Newport works were leased to William Boycott and William Fownes. Coppice woods in the Ludlow area are known to have been leased to various iron masters to provide charcoal for the industry. Cannon certainly were produced for the Royalists in Shropshire, but the numbers were undoubtedly relatively small. An order for 44 guns from iron master Francis Walker's Bouldon works near Ludlow for the defences of Bristol was probably completed during 1643, and a request for more followed later. We also have firm evidence for the manufacture of four guns which were destined for a ship at Chester, and also for the supply of shot – but nothing from which a train of modern field artillery could have been created. An interesting piece of circumstantial evidence as to what the Royalist command might have construed as Shropshire's most significant munitions product emerged in 1664. For in that year Charles II granted the Boycott family a coat of arms, upon which were no cannon, but three granadoes.

It is probably telling that whilst a significant number of leather guns, pieces by John Browne, a Parliamentarian mortar, and two guns with the arms of the Commonwealth survive from the period, there is no single piece that we can point to as definitely produced for the Royalist forces between 1642 to 1651 that still exists in collections today. This extremely patchy picture, and the almost total lack of field gun production, as opposed to fortress gun manufacture, goes a long way to explain why the Royalist commanders were so keen on the import of artillery from abroad. If there were pieces to be had – and money to buy them – foreign ordnance could have been an instant solution, purchased ready made and delivered to any point on the coast far more rapidly than a lead time involving domestic order, manufacturing time, and land transport. Needless to say things were not this simple: the enemy had control of the sea, money was extremely tight, and the guns that were for sale were not the best – nor were they necessarily compatible with anything else in the Royalist magazine.

The key markets where ordnance was to be had were France and the Netherlands, and in these areas the Queen, Lord Goring and Lord Montague

31 'Inventory of the Royal Ironworks in the Forest of Dean, 1635', reprinted in H.R. Schubert *History of the British Iron and Steel Industry*, London, 1957, pp 408–416; *Royalist Ordnance Papers* pp 8–9; P. Edwards *Dealing in Death: The Arms Trade and the British Civil Wars*, Stroud, 2000, pp 77, 79, 97–99.

were important go betweens. Initial landings of supplies were mainly on the East coast. In 1643, with better security in the South West, Royalist vessels attempted to keep open the passage up the Bristol Channel. Shipments from Europe included relatively few guns, and often the quality of other supplies was low – distinctly old stocks of cannon powder, and what one Royalist commentator was moved to call any 'old trash' that could be 'wrapt together'. Moving ordnance out of, or through, London, which might have been possible on a small scale before the shooting war started, became increasingly impossible. Improved 'stop and search' powers formally granted to the militia during 1643 gave them not merely the right but the duty, to seek out any 'provisions for war' whatever, down to searching through carriages and individual trunks. With this precaution nothing very much could come out of the city, and to make sure the job was thorough guard posts were established, housing both soldiers and civilian auxiliaries. In the small posts at Muckwell Street and Bartholomew the Lesse just four men sufficed for this boring duty; at Farringdon the full complement was 130. The civilians involved were issued with a bill or halberd to impress their authority upon the tradesmen and travellers being searched.[32]

Paradoxically some of the Royalists' best guns were those they captured from the enemy. Some were taken as early as Edgehill, but a more major windfall in this respect was the capture of the entire artillery train of the Earl of Essex after the battle of Lostwithiel in 1644. It was these guns that bolstered the Royalist army's murderous defence at the Second Battle of Newbury – where some of them were recaptured again for Parliament. Perhaps the oddest of the pieces taken by the Royalists at Lostwithiel was the so called 'Basilisco' or 'Queen's Pocket Pistol', a 12 pound piece with an amazing 23 foot long barrel. The 'Pocket Pistol' was in fact cast at Utrecht as long ago as 1544, and presented to King Henry VIII in May 1545. For both sides this century old presentation piece must have been extremely difficult to manoeuvre around the country-side.[33]

Given the difficult situation it is surprising that the Royalist Ordnance Commissioners achieved so much, the whole enterprise being what one commentator has called 'masterly improvisation'. It might also be speculated that the relatively autocratic and nimble way in which the Royalist command was sometimes able to operate compared favourably to the many committees of Parliament in the vicissitudes of war. Yet these successes would eventually count as nought against established industry, wealth, and numbers. Interestingly the real problem was not so much that the Royalists did not have enough guns, but that the types they had were unsuitable for the tasks in hand, that they were unable to supply them with sufficient ammunition, or to get both

32 *Royalist Ordnance Papers*, pp 42–44; *The True Informer*, 30 September 1643, p 11; BL E 69(14) *An Act of the Common Council ... Establishing of Watches*, October 1643, passim.
33 The Queen's Pocket Pistol, now back at Dover, is item XIX. 246 in the Royal Armouries collection.

artillery and munitions to where they were most needed at the right time. The vast majority of the King's guns were not new, were not well matched to each other, and most were tied up in towns and castles. By way of illustration it is worth noting that Parliamentarian sources claim – probably accurately – that they captured many hundreds of guns from enemy towns from 1644 to the end of the First Civil War. A pamphlet entitled *England's Jubilee* speaks of well over 300 pieces taken from the Royalists in the months leading up to early June 1646; Joshua Sprigge mentions approximately 500 for the period April 1645 to the beginning of June 1646, with an additional 400 taken by August 1646. Between them the taking of Bristol, Oxford, Exeter, Dartmouth and Pendennis Castle appears to have accounted for roughly seventy per cent of the guns lost by the King in the last year of the First Civil War.[34]

Without powder guns were useless, and both sides had problems with gunpowder, but again it was the King who had the most significant issues to overcome, and some of these problems were of his own making. Before the war it had been recognised both that supply to the crown was important, and that the gunpowder could be a lucrative product to sell. To these ends saltpetre producers had been given special powers of entry to privately owned property to collect the saltpetre that grew naturally in dung heaps, in stables and under floors. The petremen also had compulsory rights, established as long ago as the reign of Elizabeth, to allow them to hire transport for their business. The price of saltpetre was limited – whilst at the same time gunpowder itself became a regulated monopoly. The result was that though the crown profited to some degree yet another unpopular monopoly was created and placed in a few favoured hands. Moreover the regulated supply of powder rarely seemed adequate, even in peace time. A few held out against these invidious arrangements, and there were even instances where anger boiled over into actual violence. Passive resistance was widespred, being reported from as far afield as Kent, Cambridge, London and Lichfield. In Bristol a theoretically illegal powder maufactury continued to exist. Two of the prime movers in this trade were Thomas Hilliard and William Baber, with the former supplying saltpetre to the latter, 'conveyed secretly, in the night, in close sacks and barrels to Bristol'. In September 1631 the attention of the government was alerted by two informers, and following enquiries Eziekiel Wallis, mayor of Bristol, was forced to admit the existence of the illegal trade, which had been winked at due to the revenues it brought to the city. Complaints about petremen and the official system continued throughout the 1630s, prices were pegged in 1636, and Parliament only finally succeeded in overturning the 'pernicious' powder monopoly in August 1641.[35]

---

[34] J. Sprigge *Anglia Rediviva*, London, 1647 pp 334–335; BL E 509 (4) *The Jubilee of England*, London, June 1646, pp 1–3.

[35] *A Proclamation for the Prevention of Abuses Touching Gunpowder and Saltpetre*, 26 January 1623; *CSPD* CCCCXXII, May 1639, pp 262–263; CLXII, 6 March 1630, p 206; CCXXXIII, 4

When war came Charles had good reason to rue his former policy for, like so many other things, the long established gunpowder trade and its official channels ran through London: production was centred on the south east of England, and Surrey in particular. Saltpetre imports from the Indies came by sea, and the sea was largely controlled by his enemies. His servants in his own territories, the west and north of England, were forced to start afresh, import at their peril, and to trade with former 'illegals' – such as William Baber. In the meantime Parliament was faced with disgruntled monopolists and dwindling stocks; in late 1642 it faced its own crisis as the King advanced on London, some facilities had to be dismantled, and the store nearly ran dry. Nevertheless for the King's enemies there were remedies to hand, and from January 1643 the trickle of imports from abroad grew. A few weeks afterwards home production under Samuel Cordwell, John Berisford, and others was well on its way to revival. The flow of Parliamentarian powder increased to a flood in 1644, and in 1645 hit a yearly production high of 4825 barrels. To make sure that it kept coming Parliament ordered funds to be paid direct from the excise to Sir Walter Erle. Output from the centre was further supplemented by provincial powdermills in the Midlands, Gloucester and Manchester, and by imports. For the Royalists producing powder did in the end prove easier than casting heavy ordnance – but this was one more disadvantage that the King's forces could well have done without. Royalist powder magazines proved more difficult to replenish from the localities, but mills were certainly established in Newark, York, and Oxford. During the latter part of the war however these works would be snuffed out one by one, and the foreign lifeline ultimately proved tenuous.[36]

Whilst Parliament stepped up taxation and used the existing administrative and industrial assets to increase production of guns and other munitions Royalist efforts were supported by decreasing funds. Latest research suggests that Parliament spent a monthly average of over £20,000 on its navy alone during the First Civil War, with expenditure on its main field armies reaching £90,000 a month at the height of the conflict. At the same time military expenditure reached almost nine tenths of all government spending in the kingdom. Parliament was never successful in gathering all the funding that it required, and back pay and unpaid bills were a lasting legacy – but gradually financial exactions were made to bite. The machinery creaked and frequently ground exceedingly slow, but eventually it was made to work. The Royalists, by contrast, proved to have more finite coffers. Both sides were forced to conscript horses and take free quarter in lieu of ready money, but it became more obvious that the King's promises were backed by increasingly tenuous sureties. As prospects

March 1633, p 557; S. Bull 'Pearls From the Dungheap: English Saltpetre Production 1590–1640', *Journal of the Ordnance Society*, 2, London, 1990, pp 5–10.

[36] Lewis 'Office of Ordnance', pp 321–342; P. Edwards *Dealing in Death*, Stroud, 2000, pp 110–117, 179; PRO WO 55/1660; *House of Commons Journal*, 3, 26 November 1644, pp 705–706.

of recompense dwindled the dividing line between the legitimate procurement of supplies and outright plunder became more and more hazy – and a more interesting subject for Parliamentarian propaganda. Local studies of counties such as Shropshire and Worcestershire, and of Wales, have shown how the Royalist well ran dry – whilst London in particular maintained trade with the Eastern Counties and the Continent.[37]

It has been correctly remarked that not only did the Royalist ordnance procurement network lack funds, but it also lacked focus. Parliament's efforts centred on London, and through London flowed money and much of its armaments. The geographic position of London was not central to the country, but it was the wealthy Parliamentarian heartland with good access to the sea. Had London fallen it is difficult to see how Parliament's provincial centres in East Anglia and the South might have continued the war – but it did not fall. The King's position, by contrast, was diverse and fluid. Oxford was one significant centre of munitions production, Bristol another. Worcester, Weymouth and Newcastle also played their parts, but most of the Royalist towns were insecure to some degree, and Bristol in particular changed hands more than once. Scattered production created no real economy of scale, no centre of excellence, and co-ordinating supplies was difficult. For small items such as musket shot this was an inconvenience, but for the heavy industry of cannon it was a well nigh impossible situation. By the last few of months of the First Civil War it seems that the ordnance workers at Oxford had little to do: supply was all but cut off. According to one account Sir Edward Sherburne therefore formed them 'into an ordinary troop' which took its place as part of the garrison.

That the King's armies often did not have what they needed is demonstrated by many different Royalist sources. In official papers Sir John Heydon, the Royalist officer with the principal task of supplying ordnance, is continually ordered to provide guns on peril of the consequences of not doing so. Nevertheless Royalist artillery supplies had an extremely awkward habit of running out, just at the wrong moment, and as we shall see guns of relatively small calibre were forced to do duty in sieges where 'battering' ordnance should have been used. At the same time there was considerable clamour from the Royalist localities for access to the relatively small supply of artillery and small arms that the Queen was able to import from Holland. Guns were simultaneously demanded, albeit respectfully, by Yorkshire, Lancashire, and by Oxford. Similar problems were encountered by Parliament, but very often the Roundhead gunners were given the chance to start again. When supplies faltered, eventually more would come along later. When guns were captured it was possible to make or buy more. When imports were needed the Parliamentarian domination of the seas was adequate to ensure that most of the ships got through.

---

[37] See R. Hutton *The Royalist War Effort*, London, 1982, pp 86–109; J.S. Wheeler *The Making of a World Power*, Stroud, 1999, pp 80–91.

Parliamentarian central funds ran very low, but it was possible to borrow more – and tax more.

Despite the hiccup of 1645 and the King's correspondence the Brownes landed up on the winning side. Some of the Foley family of Worcestershire iron founders were on the opposite side of the line producing munitions, including some thousands of pike heads, and some iron guns and shot, for the King. Yet the awkward facts of history were no bar to Browne ambition: in the next generation, Anne, the oldest of John Browne's surviving daughters was married to Thomas Foley, son and heir to iron master Richard Foley. This cementing of mutual interest was further reinforced in the mid 1650s when George Browne bought into the Foley family business. Commonwealth, Protectorate and later Stuart gun contracts then flowed to Foleys and Brownes, with some Browne work being subcontracted to Foley furnaces. Alexander Courthope, John Baker, John Rabson, Elia Bleuett were all named as sub-contractors or collaborators in the post Restoration period. George Browne was reconfirmed as his majesty's gun founder as late as 1681. Whoever else might have claimed to have won the Civil Wars the Browne gunfounding dynasty came through virtually unscathed.[38]

[38] See also G.E. Aylmer *The State's Servants*, London, 1973, p 39.

4

Artillery Fortifications

At the opening of the Civil War knowledgeable commanders on both sides were well aware that very few of the towns, houses and castles of England were tenable in modern war. Many sieges on the Continent – in Italy, the Dutch Wars, and then the Thirty Years War – had demonstrated that medieval walls were no match for artillery. Indeed as early as 1589 Paul Ive in his *Practise of Fortification* had offered the opinion that, 'Townes enclosed with weake walles of stone, and defended with small, square or rounde towres, are insufficient to abide the mallice and offence that an enemey at this day may put in practise, the cannon being an engine of much more force than any before it invented.' It would not be exaggerating to say that the cannon had already revolution-ised siege warfare, and that in general English towns and castles were poorly prepared for what was coming. Only prodigious quantities of earth, in the latest bastioned traces, stood any chance in a protracted siege involving trains of battering ordnance. Those few places that could boast even relatively new artillery defences usually faced outward, against foreign enemies. These excep-tions to the general rule of total unpreparedness were the great ports and the border extremities: Berwick, Hull, Portsmouth, some of the Cinque Ports, and certain seaside castles of the south and the Channel Islands.

William Georges, reviewing England's defences in the reign of James I, came to the gloomy conclusion that even here the forts were not of the latest design, nor were the personnel who manned them likely to make serious resistance even if properly equipped:

> It is well worth the remembrance, and consideration that whereas we have many blockhouses and castles upon sundry parts of our coasts, where the most easy places are for an enemy to land, and make descent, the which strengths although they be not fashion'd according to the moderne fortifications, nor of so good defence, yet are of some stay ... when occasion requires, having also in them good store of ordinance, and allowance for munition, for soldiers and gunners, but so it is, that the most or many of them, are so strangely fitted with captaines, and soldiers that upon the least Alarum, or sight of an enemy, they would for fear play least in sight, or through ignorance of Martiall affaires, doe little good, if they were present.[1]

---

[1] BL Lansdowne Ms 213, f 46. A good, though now dated, resumé of literature on British fortifications is J.R. Kenyon *Castles, Town Defences, and Artillery Fortifications in Britain: A*

At best the coastal defences were a moderate obstacle to invasion – apparently most likely to come from France or Spain since the union of the English and Scottish crowns in 1603. Yet without reinforcement, and well maintained artillery, they might still fall easy prey to any invader well equipped with guns. Inland defences were even more neglected, tending to be more a matter of antiquarian interest than practicality, as was demonstrated when officers of the 'Military Company' of Norwich visited 26 of England's counties in 1635. The castles at Lincoln and Kendal were dismissed as 'much decayed'; York, Nottingham, Bristol, Queenborough on the Medway, Southampton, Oxford, Rochester and others were in various states of disrepair if not total delapidation. In North Wales other sources showed similar disrepair at many of the major castles, whilst Pembroke in the south was roofless. Another group of castles including Arundel, Winchester, Leicester, Berkley and Carlisle were all remarked on, not for their defensive potential, but for their beauty, stateliness, or quality as gentlemen's homes. The town of Gloucester was unusual in that it caught the soldier's eye as having some potential with its location 'defensively guarded by the river' and wall with six gates.

Only a handful of places were worthy of note as having any actual power of resistance, and for the most part these were on the coast. Landguard Fort was found to have 'strong fortifications' and a 'watchful garrison'. Harwich had guns but not a great deal of order, as one of the Norwich officers observed:

> I found here 10 pieces of ordinance upon the wall [of] the fort and as many more, in another place by the key side, and lying all along grouling and groaning, as if they were bed-rid, and not able to hold up their heads, ever since the other over-throat neighbouring fort [Landguard] (from whence I came last) began to flourish ...[2]

Tilbury on the Thames was another place with a blockhouse and a good stock of guns, and a potential which would only finally be fully recognised in the reign of Charles II. In 1635 the Norwich author was admitted by 'one of the drummers' who 'showed me 26 fayre peeces of ordinance, how they were planted both above and below, the magazine of ammunition, [and] the Captaines Chamber, wherin were the colours lodged that were sett up on the walles of Cales in Spain'. There were further stores of munitions at other Thames blockhouses, but at Gravesend it was the quantity of alehouses which most impressed the East Anglian visitors. Very likely it was one of these that had once been run by Master Gunner William Bourne, the inventor ballis-

---

Bibliography, Council For British Archaeology Research Report, 25, 1978. *Fort*, the Journal of the Fortress Study Group, published by the University of Liverpool from 1976 to the present, contains many more recent articles and reviews. Particularly relevant is P. Harrington 'English Civil War Fortifications' in *Fort* 15, 1987, pp 39–60.

2   BL Lansdowne Ms 213, 'Relation of a Short Survey of the Western Counties', f 3. During the Civil War at least one observer stated that Gloucester had seven gates.

tician of the reign of Queen Elizabeth who had done so much to advance ideas as diverse as experimental gunnery and the submarine. Dover was found impressive, in part because of the story that guests were told that the castle had first been built by Julius Caesar – and also because of the presence of the huge Henrician 'basilisco', now known in jest as the 'Queen's Pocket Pistol'. Of far more practical account were the modern guns in the outlying forts and bulwarks, ten pieces being counted on the 'high cliffe', and a further 20 at the other end of town near the pier. Not far away King Henry's castles at Deal and Sandown were found to be in structurally fair condition despite some alarming reports in state papers – though they were undoubtedly of old design.[3]

Further west along the south coast was Portsmouth, which was found to have a 'fort on top whereof is mounted many goodly pieces of ordnance'. This was one of the few places sufficiently security conscious for the Norfolk men to be stopped and questioned by a sentinel who was puzzled by their assiduous interest in the security of the kingdom. At Carisbrooke on the Isle of Wight the Elizabethan artillery works, improved by the Italian Gianibelli in the 1580s were discovered still to be 'spacious, strong and defensible'. In Dorset Corfe Castle, high on its natural rock, was also in 'very good repayre', but with one very obvious deficiency,

> The walls about her very strong, and large, have faire walkes, receive plat-formes, and good ordinance but their chiefest guns which were goodly brave Brasse peeces, were lately batter'd and broken in pieces, and sold, by one (you may imagine) rather of Venus, then Mars his company, much to the weakening of the whole Island.[4]

Though Plymouth retained a defensive capacity, other towns on the south coast were questionable. In the extreme south west, the Cornish Henrician castles of Pendennis and St Mawes were still garrisoned. The former had had modern angular bastions added at the end of the sixteenth century. In 1632 however the complement of Pendennis was cut from 100 to 50, and at least some of the ordnance was removed in 1639. St Mawes obviously had some structural problems for in 1634 outstanding repairs were assessed at £534 10s, and it remained vulnerable on the landward side. That same year a general proposal was made that iron guns on ships should be exchanged with any bronze guns in forts. Though bronze guns were common at sea, and iron guns were common in land defences, this clear distinction was never achieved and mixtures of bronze and iron continued to be used in forts.[5]

3   Ibid, ff 5–8. See also V.T.C. Smith 'The Artillery Defences of Gravesend', in *Archaeologia Cantania*, 89 ,1974, pp 143–153; E.C. Murray and P. Hulton *Catalogue of British Drawings*, 1960, p 175, and S. Bull 'The Key of the Kingdom', in *Army Museum 84*, Journal of the National Army Museum, 1984, pp 17–22.
4   BL Lansdowne Ms 213, f 52.
5   S.P. Oliver, citing state and other papers, in *Pendennis and St. Mawes*, London, 1875, pp 26–67, 92–97; N. Pevsner *Buildings of England: Cornwall*, 2nd edn, 1970, p 189; Department

The plot of England's defences was therefore extremely patchy at 1640. Her castles were a mixture of the ruinous and those which might be made to do some service in emergency. In towns close packed wooden framed buildings were a tempting target for modern incendiary weapons, or arsonists intent on burning out an enemy. Walls were sometimes absent, but more often old and neglected, breached or straddled by housing. Around London many suburbs would have to be partially destroyed in 1642 and 1643 to make the city defensible, and there were also troublesome buildings that had sprung up in the ditch which ringed the Tower during the decades of peace. At Chester a very significant portion of the medieval walls survived, though as late as June 1641 reports to the City Council recorded that they were in poor condition, and in places had fallen down altogether. Some towns and cities, notably York and Lincoln, did have sturdy walls. Early in the war Nehemiah Wharton also commented on the perimeters of Coventry and Hereford, with their four and five gates respectively. Even in a poor state of repair town walls were an obstacle to men and horses, if not to cannon – but in 1642 such defences were for the most part more potential than actual. Many were aware of this: Ward, in his *Animadversions of Warre* of 1639, commented that those putting 'confidence in the strength of them' were 'deceived'.[6]

It would be wrong however to assume that there was no knowledge of modern fortification in England, for not only had a good number of Englishmen served in Europe, but many experienced continental and Scottish soldiers and engineers were drawn to the growing conflict – by both mercenary and idealistic motives. Amongst these Sir Bernard de Gomme would achieve pre eminence as a builder of fortifications for the Royalists – but there were many others on both sides. The Swedish engineer Beckmann, Hendrick the Dutch engineer, and La Roche all came to the aid of the King. The German Colonel John Rosworme, fought for Parliament, as did du Boyes, John Dalbier, Joachim Haine, Cornelius Vanderboone and Humphrey Vanderblin. In perhaps the most extraordinary skill set of any person fighting in the Civil Wars Peter de Sallonova claimed to be both Master of the Ordnance and surgeon to the garrison of Weymouth, for which posts he demanded a total of £1736 in back pay at the end of the First Civil War. Robert Ellis, who planned the Royalist works of Chester was just one of several Englishmen who had fought in Europe under Gustavus Adolphus.

Moreover by the standards of the day England was a highly literate country. The works of Du Praissac, Mendoza, de Ville, Marlois and others were all trans-

of the Environment, *Pendennis and St Mawes*, 1975 pp 7–22; PRO SP 16/278, 4 December 1634.
6   The walls of York receive detailed appraisal by P. Wenham in *The Great and Close Siege of York*, Kineton, 1970, pp 4–10, whilst Wharton's comments on Coventry may be found in the reprinted edition of *The Letters of Nehemiah Wharton*, Wollaston, 1983, p 12. For Chester see S. Ward *Excavations at Chester*, Grosvenor Museum Report 4, Chester, 1987, pp 5–6, 17; R. Ward, *Animadversions of Warre*, London, 1639, p 55.

lated into English. Richard Norwood's *Fortification and Architecture Military* appeared as recently as 1639, and many of the current home grown military compendiums contained a chapter or two on the art of fortification. Many foreign works, even in the original, were at least partially accessible to non linguists since the lexis of fortification was itself a largely universal language to the competent military engineer. Words and descriptions like 'ravelin', 'court of guard', 'bulwark' and 'countermure' were a part of common vocabulary which tended to unite, rather than divide the soldiery of different European nations. Whilst many continental experts flowed into England during the period at least a few went in the opposite direction. The engineer and military theorist Thomas Malthus, for example, was English by birth though he worked in France and wrote in French. Many English Royalists in exile would put themselves at the disposal of France after 1646, and again after 1648. Spying in foreign strongholds and dockyards may have been the most glamorous way to discover the latest intelligence, but in the seventeenth century, as in the twentieth, a visit to a library was the usual way to keep abreast of rivals in military technology. The study of actual foreign sieges could be similarly rewarding and was highly practicable due to a burgeoning press: accounts of Ostend, Breda, La Rochelle, Venloo, Julich, Bergen-Op-Zoom and many others had been published – and there was little about the subject that could not be discovered. Any literate gentleman could pick up the rudiments given the will, and some, though by no means all, 'civilian soldiers' became expert. Echoes of many of the ideas they acquired still remain to be seen in the archaeology.[7]

Many of the contemporary theorists expressed their bookish notions in terms of ideals: embankments to be so many yards long; enfilading fields of fire to be from certain angles and bastions of set dimensions; stores for long sieges consisting of so much water, grain, and munitions. Abstract or fanciful as they might appear these ideas were based upon the ranges and rates of fire of musket and cannon, and upon a realistic assessment of how much food was required for a garrison to survive for given periods. Yet the approach in England in 1642 and 1643 was essentially pragmatic, and depended much on the perceived level of threat, and the ability of commanders to motivate garrisons and raise funds. Not all towns were fortified at the same time, nor in the same way. From a professional military engineering standpoint W.G. Ross appreciated this as early as the nineteenth century, remarking that walls

---

7   The 1639 English edition of Du Praissac's *Art of War* contained sections on the defence and 'expunging' of cities. Samuel Marlois *Art of Fortification* was translated into English by Hexam in 1638; Don Bernadino Mendoza's *Theorique and Practice of Warre* was an old favourite 'Englished' by Sir E. Hoby as long ago as 1597. Paul 'Ive' or 'Ivy' worked in England, his *Practice of Fortification* being published in 1589. Later influential foreign books included Adam Freitag's *Architectura Militaris*, published at Leyden in 1630, several works and versions of works by Stevin and Furtenbach, and Pietro Sardi's *Architectura Militare*, published in Venice in 1639. On Weymouth see *House of Commons Journal*, 4, 31 July 1646, pp 630–632.

were reused and strengthened with additional works wherever they existed, but where they did not 'provisional encientes' were dug and improved to modern standards as circumstances would allow. Studying the wide variety of English Civil War fortifications a century later V.T.C. Smith concluded that actually there were three main types. These were the construction of an entirely new bastioned circuit, as at Oxford or Newark; the grafting of new bastions onto old town walls, as at Worcester or Colchester; or a series of forts connected by lines of ramparts and ditches, as in the cases of London, Bristol, Plymouth and Chester.[8]

This basic typology has since been generally accepted. It is a good way to describe the broad categories, but perhaps one should be careful not to over generalise. Most English fortifications were indeed based on Dutch, French, or Swedish ideas – and major works such as those at Oxford, Bristol and Newark showed the Dutch influence particularly clearly. They also tended to be either improvements, or fresh starts. Nevertheless architects or jobbing soldiers had their own individualistic quirks. Topographic features, such as hills, rivers, and suburbs influenced designs and layouts to a significant extent, and it was an unimaginative and often unsuccessful engineer who ignored the intervention of the ground in favour of the pleasing isotropic plane of the drawing board. Large towns presented special problems in the production of continuous enceintes, and Henrician and Elizabethan works were reused or remodelled wherever possible. In all cases artillery was presumed to be the main threat, and by the middle of the war it was unusual for any significant settlement to be lacking defences, however meagre or amateurish they might be.

Though far from ideal, medieval works could be made to answer in a number of ways. Repairing breaches, flooding ditches, rehanging gates and cutting loopholes was general, and well calculated to deter or delay enemy infantry attack. Measures more specifically geared to the requirements of modern artillery included 'countermuring' – the backing of existing walls with earth and platforms, and the truncation and filling up of old, tall, medieval towers to use as mounts for guns. Excellent examples of both these techniques may still be seen at Carlisle castle, though similar works at Lathom House, Chester, and other sites have been largely expunged by subsequent building and landscaping, and even by more recent ill informed attempts to return medieval monuments to what is perceived as their 'original' appearance. At Scarborough castle probable evidence for the cutting short and filling of towers has been discovered by excavation. Ancient fortifications were also surrounded or interwoven with new earth works – as at Cambridge castle where the bastioned trace required

8   See W.G. Ross 'Military Engineering During the Great Civil War', in *Professional Papers of the Corps of Royal Engineers*, 13, Chatham, 1888, pp 142–154; V.T.C. Smith 'The Civil War Fortifications of London', unpublished manuscript held at the National Army Museum, 1978, pp 8–10, and P. Harrington *English Civil War Fortifications*, Oxford, 2003, pp 26–30.

the demolition of 15 houses in 1643. At Raglan castle the plan was particularly complex, and new bastions and curtains were conceived to cover vulnerable approaches to the old structure which was itself suitably adapted with musket loops. In perhaps the most extraordinary case the Dorset Maumbury Rings, a neolithic henge monument, subsequently used as an amphitheatre by the Romans, was transformed into a fort.

Immense amounts of material were required to stop a round shot, and the effort and cost involved in building defences should not be underestimated. Just to catch a humble musket ball needed about a foot of packed earth, but to do a proper job against the siege cannon demanded, by common consent, a 'shoulder or defence' of 'at least 11 foot high, and 23 foot thicke'. By such calculations a mere 20 feet of artillery proof banking called for the movement of perhaps as much as 5,000 cubic feet of earth – or more than 1,000 barrow loads. Small sconces might well have a trace of 600 feet, needing perhaps 150,000 cubic feet of earth. Yet this veritable mountain of backbreaking soil, shovelled and carried by hand was but part of the work. Some revetment was needed, inside, if not without the structure, and gun platforms and living accommodation would probably also be included. Even if all stone work was omitted a good deal of wood had to be cut, carted, and joined. A professional job also called for a well formed ditch, a contoured counterscarp, and entanglements of light branches, thorns, and sharpened stakes to impede infantry. Gabions or 'cannon baskets' of various sizes – probably wound from willow osiers and filled with rammed earth – provided local protection for battery positions and men detailed as lookouts. None of this was theoretical fancy, and the evidence of massive Civil War earthworks can be seen in a number of places to this day. In the instance of Taunton archaeological investigation has even revealed burnt gabions lying in the works.

The ideal method for building a modern self contained earth banked fort, capable of resisting artillery, was demonstrated at Sandown in the 1630s. Here Thomas Rudd, the supervising engineer, laid down a plot consisting of a basic square about 200 feet long on each side, furnished with projecting angled bastions to flank enemy attackers. The wet moat, fed by a ditch from the landward side, was nearly 50 feet wide – a significant obstacle to traverse when under fire. To minimise the distance that the vast amount of material had to be moved earth from the excavation of the ditch was piled up on the inner side to form the bastions. Sandown fort was designed to last, being revetted in stone – as were several of the later Cromwellian works in Scotland. Work on Sandown extended over five seasons, and fluctuated considerably in intensity. Activity ceased in the winter when the ground was hard, but the maximum strength of the workforce was achieved in the summer of 1633 when about 50 carters and 70 labourers were employed. The usual working week was six days, though a few men had to sacrifice even a part of the Lord's day during certain phases of construction when one or two lime kilns had to be kept continually alight. The labourer's pay was 9d per day, with 1s for a sawyer, and 1s 6d for a carpenter. Work periods were timed by means of hour glasses, and a drum was used to call the builders to their toil. In addition to the basic structure gun platforms were made from three inch thick planks of wood, and the banks of the fort also enclosed a barrack block, magazine, and house for the captain. The fort was complete in 1636, and the total cost of the project was assessed at £3,585. In August 1642 the keepers of the fort surrendered to Captain Richard Swanley without firing a shot.[9]

In the extremities of war urgency and lack of funding would lead to a good deal of extemporisation. The quickest, if not most perfect, way to get earthworks completed on time was to conscript the civilian population, and in many cases local authorities set the 'townesmen' – and often their womenfolk – to the task. Naturally gentlemen would usually be excused from such demeaning employment, being expected to contribute financially, or to give their time as officers in military service. In some instances the workers were paid, in others taxes were rebated against time spent. Some of the work was effectively slave labour, executed against promises which were never honoured. The degree to which men worked willingly must have varied considerably, depending on commitment to the cause, likelihood of pay, the imminence of the harvest, and other factors. Lithgow would have us believe that in the case of London the populace went to their work with joy in their hearts and fire in their bellies, and even some of the better sort taking part in manual labour:

> The daily musters and shows of all sorts of Londoners were wonderous commendable, in marching to the fields and outworks (as merchants, silkmen, macers, shop keepers etc) with great alacritie, carrying on their shoulders yron mattocks, and wooden shovels; with roaring drummes, flying colours, and girded swords; most companies being also interladed with ladies, women, and girles, two and two, carrying baskets for to advance and labour.

Only a tiny fragment of all this work now remains in the form of a denuded bank within Hyde Park.[10]

In fact the capital's defences were improved in stages, 'directions for the defence of London' being issued by Parliament as early as August 1642 – though not very much was achieved until later in the year. In October, when it seemed the King's army might break through, fresh instructions were given to 'fortifie all the passages' into both the City and the suburbs. At this time it appears that there were additions and repairs to the existing medieval defences, barriers and chains were put up across streets, and earthwork forts commenced.

---

[9] See J.D. Jones 'The Building of a Fort at Sandown, Isle of Wight, 1632–1636', in *Proceedings of the Isle of Wight Natural History and Archaeological Society*, vol 6, part III, pp 166–188, and A. Cantwell and P. Sprack 'The Sandown Bay Defences', in *Fortress, the Castles and Fortifications Quarterly*, number 7, 1990, pp 51–59.

[10] W. Lithgow *Present Surveigh of London*, London, 1643. Details of London and other works are given in Ross, 'Military Engineering', pp 202–230. See also J. Vicars *England's Parliamentary Chronicle*, London, 1646, pp 206–207.

The following February an 'Act of Common Council' instigated further works. These were approved by Parliament in March 1643, which then granted the Lord Mayor and Boroughs specific powers to 'entrench and stop all highways and byways' as they saw fit. According to the Venetian ambassador it was engineers from Holland who oversaw the works which proceeded with 'incredible cost and effort', and to his surprise the digging did not even stop on Sundays. Anything up to 20,000 people were employed at any given time with the Livery Companies vying with each other to make the most significant contribution – a competition apparently won by the weavers who claimed to have furnished 9,000 workers on one particular day. By late May the vast undertaking was virtually complete, with a total enclosed circuit of about 18 miles and a ditch that recent archaeological investigations have suggested to be about 18 feet wide. Much of London's anti artillery defence was the familiar earth and turf revetted with wattles, but in places, such as the major forts, some stonework was also used. The papers of the Ordnance Office show that 139 guns were supplied for the defence of London, the vast majority of these during 1643. To keep the works in good repair was a vast undertaking in itself, and a tax of 2d in the pound was introduced for this purpose. Arguably one of those worst hit by these impositions was Miles Brand, the lessee of Whitechapel Mill, whose tenements were demolished to make way for the defences and his mill rendered useless. Nevertheless he still had his taxes to pay, and his landlord sued him for unpaid rent.[11]

When Northampton's defences were strengthened following an order of May 1643 the mood was probably less upbeat than in London. The walls were in particularly poor state of repair, and the work was urgent. Initially the impressment quota was set at one person per household, labouring from one to six in the afternoon – presumably so as to allow families to earn their daily bread or tend any livestock in the mornings. In June a more complex direction made each ward of the town take to the works in rotation. Activity still continued in August 1643, and one of the major jobs completed was the cutting down of trees which were thought likely to shelter enemy troops from view in the event of attack. At Tenby the governor might have lacked such finesse, but in 1644 his defence works had a certain grim practicality. He simply had the main gate blocked, 'with dung and rubbish that grew hard and compacted' – and on the outside placed cannon baskets so close that a single man was hard pressed to worm his way between them to the gate. At Carmarthen a part of the substantial new town ditch survives to this day. Excavations in other places have demonstrated that it once varied from fifteen to almost 40 feet wide, and was anything up to 20 feet in depth. At Reading, towards the end of 1643, a contemporary account suggests that no less than 5,000 people from the surrounding areas of Berkshire were employed building the fortifications.

---

[11] See S. Porter *London and the Civil War*, 1996, passim, and D.E. Lewis 'The Office of Ordnance', unpublished PhD thesis, Loughborough, 1976, p 334.

Given the urgency of the situation some even laboured on during the night. Opening the fields of fire from the new works entailed the burning of three villages.

Few garrisons or towns were too small not to have any defensive provision, and archaeological records alone note about 200 Civil War works, some material evidence of which has survived into modern times. More exist only in the contemporary paper record, and some are doubtless now lost to us entirely. Spots as apparently as insignificant as Great Chalford in Wiltshire were given defences by Parliament, whilst gentlemen's homes which were deemed particularly strategically important might have apparently disproportionate efforts lavished upon them. At least £1,000 was spent on the defences of Basing House in Hampshire, an investment which turned out to be thoroughly justified. Shelford Manor, effectively an outstation to Newark, was entrenched with 'a great ditch without, in most places wet at the bottom', and 'a very strong bulwark'. Significant towns often received commensurately greater works. At Barnstaple the 'great fort' to house 28 guns is supposed to have cost £1,120; an entrenchment around the town £450; and improvements to the castle, including 16 gun platforms, a further £660. The huge and magnificent earthworks at Oxford, set about with 'many strong bulwarks', storm poles, and flooded obstacles, were something of a bargain at £30,000, though this probably does not include the hidden cost of conscripting males from 16 to 60, who were fined for any non attendance. Unusually the works of Oxford were later memorialised in paint, being pictured in Jan de Wyck's impressive picture, *The Siege of Oxford*. London certainly spent in excess of £12,000 as early as mid 1643. Given the final vast extent of London's works this initial expenditure can only have been a tiny part of the final total cost.[12]

The cost at Portsmouth is similarly unclear, though it must have been large, Clarendon being moved to describe it as 'the strongest and best fortified town in the kingdom'. It already possessed medieval works, and in 1640 was unusual in boasting a permanent garrison of 135 men, including Master Gunner John Lobb and 29 other gunners. This was subsequently much increased, and in the run up to hostilities, the governor, George Goring, appears to have courted both sides, extracting a promise of £3,000 and warrants for £5,030 from Parliament in July 1642. Significant sums of real money came from the King, with a rumour circulating of a delivery of £9,000 in silver, part of which was suggested simply to have disappeared into Goring's own pocket. The Castle defences were however mounted with at least 14 guns, the majority of which

[12] J.C. Cox (ed) *The Records of the Borough of Northampton*, Northampton, 1898, vol 2 pp 438–452; F.J. Varley *The Siege of Oxford*, Oxford, 1932, pp 19–24, 106–121; R.W. Cotton *Barnstaple and the Northern Part of Devonshire During the Great Civil War*, Barnstaple, 1889, pp 111–116; C. Trenchard *The Siege of Bridgwater*, Bridgwater, 1929, pp 16–21. BL E 42 (13) *A True Relation of the Routing of His Majesties Forces in the County of Pembroke*, April 1644, pp 2–7. Ross, 'Military Engineering', p 151; L. Hutchinson, *Memoirs of the Life of Colonel Hutchinson*, reprinted London, 1846, pp 284–287.

were 12 pounders. Critics were alarmed that Goring also ordered the removal of brass ordnance from ships, and placed it in landward facing defences. In the event some of the gunners deserted to Parliament, and the town's provisions proved inadequate.

In September Portsmouth was battered from across the water by Parliamentarian guns at Gosport, even as some of the defenders were labouring on new trenches at the Mount. One shot scudded through the town and ricocheted around inside the church, whilst other balls smashed one of the bells, and damaged nearby buildings. The explanation given for this apparently sacrilegious bombardment by Parliamentarian John Vicars was that the Royalists were using the church tower 'as their watch tower'. Parliamentarian troops equipped with scaling ladders, under the splendidly named Brown Bushell, rapidly overcame some rather half hearted resistance at Southsea Castle, despite a supporting bombardment from other parts of the defence. Morale raising appeals from Goring fell on deaf ears and Portsmouth was soon surrendered.[13]

The significant Civil War defences at York were still much apparent in the 1720s when Daniel Defoe regarded them as a charming relic of a former age. The earthworks here were however very much additions to the medieval walls and towers, which by themselves created a fortified circuit of over 5,000 yards. Repairs of the old works and the construction of new was commenced in September 1642. Three sconces were erected to the west of the City, and these were capable of containing substantial garrisons, 120 men being mentioned as the number housed in that at Bishopsthorpe Road. Further works at Clifton are believed to have been linked by trenches and breastworks. To the south of York a battery on Lamel Hill was the later work of the Parliamentarian besiegers, but to the east another Royalist fort has been identified on Baile Hill, atop a Norman motte. Another earthwork to the north of the City probably started life as a Royalist defence – later put to use by the enemy. The basic plan of the defenders was to regard the renovated walls of York as a back stop, in front of which were built artillery forts. The duty of these new constructions was to keep enemy guns well away from the medieval walls and castle – and thereby prevent them being breached by round shot. The town's artillery appears to have been made more self sufficient by the conversion of a mill near the castle to the production of gunpowder. Sadly evidence of earthworks that had survived well into the twentieth century was destroyed during building work in the 1930s and 1950s.[14]

Initially the plan of new works bolted onto old was repeated at Royalist Newark, where the castle formed an effective strong point, but the medi-

13 J. Webb *The Siege of Portsmouth in the Civil War*, Portsmouth Papers, number 7, revised edn 1977, pp 3–19; B.H. Patterson *A Military Heritage: A History of Portsmouth and Portsea Town Fortifications*, 2nd edn, Portsmouth, 1987, pp 8–23. J. Vicars *England's Parliamentary Chronicle*, pp 157–161.

14 York is discussed at length in P. Wenham *The Great and Close Siege of York*, Kineton, 1970, pp 4–8, 143–154. See also BL E 81 (17) *The Kingdom's Weekly Post*, 10 January 1644.

eval walls had been rendered much less effective by later development that straddled or beached them. Nevertheless at least some of the old walls were improved by piling earth behind them. The first new earthworks, as shown in a plan in Newark Museum, were constructed in 1642. These were a relatively slender affair with what has been described as 'irregular projections' rather than true bastions. Nevertheless Newark was able to withstand an attempt made upon her in February 1643. As reported in *Certaine Informations* the following month the Parliamentarians actually succeeded in seizing one of the bulwarks, but were pushed back leaving a couple of guns behind them. Thereafter a far more substantial circuit of defences was constructed. This included 'horn-works' or 'crownworks', different terms for external extensions to the lines of defence. Eyewitness John Twentyman observed that the new works were 'very high and strong', one of them, the 'King's Sconce', being erected on the land surrounding Twentyman's own dovecote. Other significant structures included the 'Goat Bridge Hornwork', 'Spight's Bulworke', 'The Great Bullworke', 'Millgate Hornwork', the 'Queen's Sconce' and a number of smaller bastions, batteries, and 'ravelins' (detached triangular bastions). The Queen's Sconce in particular remains an impressive monument, covering a little over three acres. Its vast ditch, up to 70 feet wide, is 12 to 15 feet deep, with a flat bottom and steep sides. Its corners feature large angle bastions with vastly thick walls of earth. Each side of the sconce is about 400 feet long, and the rampart rises to 30 feet above the ditch bottom in places. Working from the present dimensions, and allowing for erosion, we can calculate that digging the ditch and using the spoil to erect the bastions might well have required the shifting of half a million cubic feet of earth. Taken as a whole the Newark defences served effectively to make the town a very tough nut to crack. Together with the copious siege works later erected by the Parliamentarians the Newark complex eventually comprised one of the most comprehensive – and ultimately best preserved – collections of Civil War earthworks in the country.[15]

As we have seen the Parliamentarian town of Gloucester began the war with some protection from the river Severn, and from its medieval walls, apparent in John Speed's map of 1610. Nevertheless to achieve a credible defence capable of resisting modern siege weapons was a considerable challenge, particularly when over a hundred of Gloucester's citizens were thought to be Royalist sympathisers. Yet the committee had to start somewhere, and one of the first measures was the mounting of a good watch – with the town gates locked between 9pm and sunrise. A supply of horses was found for reconnaissance. Next £100 was raised for the purchase of three cannon, hand tools and barrows. Since suburbs had grown up outside the walls, and these would be untenable under

---

15 The Newark works are fully described in *Newark on Trent: The Civil War Siege Works*, Royal Commission on Historical Monuments, London, 1964; see also BL E 93(18) *Certaine Informations*, 13–20 March 1643, p 66; P. Young and W. Emberton *Sieges of the Great Civil War*, London, 1978, pp 127–136, and P. Harrington *English Civil War Archaeology*, London, 2004, pp 29–31.

siege conditions, another committee was appointed specifically to deal with the rehousing of displaced inhabitants. The Chamberlain's accounts mention the engagement of carpenters, labourers, smiths and other tradesmen. Nicholas Williams was employed to make gun carriages, whilst a man called Pegler fabricated their wheels. Amongst other items purchased were five powder horns for the ordnance, a linstock, and a 'form' – presumably for the making of cartridges. As costs escalated local taxes were gradually reassessed upwards.[16]

A great deal was achieved: existing walls were repaired, new sconces were constructed at either end of Alney Island, and sluices were opened to add flooded areas to the obstacles facing any attacker. A significant new earthwork was constructed at the Vinyard, Over. John Corbet records that the East and South ports of the town were blocked, 'and rammed with a thickness of earth cannon proofe, and the walls on that side from port to port were lined to the battlements, since there we thought to receive the main shock'. Impressive new bastioned lines were also added to the perimeter, again mainly to the south and east sides of the town, though not all of these were completed in 1643. Just how massive Gloucester's works were has only recently become fully apparent as a result of archaeological excavation. The ditch at South Gate bastion was about 33 feet wide and 14 deep, and the bastion itself was well over 300 feet wide. At least some of the works were also protected externally by pointed wooden 'storm poles' to deter infantry from swarming over the top.[17]

Newcastle had some work on its defences from 1638 in expectation of Scottish attack, with Sir Jacob Astley and the engineer du Boyes employed about the business. Though Astley realistically advised that the town could not be held indefinitely as it was overlooked by hills, he recommended that repairs on the gates be completed and then 20 guns should be placed on the towers, walls, or 'convenient batteries'. At least one fort was constructed outside the town and 'Carr's Battery' within. During 1643 and 1644 more defence works were commissioned by the mayor John Marley, who had the ditches and castle improved, whilst the old walls were reinforced with material from a huge dung heap. His most useful contribution was a series of modern earth works consisting of redoubts, bastions, hornworks and 'demi lunes'. The complete circuit enclosed by medieval and new fortifications extended for at least two miles. Parts of the Newcastle defences have been excavated in recent times,

[16] J.R.S. Whiting *Gloucester Besieged*, Gloucester, 1975, pp 7–8; T.D. Fosbrooke *An Original History of Gloucester*, Gloucester, 1819, pp 12–65; GRO Gloucester Borough Records F4/5; R. Atkyns *The Ancient and Present State of Gloucester*, 1712, passim. I am particularly grateful to clay pipe collector Mr P. Christmas, then of Gloucester, for many enjoyable field trips to the town during the period 1981–1991.

[17] J. Corbet *An Historicall Relation of the Military Government of Gloucester*, London, 1645, p 41. A lucid explanation of the archaeology is given in M. Atkin and W. Laughlin *Gloucester and the Civil War*, Stroud, 1992, pp 44–74. See also C.M. Heighway *The East and North Gates of Gloucester*, Western Archaeological Trust, 1983, passim. A number of useful tracts are reprinted in J. Washbourn, *Bibliotheca Gloucestrensis*, 1823.

with a 20 foot wide ditch, partly revetted in stone, being one of the main features discovered. Small finds associated with these defences included shot, part of a hand grenade, and powder charges from a bandolier.[18]

Newport Pagnell is unusual in that it appears to have been heavily fortified to modern standards by Parliament comparatively late in the war. At about Christmas 1643 orders were issued that the eight counties of the Eastern Association should contribute to a garrison here, and some time during 1644 the Dutch engineer and 'master of fireworks' Vanderboone completed an earthwork enclosure of the town. This included eight bastions and three entrances, as well as a substantial ditch which was probably flooded.

In the instance of Chester, in early 1643, the new Dutch style earthworks were laid out by Royalist engineers, 'who caused according to the modern way of fortification to be cut a trench and mud wall to be made from Deeside without the Barrs to Deeside at the new tower ... and turnpikes at all the outworks as Barrs, Cowlane end, without the Northgate and at the Mount at Deelane end, by little St John's, besides severall mounts, pit falls and other devices to secure the outworks and annoy the enemy's approach to the City'. At least seven of the new works were designated 'mounts' – as for example 'Reed's Mount' and 'Cock Pit Mount' suggesting that they were dedicated gun platforms. Altogther the new lines stretched upwards of two miles, and showed how cleverly the planners took advantage of the town's position within the bend of the river Dee to create as large an enclosure as possible whilst maintaining economy of effort. The new works also had the effect of creating a double skin to the existing defence on the northern and eastern sides of Chester, where the old walls now formed an inner citadel. The Castle, in the extreme southern corner overlooking the river, now had potential as a literal 'last ditch' redoubt.

In aiming to create a vast enclosure the Chester Royalists may actually have been too successful, because improvements of 1644 not only appear to have strengthened the works, but rationalised and shortened their compass – apparently to save on manpower. Nevertheless ditches were deepened, further mounts constructed, and a form of covered way dug to facilitate the movement of ordnance. Though Chester was besieged at great length, Lord Byron also added a detached fort on the other side of the Dee in mid 1645. It is thought that this Hanbridge work took the form of a sconce with bastions, and mounted cannon. Assuming a main ditch just six feet deep and 20 feet wide, and as few as ten significant forts or batteries, it would be safe to presume that eventually the amount of earth moved to complete Chester's various defences far exceeded three million cubic feet.[19]

---

[18] M. Ellison and B. Harbottle 'The Excavation of a Seventeenth Century Bastion in the Castle of Newcastle Upon Tyne', in *Archaeologia Aeliana*, 5th series, vol 11, Newcastle, 1983, pp 135–263.

[19] BL Harleian Ms 2155; W. Cowper, *Plan of the Royalist Works*, CRO DCC26; S. Harrison (et al) *Loyal Chester*, CRO, 1984, pp 20–25; Ward *Animadversions of Warre*, pp 4–11.

Almost at the other end of the scale Skipton Castle in Yorkshire, owned by the Royalist Clifford family, was a medieval structure, made answerable to the moment in a very different way. Sods were laid against the walls to absorb cannon shot, and carters delivered 867 loads of stone for upgrading the old defences. The castle stores were already full of ordnance, predominantly Tudor, but much of it was still serviceable. The guns numbered 15 pieces, seven of them iron guns, including a 27 pound demi cannon. Some of the brass pieces were historical curiosities, being three of the so called 'seven sisters' – 18 and 19 pound pieces brought back from the battle field of Flodden in 1513. Amongst the smaller guns was a 'murderer' – an old wide bored weapon designed to fire case or other pieces of small shot against infantry at close range. Barrels of powder were obtained from York along with small arms and other equipment, and Scottish engineer and gunner Duncan Liddell was retained at a generous £3 a month as resident expert, seconded by three other gunners on lesser wages. The garrison was brought up to strength with 127 common soldiers, and Earl Henry ran up debts of over £1000 with tradesmen and craftsmen for work and victuals.

Though the scope for modern earthworks at Skipton was limited, considerable pains were taken to remount the artillery. Guns were hoisted up to the top of a number of towers, but the *pièce de résistance* was at the south east corner of the fortress. Here a 'great mount' was erected and the biggest gun, the two ton demi cannon, was hauled up onto the platform. This mount alone cost £8 to build, but it was money well spent for, when the Parliamentarians first approached in 1643, they were kept so far back from the walls by the thunder of cannon that they were unable to inflict any damage. Only in August 1645, long after much of the north had been suppressed in the wake of Marston Moor, did a Parliamentarian force succeed in installing batteries to fire on the castle – and with the guns 700 yards away at that. The finding of cannon balls ranging in size from 18 pounds down to 3 ounces in and around the castle and town does however attest to a fair exchange of fire, the Royalists being 'very potent' within their stronghold. This first siege was abandoned in October, before fresh forces started a new attempt in November. Skipton finally capitulated only shortly before Christmas, 1645. Even then the surrender was honourable, with the Royalists allowed to march out – colours flying and drums beating.[20]

Worcester, which has the dubious distinction of being fought over in the Third Civil War as well as being besieged, is interesting in that a series of excavations over a period of decades have helped to demonstrate that at least a part of its ditch defences was contoured in the latest continental manner. Though the actual depth of the ditch below the original ground level may only have

[20] *Articles Agreed Upon Betweene Coll. Richard Thorneton, Commander in chiefe of the Forces before Skipton Castle … And Sir John Mallory, Knight*, 1645; R.T. Spence *Skipton Castle in the Great Civil War*, Skipton, 1991, pp 12–55; 81–100.

been eight feet this was much improved by the height of the rampart that it enclosed, and a 'glacis bank' around the outside. This outer bank to the ditch reinforced it against erosion, but also presented any attacker with an extra steep step down, which he would have had to negotiate whilst fully exposed to the observation and fire of the defence. It is also probable that the rampart itself was furnished with a fire step, and possibly sharp 'storm poles', that would have made climbing out of the ditch and over the rampart especially difficult.[21]

A number of very detailed financial accounts for Civil War town defences survive. Some of the most comprehensive are those of Exeter, relating to the period from the end of 1642 to the late summer of 1643. A summary drawn up in mid 1643 states that by that time the town had expended at least £18,479 on its own defence, of which £4,374 had gone into physical construction. Digging and carrying turf for artillery works was one significant element, carpentry and masonry another, with planks being gathered and sawn, stone carted and laid. Some of the rock was carried by 'divers women' to the town walls, who were collectively paid 5s 8d for their trouble. The town ditches were deepened and reprofiled by teams of townsmen summoned by beat of drum. At Southernhay trenches were dug, and new works, including barricades and a turnpike, appeared at Exebridge. The old castle was also put back into a decent state of repair, a vital detail being the recommissioning of the well – which was cleaned out and given new ropes and iron work. Impromptu cover for the defenders included 17 'packs of woolls', retrieved from the cellars of Robert Robins and set upon barricades and the bridge. The danger from fire was not neglected: parts of the suburbs were barricaded off, and stocks of hay and straw moved away from the Guildhall.

Exeter's store of guns, probably only six in number initially, appear to have been increased to 25. Southgate was reinforced to take some of the artillery. Timber to make 'carriages for the great guns' was bought from 'Mr Anthony', whilst deal boards to provide running surfaces for the pieces within the batteries were found by Richard Hornabrook at a cost of £1 9s 6d, and John Baker for £15. That at least a portion of Exeter's gunpowder was locally made is suggested by an account entry for 12s to Emmanuel Dart, who carted water 'to make salt peter'. In January 1643 the total powder requirement of the town magazine was assessed as 80 barrels, whilst 40 cwt of match was needed to complement 30 cwt of 'musket bullets of several sizes' and four cwt of 'carbine bullets'. Round shot for the cannon were obviously critical as it was decreed that 1000 should be put into store, 'of severall sizes per the Gunners direccon'. All in all £3,769 was expended on ammunition, but the biggest single item in the town defence budget was soldiers' pay – a total of £9,442 in less than nine months. Part of this was spent on individual sentries to 'watch and ward' over the defences, usually armed with 'firelocks', at '8d a time'. Once Exeter was besieged the guard regime was tightened, with additional searches of walls and

21 P. Harrington, *English Civil War Archaeology*, London, 2004, pp 25–26.

houses, and each of the sentries inspected before going to his duty. Every man was expected to go on watch with four rounds of ammunition, and no bells were to be rung in Exeter except as an alarm, or to call the sentinels to duty – the church steeple itself doubled as watch tower.[22]

Though less well documented it is clear that further large sums must have been spent on Exeter in the latter part of the war – with various references to new works and trenches. The garrison may ultimately have commanded as many as 75 guns, this being the number specified by Joshua Sprigge as captured when the town fell. Under Royalist control more than £345 was spent on repairs to the city walls in 1644 alone. In 1646 Parliamentarian besiegers erected new forts and works outside the town to contain it – another expensive undertaking, though not one which was immediately paid for by the people of Exeter. By the time the town capitulated on 9 April 1646 the total bill for its defence is unlikely to have been much less than £40,000.[23]

We cannot tell exactly what the earthworks at Carlisle cost, and some of the defences there predated the Civil War. However we do know that £463 10s was expended in simply provisioning the garrison during the siege of 1644 to 1645. According to contemporary account this was gathered from local knights, gentlemen and other worthies. Of 126 contributions one was a combined effort by the Dean and Chapter, and a handful of others came from the sequesters of estates, or the representatives of estates – but the vast majority was donations by named individuals. Several were important Royalists whose names we recognise as leading regiments during the wars, each of whom gave sums from ten to twenty pounds. Many minor gentry and clergy committed anything from one to five pounds; the only woman named, Lady Curwen of Rottington, gave £4.[24]

Though every fortification of the period differed in detail there are a number of general observations that can be made. Most importantly in all but the most trivial of new structures the form was dictated by artillery – an ability to resist round shot, or to mount defensive pieces, or both. Less obviously it emerges that most of the defences were locally, not centrally, executed – and for the most part were certainly not paid for directly by either Charles' treasury or the London Parliament. De Gomme, as the King's 'engineer general', drew up many plans, but in a number of instances it is clear that what he was recording was either something that already existed, or that he was seeking to improve

---

22 Devonshire Records Office DD36995, Misc 6, and DD391, all transcribed in M. Stoyle *Exeter City Defences Project*, Exeter Museums Archaeological Field Unit, Report 88.12, December 1988, pp 1–54.

23 M. Stoyle *The Civil War Defences of Exeter and the Great Parliamentary Siege of 1645–1646*, Exeter Museums Archaeological Field Unit, Report 90.26, 1990, pp 12–36; J. Sprigge *Anglia Rediviva*, London, 1647, pp 334–335; BL E 84 (6) *Speciall Passages*, 27 December 1642 – 3 January 1643, p 174; E 84 (24) *A Famous Victory Obtained Before the City of Exeter*, January 1643, passim.

24 I. Tullie *Siege of Carlisle*, reprinted by S. Jefferson, Carlisle, 1840, pp 39–42.

on pre-existing structures. The case of Bristol is perhaps the most obvious in this respect. In 1643 the town was protected by a mixture of ancient features and new Parliamentarian works, and in 1644 its fortification was made better by Royalist hands. The report to which de Gomme appended his name after Bristol was retaken by Parliament in 1645 is essentially an apology explaining why poor works could not be held in the face of a superior enemy. The fact that the Royalists ordered the iron master Francis Walker to cast 30 extra guns culverins, demi culverins and sakers specifically for the defence of the town, just a month after they had seized it, would seem to suggest that there were also others who did not think Bristol was strong enough. Similarly de Gomme's plan of Liverpool does not demonstrate that workmen from Rupert's army built the defences of the town under his direction – rather that they sought to improve on what they found there, and his plan may, or may not, have been fully carried through at this time. Some of his best known work, such that at Tilbury and Portsmouth, obviously post dates the Civil War period.[25]

In the early part of the war lack of central direction in fort planning and building is even more apparent amongst the Parliamentarians. In the 1630s Francis Conningsby, Surveyor General of the Ordnance, had expanded his role to include that of Commissary General of fortifications – making surveys and returns on the state of works. After 1642 such a comprehensive approach was clearly impossible for Parliament's London Ordnance Office, and as far as we can tell was never even attempted by the new surveyor George Payler. The most that the Parliament officers appear to have been able to achieve was to recommend suitable engineers to the localities, and, sometimes, supply them with hardware. Frequently the approach was entirely ad hoc. In the case of Manchester, for example, the German engineer John Rosworme appears to have been appointed entirely upon the initiative of the local committee, and no assistance from London – let alone any instruction, was forthcoming for at least a year. At Barnstaple, Parliament may have voted £200 for the town's protection in January 1643 but, as we have seen, local expenditure on artillery works exceeded £1,600. In a number of cases Parliamentarian towns appear to have built first, then applied belatedly to the centre for financial contribution. Even in the crucial instance of Gloucester it appears that Parliament made promises which would not actually be fulfilled until long after the event. In November 1642 the MPs in London earmarked £1,000 for the town's garrison, and a further £500 was set aside in January 1643. As far as can be ascertained little, or none, of this was actually paid until 1644. For the most part Parliamentarians in the provinces appear to have used what was to hand, or planned

---

[25] A.D. Saunders *Tilbury Fort*, London, 1977, passim. The De Gomme plan of Liverpool is BL Add. Ms 5027, f 69. Other drawings by him are contained in Add Ms 16370, including Tilbury (ff 2–10); Plymouth (f 43); battle of Newbury (f 61); battle of Naseby (f 62); battle of Marston Moor (f 65); Elizabeth Castle, Jersey (f 87). On Bristol's guns see Gloucester RO D115/15.

and paid entirely for their own defence works. Such similarities as do exist between the various defence plans are therefore not usually due to either King or Parliament, but to a common approach amongst professional engineers with shared knowledge, or to the same engineers working in different places. Proof of this contention seems to be provided by the plans and fortifications themselves – because there is much commonality between Parliamentarian and Royalists structures, and little that we can point to in their execution as specific to one side or the other.[26]

---

[26] Ross, 'Military Engineering', pp 145–150; H.C. Tomlinson 'The Ordnance Office and Fortifications: An Administrative Survey', National Army Museum, unpublished typescript, pp 3–15. See also Hutton and Reeves 'Sieges and Fortifications', in J. Kenyon and J. Ohlmeyer (eds) *The Civil Wars*, Oxford, 1998, pp 195–233. Gloucester payments are mentioned in the GRO Gloucester Borough Records 3/2 ff 235, 236, 317.

5

Artillery and Sieges

> It was more than admirable to behold the desperate courage both of the assailants and defendants, the thundering cannons roaring from our batteries without, their's roaring from the castle within; the thousands of musket balls flying at each others faces, like the driving hailstones ... the clangor and carvings of naked and unsheathed swords; the pushing of untrailed pikes, crying for blood, and the pitiful clamour of heart fainting women imploring mercy for their husbands.
>
> (William Lithgow, describing the siege of Newcastle, 1644)[1]

Sieges were every bit as important as battle in the Civil Wars: many casualties were caused, and much of the cost of the war was absorbed in defending and attacking towns and castles. Holding cities dominated trade, allowed regulation of taxation, and controlled major route ways – thus shaping campaigns. Many battles occurred when, and where, they did because armies were deployed to capture or relieve towns and were confronted en route to their objective. Moreover at any given moment until the final stages of the First Civil War, roughly ten times as much ordnance was tied up in static defences around the country as was actually in the field as part of 'marching trains' of artillery. Though it would be wrong to say that sieges of the Civil War were stereotypical, there were methods of reducing fortresses which were widely employed and commonly understood. These were often patterned on long practised continental methods. Many sieges therefore tended to follow a series of recognisable phases. The artillery had a particularly significant role to play in determining whether sieges were possible, the timing and importance of each phase of a siege – and indeed ultimate success or failure. Similarly there were customs of war that were generally expected to be adhered to, and were often referred to as 'laws of war' – even if these rules were not exactly codified, nor ratified by explicit convention. Again the artillery played a crucial part in what could be expected from those attacking or defending.

Most sieges began with the appearance of a detachment from a hostile army near a town or castle. Usually those about to be besieged would now be offered the chance to surrender, or to change sides. An emissary would approach the

[1] W. Lithgow *Experimental and Exact Relations* ... [of the] *Siege of Newcastle*, 1645.

gates accompanied by a drummer, and perhaps a flag of truce. The demands and terms of the aggressors would then be delivered, sometimes with an ultimatum as to how long the defending party would be given to respond. If those inside were uncertain of their ability to resist the siege might be stillborn, and immediate capitulation followed. At Arundel Castle in 1643 it was a show of strength by Sir Ralph Hopton that proved convincing. Following an approach march by night, he came, 'in the morning with shew of as much terror to the castle and new endeavours upon it as he could make'. After this intimidating performance the 80 man garrison marched meekly out, on 'reasonable' conditions. The same year the Parliamentarians used a different stratagem, taking advantage of wavering resolve to grab an easy victory at Lowestoft, where

> The Colonel summoned the town, and demanded, if they would deliver up their strangers [out of town Royalists] the Town and their army? Promising them favour, if so; if not, none. They yielded to deliver up their strangers, but not so to the rest. Whereupon our Norwich dragoons crept under the chain before mentioned; and came within pistol shot of their ordnance; proffering to fire on their canonneer – who fled; so they gained the two pieces of ordnance, and broke the chain; and they and the horse entered the town without more resistance.[2]

Occasionally those inside a town pretended that they had been the covert friends of the besiegers all along; such was the case at Preston in 1644 when it was threatened by a massive and victorious Royalist army. The mayor and other officials even greeted Prince Rupert with an invitation dinner – a couple of them were thrown into prison for this cheek, but the town was saved the devastation so recently visited on Bolton and Liverpool. Sometimes, as at Lathom, wily defenders stalled for time, attempting to save themselves by pedantic point by point negotiations, giving a few extra days to any relieving force near enough to come to the rescue. Bold and less subtle garrisons sometimes gave the enemy messengers a difficult time, berating them, or rough handling them off the premises. At other times they made their feelings clear as the enemy approached. This was certainly the case at Lyme in 1644 when the Parliamentarians, 'not a jot dismayed', yelled their defiance at the Royalist soldiers outside.

Assuming the summons was refused, and not merely bluff on the behalf of the aggressor, the besieging army now arrived in strength and began the first stage of its preparations. This was usually to surround the target so as to deny it supplies or communication with the outside world. Thorough besiegers would now also begin to dig continuous encircling trenches, outside the effective range of the garrison's guns, or at least out of easy line of sight. Lines of

---

2   T. Carlyle (ed) *Oliver Cromwell's Letters and Speeches*, London, 1866, vol 1, pp 108–109, letter by John Cory; C.E.H. Chadwyck Healey (ed) *Bellum Civile: Hopton's Narrative*, reprinted in Somerset Record Society, 18, 1902, p 69.

'countervallation' faced inwards towards the town or fortress, lines of 'circum-vallation' faced outwards, so as to protect the backs of the besiegers against any interference from outside. Forts or sconces might well be provided for the additional security of the attackers, and a place of retreat for the workmen. As might be imagined lines of circumvallation might well be hundreds of yards beyond the town walls, and, in the case of attempting to take in a major town such as York, Newark, or Oxford, might have to stretch for many miles.

Unless attackers were numerous and well supplied unbroken trench lines might prove beyond their capability – in such instances dangerous gaps in the besiegers' grip could emerge, and be exploited by the defenders. It has been suggested that English besieging armies were less exacting than their Dutch counterparts, and this may have been the case, especially early in the war. Being a trench digging 'pioneer' was certainly judged an inferior calling to that of the real soldier, and even the New Model Army had only one permanent company of pioneers – relying largely on conscripted labour, or what might be now called the multi-tasking of its infantry. Nevertheless it is also true that English and continental conditions varied – the 'front line' between the King's territory and that of his enemies was long, intricate, and frequently blurred; and the supply of materials was often uncertain. Moreover the Low Countries were essentially small, flat, and densely populated – uncomplicated by signifi-cant hills or a vast coast line.

As digging commenced the train of battering guns was called up, and gun positions identified. The first batteries would now be raised, usually several hundred yards from the enemy. From here cannon might begin to harass the defence, or cover the ground leading up to the outer walls of the town or fort with their muzzles. Batteries and posts for sentries could be partially prefab-ricated by the construction of cylindrical 'cannon baskets' or 'gabions' behind the lines, these being pushed into position and filled on the spot to provide protection. 'SR' writing from the lines before Oxford in June 1646 recorded how 'neer 80 cannon baskets, and faggots in abundance' were prepared 'to raise the batteries', following which the 'great pieces' played on both sides, without injury to the attackers. Where opportunity allowed however siege batteries became full blown works in their own right. Hexham described an ideal design consisting of an oblong area enclosed by a ditch, within which was an earth-work with wooden platforms and embrasures for the guns. Refinements might include a covered magazine at the back of the position and wooden shutters in front of the guns which could be closed during loading. The heavy recoil of the guns would push the pieces back up their inclined platforms, and the gun team's job of pushing them back into the firing position was aided by gravity. According to the author of the Coates Manuscript the dimensions for battery platforms were: 'for everie peece of batterie' or 'whole cannon', 14 or 15 feet wide by 30 feet deep, reckoning from 'the loophole back'. This would allow 12 feet for the gun, six for her carriage, and a further 12 for the recoil. As mortars fired at high elevations and required no direct view of the target they needed no elaborate battery – and were usually placed in pits. The French author St Julien shows a mortar pit which is rectangular with all round cover, but circular examples are also mentioned. Sometimes an opening cannonade was sufficiently awe inspiring, or lucky, to bring the fortress to its knees in short order. Such was the case at Sherborne in 1642, where, 'after some 40 shots made by the Earle of Bedford against the castle a fortunate shot was made, which took away the main battlements of the castle, where one of the pieces was planted, so that the ordnance fell to the ground with a great part of the wall'.[3]

Though engineers might reconnoitre during the day, laying plans with the aid of maps and telescopes, the actual excavation of 'approaches' was usually started at night. A line of soldiers or conscripted civilians would begin to dig a trench perhaps two hundred yards away from, and roughly parallel to, the defences they were attacking. Earth would be thrown up to the front as they dug, so obscuring their activity as quickly as possible. Cover of darkness would ensure that the workmen were very difficult to see, let alone shoot, and a prudent besieger kept a company or two of infantry ready to intervene just in case the defending general took it into his head to order a sally to disrupt the work. If all went well the diggers would be hidden from the besieged before daylight, and work could continue unhindered. Where saps were required to get closer to the enemy fortification the sappers could now work in teams, with some of the men pushing a heavy roller, or erecting screens to conceal the diggers from enemy observation and fire. Occasionally sappers were specially equipped with purpose made heavy helmets and breastplates which might protect them as their heads bobbed up and down in their works. So it was, little by little, the besiegers dug ever closer, their trenches zigzagging to prevent enemy fire slamming straight down the cavity, and thereby providing as much cover for the occupants at possible.

However careful soldiers in siege works could still face sudden death at the hands of a patient sniper, waiting for the right opportunity. Thomas Raymond, an Englishman at the siege of Rijnberg in 1633, recorded that several of his own company were picked off in 'peeping' over the parapet of their works. The enemy had placed 'rogues' armed with fire locks, 'lying close to the ground', ready to dispatch any observers. These snipers were so vigilant that if so much as the 'topp of an old hatt' appeared between the cannon baskets it soon collected three or four holes. If the defenders had any riflemen these could shoot from vantage points further off, from loopholes or between chimney pots high up on buildings overlooking the ground. Rifles or 'screwed' pieces had been in existence for about a century before the Civil Wars – but being expensive, and slow to load, had found little employment on the open battlefield. In sieges

---

3 BL E 118 (9) *Propositions Propounded by the Marquesse of Hartford*, September 1642, p 3; BL E 511 (10) *Perfect Occurences*, London, 12 June 1646, sig A4; St. Julien, *La Forge de Vulcain*, La Haye, 1606, p 123.

where the shooter could pop down behind the battlements to recharge his piece at leisure they could become a deadly menace.[4]

With the works now very close, perhaps little more than one hundred yards from the fortification, the time had come to establish batteries able to concentrate their fire on very narrow sections of the walls. Whether to focus the attack on a bastion or a section of wall was a matter of judgement: walls were usually easier to demolish than bastions, but might be subject to enfilading fire from other works. The cannon for battery might be mounted at night, or pushed up one of the approaches if there was one big enough. Though one big, or 'Royal', battery had been the fashion in the sixteenth century by the time of the Civil Wars it was more normal to set up two or more gun positions, so that they could fire on a wall from different angles, or tackle a troublesome bastion from both sides. Authorities suggested that smaller guns of relatively high velocity were particularly adept for counter battery fire – smashing or dismounting the defenders' guns. Conversely the best battering pieces were the full and demi cannon whose heavy balls transferred the maximum shock to masonry, and ploughed out satisfyingly large holes through embankments showering earth asunder in the process. In Robert Norton's ideal siege batteries, doubtless rarely achieved in practice, there were no less than 18 guns – eight cannon, six culverins and four demi-culverins. The cannon were situated at right angles to a wall, battering and shaking it 'by reason of their weight of shot'. The culverins were placed to play 'transversely', to cut out what the cannons had battered. The demi-culverins focused meanwhile 'upon the flankers and defences', to hinder the enemy from making a sally, and engaging their artillery. According to Thomas Smith the best way to demolish a wall with the heavy ordnance was first to level the guns 'something under the middle part of the wall' for the first rounds and then aim two or three feet higher. Having smashed the lower part of a wall, the rest would fall 'of necessity'. Ideally the siege guns would fire simultaneously, rather than one after another, for maximum impact.

Where the right types of guns were used with skill and determination the result could be catastrophic. Newcastle certainly suffered spectacular damage, as recent archaeological examination of its walls has confirmed, a stretch of wall about 180 feet long having to be reconstructed after the siege. At Chester there was damage to both walls and towers, that at Barnaby's Tower being particularly well recorded. Lower parts of the structure still bear the impact marks of about 18 ball strikes, whilst the upper part appears to have been totally rebuilt after the war. Laugharne castle in Pembrokeshire suffered a significant breach, and it appears that much of the front of the gatehouse was shot away, and, as well as finding cannon balls in the ground, archaeologists have discovered them embedded in parts of the upper masonry. The fourteenth century shell keep of Sandal castle was so heavily bombarded that several breaches were made, and

---

[4]   G. Davies (ed) *Autobiography of Thomas Raymond*, Royal Historical Society, Camden Third Series, 28, 1917, p 39.

in the end the defenders had to dig a trench through the rubble of the keep to maintain communications between two of the towers that they were still able to occupy. About 50 round shot have since been recovered from the castle's Well Tower. At Winchester in 1645 the guns of the New Model Army just kept battering until they created a beach in the walls which their chaplain thought wide enough that '30 men might go abreast' through the gaping hole. Mortar shells followed, blowing away the defenders' flag pole, and sending splinters slicing off the legs of one of the garrison at the thigh. In the end the cannonade went on from Saturday morning, then relentlessly through the Lord's Day until at eight at night when the Royalists sued for surrender.[5]

Such were the ideal deployments of siege guns, but topography and opportunity were used wherever possible by both defender and attacker. In some cases hills allowed guns to be pushed relatively close to the enemy without danger, in others, as at Reading, guns were pulled up into church towers where advantage might be had from added height. This however was a potentially risky business, as was reported by Robert Codrington: 'they [the Royalists] had planted some ordnance in a steeple, believing that from that height they might play upon our men with more advantage, but our canon was levelled against it with such dexterity that both the canoneirs and [their guns] were quickly buried in the ruins of the steeple'. At Colchester in 1648 the defending Royalists managed to mount a brass saker in the 'frame of the bells' within a church tower, positioned so as to flank the enemy trenches, and so 'did them much injury'.[6]

Competent commanders would rarely sit and wait for their fortifications to be devastated. As sieges progressed plans of attack became more obvious, and the resources of the besiegers became more stretched, so sorties from within the defences became ever more desirable as a way to impede the designs of the assailants. Sallies from towns and forts were commonplace; some turned into bloody fiascos, others made huge contributions to the defence, especially when enemy guns or mortars could be captured or magazines blown up. In a particularly dramatic episode at Carlisle the Royalist defenders mustered five parties of cavalry, and a company of foot under Captain Dixon. Whilst the cavalry rode bravely upon the enemy – right up to the range of pistol shot – and engaged them at close range, the infantry took the opportunity of this diversionary raid to concentrate on the Roundhead pioneers. One of Dixon's company 'threw in a fireball, which fell amongst their powder, and blew up spades, mattocks and men. So at once they leaped out of the work'. Some of the horse now turned

5   See C. Duffy *Siege Warfare: The Fortress in the Early Modern World*, London, 1979, pp 89–100, and J. Burke 'The New Model Army and the Problems of Siege Warfare', in *Irish Historical Studies*, vol 27, number 105, 1990, pp 1–29; J. Sprigge *Anglia Rediviva*, London, 1647, pp 129–131; Smith *The Art of Gunnery*, 1643, p 45.

6   R. Codrington *The Life and Death of the Illustrious Robert Earle of Essex*, London, 1646, p 26; M. Carter *A Most True and Exact Relation ... [of] Kent, Essex and Colchester*, London, 1650, pp 162–163; BL E 458 (21) *The Moderate Intelligencer*, London, 8–15 August, sig E–E4v.

on the hapless workmen, and rode them down, doing 'lamentable execution'. The King's foot secured 39 prisoners, some of whom were 'pitifully burned', then they levelled the work that the enemy had been attempting to construct, and secured the town's water supply.

Defenders might also redeploy their artillery within their works, and thus besiegers could suddenly find themselves outgunned. Just such an eventuality occurred at Colchester whilst Parliamentarian gunners were busy destroying St Mary's church with two demi cannon. The Royalists within the town reacted quickly and, with 'as much speed as could be', set up a battery 'upon the curtain', from whence they killed one of the besiegers' gunners and 'six men more' forcing them to desist. One witness reported a soldier shot in two, another with his legs neatly amputated whilst 'lying in his hut'. The Parliamentarian's key antagonist was said to be a cunning one eyed gunner, whose most devious ruse was to set up his piece during the day, then fire it off under cover of darkness, taking the besiegers by surprise. This redoubtable character, described as an 'absolute gunner', and 'the best in England', was eventually reported killed by a cannon ball 'in the belly'. The demise of this man was noted in several independent sources – and so was probably not mere Roundhead propaganda. With gun batteries hammering at the walls from point blank range and mortars being moved into position all but the staunchest defenders would now decide that the time for surrender had arrived. Such was the case with the capitulation at Raglan in August 1646 – as Colonel Morgan reported to the Speaker of the Commons, 'truly, had this happy conclusion not been made our mortar pieces would have played very suddenly, and we were come very near with our approaches'.[7]

Mortars were not used at every siege – but they were the one instrument unimpeded by earthworks, since their high trajectory shells could sail clean over the top into vulnerable buildings behind. Exploding granadoes might shatter structures and people alike, whilst 'fire balls' or incendiary missiles threatened to burn the entire fortress or town rendering all resistance futile. Perhaps the most vivid description of being on the receiving end of granadoes comes from the Royalist defence of Chester:

> Eleven huge granadoes like so many tumbling demi phaetons threaten to set the city, if not the whole world on fire. This was a terrible night endeed, our houses like so many splitt vessels crash their supporters and burst themselves in sunder through the very violence of these descending firebrands. The Talbott, and house adjoyning the Eastgate flames outright; our hands are busied in quenching this whilst the law of nature bids us leave and seek our own security. Being thus distracted another thundercracke invites our eyes to the most

7   Letter from Morgan reprinted in H. Cary *Memorials of the Great Civil War*, London, 1842, p 147; BL E 452 (4) *Denbigh Castle ... also the Last Fight at Colchester*, 11 July 1648, pp 5–6; E 452 (41) *Joyfull Newes From Colchester*, London, July 1648, p 2; E 456 (5) *Another Great and Bloody Fight*, London, 1648, p 2; I. Tullie *A Narrative of the Siege of Carlisle*, ed. S. Jefferson, 1840, pp 37–39.

miserable spectacle that spite could possibly present us with – two houses in the Watergate shippes joynt from joynt and creates an earthquake, the main posts josell each other, whilst the frightened casemates fly for feare, in a word the whole fabrick is a perfect chaoes lively set forth in this metamorphosis. The grandmother, mother and three children are struck stark dead in the ruins of this humble edifice, a sepulcher well worth the enemye's remembrance. But for all this they are not satisfied, women and children have not blood enough to quench their fury, and therefore about midnight they shoot seven more in the hope of greater execution, one of these last night in an old man's bedchamber, almost dead with age, and send him a few dayes sooner to his grave then perhaps was given him.[8]

Interesting archaeological evidence of the effectiveness of mortars has come to light at Sandal Castle in Yorkshire, besieged by Parliament in 1645. Here excavations unearthed nine burials, one thought to be that of Major Ward the garrison commander. Three of the others were associated with metal fragments, leading to the suggestion that they were victims of mortar bombs. At Lichfield, a town that faced three sieges, the very fear of mortars was turned to advantage. Here Parliamentarian defenders 'mounted three or foure leather buckets upon wheels like a mortar piece', apparently threatening the Royalist batteries, and these in their turn immediately vented their fury upon it – thereby wasting both their ammunition and time which would more profitably have been spent engaging other targets.[9]

Perhaps the key problem with mortars was that there was seldom enough of them, nor their ammunition, and supplies from London were often slow to materialise. Colonel Birch, the besieger of Goodrich Castle in 1646, was one Parliamentarian commander not prepared to wait. He had the famous 'Roaring Meg' – a 15 and a half inch type 'carrying a shell of 200 pound weight' – cast locally, adding it to one that he already possessed and his existing gun battery. Despite also having granadoes cast in the Forest of Dean he very quickly realised that his ordnance would 'spend more powder than is here to be had'. A further 80 barrels were soon ordered from the Ordnance Office in London, and at last he 'tore' the castle. The defenders were alive to the threat, and struck back with a sally which almost succeeded in destroying the mortars, as they might since it was these which were doing most of the damage. As the Parliamentarian observer 'E.S.' reported in the *Perfect Occurences*,

> There is one of our Gunnes cracked at the mussle, I am afraid she will not prove usefull. But they are now very quiet within yet will not yield. Our ordnance are small, and have done but little execution as yet: what hath beene

8 BL Harleian Ms 2155, reprinted in R.H. Morris *The Siege of Chester*, Chester and North Wales Archaeological Society, 25, pp 234–235.
9 K. Manchester 'Paleopathology of a Royalist Garrison', in *OSSA. The Journal of the Osteological Laboratory*, 5, Stockholm, 1979, pp 25–33. On Lichfield see BL E 99(28) *Honour Advanced*, April 1643, pp 1–4.

performed, it hath beene with our mortar-peeces. Colonell Birch hath sent to
the Generall for two great gunnes.

Roaring Meg is probably the only English Civil War period mortar to survive
to the present day. Brought into Hereford after the siege, it was later upturned
and embedded into the ground doing duty for many years as a corner post
at the junction of Gwynne Street and Bridge Street. In 1839 it was uprooted
again and moved to Castle Green. From thence it was later moved to Hereford
Museum, but in 2004 it was moved back to be displayed at Goodrich.[10]

Granadoe supply for mortars bedevilled both sides for a long time. Amongst
the Parliamentarians the Earl of Essex received 498 granadoes for his mortars
from August to December 1642. Thomas Wright, acting as 'firemaster' under
Major General Browne, was allotted just 20 for his part in the siege of Banbury
Castle in 1644. The New Model Army were given 300 large granadoes and 300
of 'saker' size at Christmas 1644, whilst Manchester's artillery handed in only
20 at the time that it was incorporated with Fairfax's army. A new mortar piece
delivered to the New Model Army in May 1645 came ready equipped with
60 shells. Yet even these were numbers that the Royalists could not match: 75
shells accompanied the Queen's mortars when they left Oxford. A 'marching
train' of 19 guns and a mortar planned in May 1645 had just 30 granadoes.
What appears to have been the biggest Royalist order, for 260, was placed in
January 1645, though we cannot confirm that this was completed. It does
seem however that by the time of the Third Civil War in 1651 Parliament had
solved the problem. A supply of 600 shells went with the three mortars which
accompanied Thomas Wright to Jersey that year.[11]

Sometimes defenders persisted in their defiance for weeks or months under
the optimistic delusion that relief was just around the corner. Others simply
did not know when they were beaten. Corfe castle suffered virtually everything
that besiegers could throw at it through two sieges; its fragmentary remains
bear testament to the impact of mines, artillery, and post combat 'slighting'.
The litter that archaeologists picked their way over during the 1990s included
debris of every description from broken pottery and the remains of a mortar,
to bar shot and cannon balls of a variety of calibres, up to and including 32
pounds weight. Royalist accounts of the siege of Newcastle had it that '1000
great shot' fell into the town, 'wherof many were 31lb weight, and 60 Grenadoes, being some 12 stone and 8 pound, by all of which they killed but 35
men, women and children'. At Hawarden Lady Neale pledged to her husband

[10] BL E 511 (22) *Perfect Occurences*, 16 June, 26 June and 15 July 1646; and E 511(28), 31 July
1646; L. Hutchinson *Memoirs of the Life of Colonel Hutchinson*, reprinted London, 1846, p
285.
[11] PRO WO 47/1, ff 81, 94, 157, 216, 229, 232, 245; Roy, *Royalist Ordnance Papers*, vol 1, pp
100, 107–108, 111, 139, 156–157, 268–269, 427; S. Bull *Granadoe!*, Leigh-on-Sea, 1985,
passim; D.E. Lewis 'The Office of Ordnance and the Parliamentarian Land Forces', unpublished PhD thesis, Loughborough University, 1976, p 333.

that she would hold out as long as there was food – even in the face of cannon. Conversely Shelford Manor, near Newark, is reported to have been optimistic of holding out so long as there was 'no cannon brought against them'. Famously the starving townspeople of Colchester ate their horses, their dogs and cats. Also at Colchester, Worcester, and a number of other towns many hapless civilians, accounted useless mouths to feed, were first driven out of the besieged town by the defenders – then promptly driven back by the besiegers, who perceived that the quicker the supplies of the town were exhausted the sooner the struggle might end. As one pamphleteer observed 'Captain Storm' did his work without, but 'Captain Hunger' did his work within.[12]

Undertaking a storm was one of the most nerve wracking services a soldier in the Civil Wars might perform – for all he knew the enemy would be ready and waiting, guns and muskets trained on the breach, ready to send him to kingdom come. Muskets and case shot were relatively inaccurate tools of destruction, but blasted into a narrow defile they could scarcely miss at close range. The defenders might also have retreated securely into fresh works, just inside the old, whose battered condition now tempted the attacking general into a full scale assault. If there was no breach the troops might have to carry ladders with them, making themselves slow moving, clumsy targets on the way in, and sitting ducks when climbing. At Lincoln in 1644 the storm appeared to be going well – until it was discovered that the scaling ladders were embarrassingly short. Traditionally dismounted cavalry were given the dubious honour of being first into the breach – they often had a breast plate and helmet which fitted them particularly well for close action, and doubtless the infantry, who usually bore the brunt of the trench warfare which preceded the storm, were happy to finally let their mounted comrades in on the action. The weapons of the storm were half pikes, grenades, hatchets and edged weapons – ideally suited to the scrum of close combat where hand to hand fighting rarely allowed time or space to wield a full size pike, or recharge a musket.

The Royalist storming of Bristol, in July 1643, proved to be one of the bloodiest actions of the war. First 'waines full of faggots' were run into the ditches to help the soldiers cross the void, then the infantry set to, 'fire pikes and granadoes in their hands'. Prince Rupert thought that the most devastating blow would be a double one, with assaults from both sides of town, but it was not as easy as predicted, as Clarendon reported:

> The next morning, with no other provisions fit for such work but the courage of the assailants, both armies fell on. On the west side, where the Cornish were, they assaulted in three places. These three divisions fell on together, with that courage and resolution as nothing but death could control. Though the middle division got into the ditch, and so near filled it that some mounted the

12 BL E 42 (26) *Mercurius Aulicus*, 30 March 1644, pp 913–914; *A Great and Bloody Fight at Colchester*, London, 1648, passim; BL E 461 (24) *A True and Exact Relation of the Taking of Colchester*, London, 31 August 1648, pp 1–6.

wall, yet by the prodigious disadvantage of the ground, and the full defence the besieged made within, they were driven back with a great slaughter; the common soldiers, after their chief officers were killed or desperately wounded, finding it a bootless attempt. On Prince Rupert's side, it was assaulted with equal courage, and almost equal loss, but with better success; for Colonel Washington, finding a place in the curtain weaker than the rest, entered ... The enemy, as soon as they saw their line entered in one place, either by fear or command of their officers, quit their posts; so that the Prince ... marched up Froomgate, losing many men and some very good officers by shot from walls and windows. All men were much cast down to see so little gotten with so great a loss.

According to Nathaniel Fiennes' report to Parliament the Royalists acted like maniacs at Bristol, running desperately up to the gun embrasures and fort palisades, not desisting until 'they were knock'd down with stones and halberts'. Some, including Sir Nicholas Slanning, were simply blown off the works by case shot – which in his instance led to a smashed thigh, later proving mortal. The numbers of guns captured at Bristol certainly numbered about hundred – the Royalist news sheet *Mercurius Aulicus* mentions a figure of 130, whilst an official survey listed more than 90. That this high number was perfectly feasible was demonstrated in 1645 when Parliament retook the town, at which time Parliamentarian sources claimed to have captured over 150.[13]

What might happen to the defeated in siege warfare varied from little or nothing through to bloody slaughter. Yet in the context of the times this was no contradiction: both sides had a good inkling of what they might face in specific circumstances. Whilst the rules of conflict had not been formally ratified, jurists were publishing a growing body of opinion on international law and war. Particularly influential were the Italian Alberico Gentili (1552–1608), who worked in England during the last twenty years of his life, and Dutchman Hugo Grotius (1583–1645). Grotius published his *De Jure Belli ac Pacis* whilst he was an exile in Paris in 1625, a noteworthy attempt to define what constituted a just war, and to mitigate its deleterious impacts. Gentili offered more specific advice on sieges in his *De Jure Belli Libri Tres*. Here he cited precedent of the Ancients and their siege weapons, such as the battering ram, by way of comparison for the conduct of modern artillery.

In Gentili's view, based on scripture, 'to resist one who is stronger' was a sin, therefore it was permissible to punish 'obstinate rustics' who made it necessary to bring artillery against even the weakest places. Conversely it was good practice to grant better terms to those who surrendered without a fight. On

---

13   BL E 47 (2) *A True Relation of the taking of the City, Minster and Castle of Lincolne*, London, 1644, p 3, and E 47 (8) *A Particular Relation*, London, 1644, p 8. Clarendon *History of the Great Rebellion*, ed. R. Lockyer, Oxford, 1967, pp 147–148; BL E 64 (12) *A Relation Made to the House of Commons by Col. Nathaniel Fiennes*, August 1643, p. 7; BL E 92 (25) *Mercurius Aulicus*, Oxford, 1643, p 133, and R. Robinson *The Sieges of Bristol During the Civil War*, Bristol, 1868, passim. See also Appendix VI

this point it was Caesar himself who was given as precedent, since he offered to spare the lives of those who would render their city 'before the [battering] ram had touched the walls'. For Gentili there was a direct parallel with modern guns, for now, 'if bombards are brought up to weak places, no room seems to be left for surrender'. Moreover, once the artillery was in position, forces or persons attempting to bring succour to the enemy could be the target of reprisals – that might under other circumstances be regarded as unnecessary cruelty. Nevertheless parties negotiating from a position of weakness had no compulsion to reveal their disadvantageous situation, nor were those who captured towns under any universal compulsion to spare prisoners their lives – though they should stick to any agreement so to do.[14]

In the England of the 1640s such notions, plus observation of European and Irish horrors, translated into what was effectively a code of expectation between the besieger and the besieged. Many times bloodshed was avoided by negotiation and surrender at an appropriate moment – usually at a point far enough down the line to convince one's own comrades that treachery played no part, but soon enough to evade slaughter. Whether or not the besiegers' artillery had arrived, and whether it had opened fire, were key indicators of what might be granted. Honourable surrender could however be given at any point that the besiegers believed it was in their interest to accept it, and in such cases there was a sliding scale of what the defeated party might salvage.

At the most equable end of the spectrum the defenders could be allowed to march out, fully armed – occasionally even retaining their artillery – and rejoin their army elsewhere as full combatants. There were many such honourable surrenders: at York in July 1644, the besieged Royalists were allowed to come out under their own colours carrying their muskets, and head for Skipton, though their cannon were forfeited. Despite this brave martial show Simeon Ashe recorded that many of the men were drunk when the time came to leave, bringing their many wounded with them. Contrary to the agreement some of the Royalist wagons were also plundered. Similar terms were granted on the surrender of Pendennis Castle in August 1646, when the Royalists came out 'with flying colours, trumpets sounding, drums beating, matches lighted at both ends, bullets in their mouths, and every soldier twelve charges of powder'. The Pendennis garrison were also allowed to keep their personal goods, but in this instance most weapons, including the artillery, were immediately handed over following this dramatic exit.[15]

Further down the scale of mercy horses and private possessions might be forfeit – and agreements imposed regarding exile, or promises extracted not to take up arms again. Certain notorious commanders – or soldiers guilty of particular offences – might be singled out for punishment or death, whilst

14   A. Gentili *De Jure Belli Libri Tres*, 1589, reprinted Washington, 1924, pp 340–360.
15   J. Sprigge *Anglia Rediviva*, London, 1647, pp 305–306; *Articles Agreed Upon … About York*, London, 1644.

others were imprisoned or spared. In this respect summary justice became more common in the Second Civil War and in the later Irish campaign, where the defeated were seen to have wilfully re-ignited a conflict already lost, or to have breached their former paroles. The deaths of Sir Charles Lucas and Sir George Lisle those 'mere soldiers of fortune' in front of a firing squad, after the fall of Colchester in 1648, may be interpreted in this light. The Parliamentarians had already been forced to use their siege guns, and parts of the town had been burned. Lucas had already been captured at least twice in the First Civil War, at Marston Moor and Stow on the Wold.

In the most extreme cases it was acknowledged that once a breach had been made in the walls of a fortress, and a storm attempted, the attacker was not obliged to spare any person or property. Lord General Fairfax therefore showed a degree of leniency to Bridgwater in July 1645. There had been exchanges of red hot shot, and parts of the town had burnt, but the Royalists still refused to capitulate. Fairfax's men had been forced to storm the ditch, and mount the enemy's works with 'undaunted courage'. Even so the Royalists were spared. They were also allowed the clothes they stood up in, but whilst all were given 'civil usage for the time being', gentlemen were ultimately to be 'disposed of as the Parliament should appoint'. In practice genuine cold-blooded slayings, particularly of civilians, were actually quite rare. Many thousands did die in bombardments, stormings, and fires – but the deliberate killing of non-combatants in particular was noteworthy because it was so uncommon. Probably the most notorious incident during the storming of a town in England was the seizure of Bolton in 1644, where very large numbers were undoubtedly killed. Even here however the vast majority were combatants, many of them cut down whilst routing away from Rupert's victorious army. Bolton parish registers record the names of just 74 known civilians who died, and almost all of these were male adults.[16]

At times the commanders were caught squarely between their duty to their King or Parliament, and their honour in adhering to accepted laws of war and siege. In April 1643, for example, Colonel Fielding was in the midst of surrendering Royalist Reading when the King's instructions for him to make an attack were relayed. He refused to do so on the grounds that he 'could not forfeit his honour', as he had made pledges during the truce. Later Fielding was court martialled by his own side, condemned to death, and led to the scaffold – but finally pardoned. At Liverpool in 1645, General Meldrum, the besieging commander, was theoretically bound by a recent Parliament decision not to grant mercy to Irishmen caught under arms in England. He professed himself conveniently uninformed of these strictures – releasing almost all the English Royalists to their homes, and permitting the Irish to depart having taken an oath not to take up arms again.

---

[16] Ibid, pp 66–74, and *Sir Thomas Fairfaxes Entering Bridgewater By Storming*, London, 1645, passim.

Sometimes very specific 'customs war' relating to the artillery were imposed by the decree of the victor. Soon after the storm of Bristol in 1643, for example, King Charles gave the following warrant to Lord Henry Percy 'Generall of our Artillery':

> Wheras by the custome of warr those places which doe stand out after summons given, doe forfeit their bells to the Generall of the Ordinance And whereas our Citty of Bristoll by their standing out after such summons have encurred the said forfeiture, Theise are therefore to lett you knowe the said forfeiture belongs unto the said Generall as his right, by vertue and authority given to him by us, soe that he may justly clayme the said bells, or if he thinke fitt take such other compositions as shall be agreed upon.

Similarly, after the surrender of Banbury in 1646, Parliament ordered that the engineer in charge should be paid a bonus of £50.[17]

It would be redundant to relate the role of artillery in every siege of the Civil War but it is apposite to supply concrete examples of the different types of siege scenario which occurred – and the actual performance of guns in given circumstances. The case studies – Basing House, Pontefract Castle, Lathom House and the town of Gloucester, plus a selection of coastal locations – provide a cross section in terms of scale and geography, encompassing defended noble houses, a medieval castle, and towns. They also give examples where Royalists besieged Parliamentarians, and vice versa, and illustrate situations in which artillery was either plentiful, or scarce.

BASING: SAPPER, SIEGE GUN AND MORTAR IN ACTION

As Parliamentarian contemporary Joshua Sprigge observed, the Marquis of Winchester's Royalist stronghold at Basing House in Hampshire was of significance because it threatened communications from London to the West – and was potentially 'a great annoyance'. It was therefore fortified by the King's supporters early in the war. Though known as a 'house' its compass should not be underestimated, for it is calculated that its plot covered over 14 acres. The latest artillery works here were added as new layers atop iron age, Norman, and sixteenth century defences. Even today – following war, sacking, and four hundred years of erosion and later development – evidence remains of at least three significant bastions and other earthworks. Recent archaeological excavations have helped to determine the extent of the Tudor mansion and other structures on the site. Though the towers of Basing were very vulnerable to artillery, much of the stronghold was not, being enclosed by a mile long wall, nine feet thick, with a rammed earth core. Such an obstacle could stop smaller artillery projectiles, and take limited punishment from the heavier varieties,

---

[17] Gloucester RO D115/ 6; BL E 509 (4) *Perfect Diurnall*, 11–18 May 1646, p 1168.

if the defenders were allowed time to make repairs. The much more massive main bastions could stop almost anything.

In 1643 the first attempt on Basing by Sir William Waller proved unsuccessful, and part of the problem was undoubtedly lack of ordnance. The Royalist journal *Mercurius Aulicus* reported that Waller had been able to deploy 'five small pieces' and 'two demi cannons', and was reinforced in mid November by 'fireworks' from London. Short bombardments were followed by three assaults. Yet the house proved too strong, as was related by a soldier in Waller's own command, being

> very strongly fortified the walles of the houses are made thick and strong to beare out cannon bullet, and the house built upright, so that no man can command the roofs, the windowes thereof are guarded by the outer walles, and there is no place even in the house save only for certain drakes which are on the top of the said house wherewith they are able to play upon our army though we discern them not. The house is as large and spacious as the Tower of London, and strongly walled about with earth raised against the wall, of such thicknesse that it is able to dead the greatest cannon bullet, besides they have very great store both of ammunition and victualls, to serve for supply a long time and in the walls are divers pieces of ordnance about the house.[18]

In short Basing was well supplied with food as well as guns, and stoutly protected by artillery defences of banked earth. The ordnance that the Royalists deployed from within was used to devastating effect. In a counter to an early attempt upon the house they had deployed 'a small peece upon the rampier, loaden with case shot', and the gunner 'spyed his time and fired her, which slew about a dozen of them, hurt many more and made the rest of them take their heels'. Nevertheless the enemy was not about to give up at the first attempt, and now subjected the house to what one contemporary described as, 'the fury of the most violent assault that ever was'. The great guns of the Parliament army now

> made such a loud and continual thunder for two full howres, that the like, as soldiers affirm, hath never or very rarely bin heard. The rebels boldly advanced through the wood, and drawing two drakes, and two loads of ladders with them, within a few yards of the house walls; and in despight of the castle, presse into the ditch, drive the garrison soldiers over the lower half moone, raise one of their ensignes in the ditch, and clap a great petard on the jaume of the gate having intelligence (by two who crept out of the garrison) of the weakest place, the gate itself being so dammed up within, that it was not to be forced.

---

18 Report reprinted in J. Adair (ed) *They Saw it Happen: Contemporary Accounts of the Siege of Basing House*, Hampshire County Council, 1981, p 17. See also P. Harrington *Archaeology of the English Civil War*, Princes Risborough, 1992, pp 13–14, 24–25, 37, and Sprigge *Anglia Rediviva*, pp 127, 137.

Even this was to no avail. This time the assault was thwarted principally by a sniper, 'an ingenious and vigilant' German within the garrison, who picked off several attackers shooting through a new loop hole cut in the wall.[19]

The second siege, of 1644, was a far more considered and systematic affair in which the besiegers took time and pains to bring to bear the full panoply of current military science. By June their siege works had been brought 'to some perfection' – with a culverin shooting from behind protective 'cannon baskets' or gabions, whilst a sconce, platform and further trench lines were still being constructed. Though the defenders proved able to dismount one gun with counter battery fire, the attackers were able to creep ever closer, extending their works

> within halfe musket shot … pouring their lead into the garrison, they spoil us two or three a day, burning our workes, and shoot the Marquis himself through his clouths, the carriage of their peece being repaired, they now renew their battery on the House to the detriment and toppling of our towers and chimnies.

By 20 July the defenders' situation had deteriorated still further, for having refused another ultimatum to surrender they were subjected to mortar fire. This was apparently delivered by two weapons, a ten inch mortar and a six inch mortar, whose shells weighed 80 and 36 pounds respectively. A diary of one of the garrison reported that the parliamentarian

> lines are much advanced and their sconce flanking their battery in the parke [is] finished, the Marquisse himself hurt by a shot and two men killed by chance shot and the cariage of our falconet broke from their culverin. The following night being darke and stormy we despatched our messenger. Eight prisoners taking their opportunity to doo the same for themselves to their leaguer, making our allowance of great shot to be the next day dubled and at night more grenadoes.[20]

Fortunately granadoes appear to have been in short supply, for they were supplemented with large stones. Gradually growing in familiarity with the menace, the diary writer and his comrades began to call the mortar shot troublesome 'bawbles'. Despite this brave face the mortars still did damage, setting light to a barn and destroying provisions. Next the besiegers pulled a culverin up the tower of Basing church, and from here battered a tower in which Royalist snipers were deployed.

It was probably continuing hope of relief that steadied the morale of the garrison. A sally enabled them to smash up some of the enemy works, and perhaps more importantly, capture a mortar. Even so the outcome hung in

---

[19] BL E 77 (18) *Mercurius Aulicus, Oxford*, 12–19 November 1643, pp 656–650.
[20] 'Siege Diary', in Adair, *They Saw it Happen*, pp 33–38; BL E 77 (15) *Mercurius Civicus*, 23–30 November 1643, p 312.

the balance. Further artillery work by the Parliamentarians was recorded on
19 August, with 48 rounds fired from a demi cannon in a work by the woods
and other guns. In successive days another 160 large roundshot fell upon the
garrison, 'with which and with grenades they killed two men, and mischieved
two more, break our best iron gun, and make a breach in one of our square
towers'. Holes began to appear in the walls and earthworks, and only by both
officers and men energetically 'putting hand to spade' was the damage recti-
fied. The bombardment continued, the missiles now including not just solid
ball but 'crossbar' shot, logs bound with iron, stones and grenades, all of
which were tried and tested anti personnel weapons. Arrows also flew over the
banking carrying messages containing incitement to surrender and mutiny. By
25 August the Parliamentarian works had crept forward to 'within pistol shot',
and musketeers also came up, pushing a bullet proof screen in front of them.
More calls to surrender led to more defiance, and in turn to more bombardment. A cannonade of 120 shot reduced one of the great brick towers of Basing
to rubble, so clogging the defence works that the Royalists were forced to build
a new traverse behind the crumbled walls. One Parliamentarian cannon now
became so overheated it was 'at fault' and had to be withdrawn. So heavy
was the expenditure of shot that the besiegers may well have begun to run
short, for on 27 August the Committee of Both Kingdoms gave orders for the
delivery of 400 culverin and 150 demi cannon balls, to 'Nicholas Love esquire,
before Basing'. On 5 September a fresh sally was mounted by the defenders,
but though a troublesome demi-culverin was temporarily seized three Royalists
were struck down dead by case shot.[21]

However deliverance was at hand. Clarendon has it that it was Charles'
Council that prevailed upon the King to send a relief force, and so it was that
Colonel Gage stole out of Oxford, by night, with a small body of cavalry.
Travelling via a wood near Wallingford where they halted for a while, then,
'the troops marched through by lanes to Aldermaston, a village out of any great
road, where they intended to take more rest that night. They had marched
from the time they left Oxford with orange-tawny scarfs and ribbons, that
they might be taken for Parliament soldiers.' Though they momentarily forgot
themselves long enough to attack some enemy troopers on the way, and were
forced to engage in a cavalry skirmish they made it through to Basing which
was successfully replenished with ammunition and other supplies. By such
cloak and dagger derring-do Basing was saved; but only in the nick of time,
since tried and tested siege methods had seemed about to decide the fate of the
house, had it not been for Colonel Gage.[22]

21 PRO WO 47/1 f 92. See also W. Emberton, *Love Loyalty: The Close and Perilous Siege
of Basing House*, Basingstoke, 1972, passim. I am grateful to my former colleague at the
National Army Museum, Andrew Robertshaw, now curator of the Royal Logistics Corps
Museum, for information on Rawdon's regiment at the defence of Basing.

22 Clarendon *History of the Great Rebellion*, ed. Lockyer, pp 229–233. For details of Gage see P.
Newman *Royalist Officers in England and Wales*, New York, 1981, pp 146–147.

Basing was finally overcome in the autumn of 1645, and again it was systematic besieging, based on the destructive power of artillery, that did the job. On 1 August 1645 the Parliamentarian Hampshire Committee submitted an impressive, not to say optimistic, list of forthcoming requirements to Parliament. This included two demi cannon, two culverins, three demi culverins and three sakers, all with shot; plus a ten inch mortar, 200 'granado shells', 2,000 shovels, picks and mattocks, 300 axes, 600 hand baskets, 100 barrels of powder and three tons of match. Though some materials were not immediately available, part of the list, including the roundshot, was found. There can be little doubt that much of this was destined for the besieging of Royalist properties in the county – notably Basing. Dutch engineer Colonel Dalbier led the battery of the house, as a Parliamentarian account explained,

> after many shots against the midst of the house, which loosened the bricks and made a crack in the wall, he made another shot or two at the top of the house which brought down the high turret, the fall whereof so shook that part of the house, which before was weakened that the outmost wall fell down at once, insomuch as our men could see bedding fall out of the house into the court.

There was no immediate surrender so, following a signal fired by four cannon, Oliver Cromwell led the storm of Basing, at the head of veteran troops, on 14 October 1645. The men fell on with 'great cheerfulness and resolution', the soldiers of Colonel Pickering, Colonel Montague and Sir Hardress Waller being in the vanguard. Montague's and Waller's

> assaulted the strongest works, where the enemy kept his court of guard, which with great resolution they recovered, beating the enemy from a whole culverin, and from that work; which having done they drew their ladders after them, and got over another work, and the house wall, before they could enter: In this Sir Hardresse Waller performing his duty with honour and diligence, was shot in the arm, but not dangerous. We have had little losse; many of the enemy our men put to the sword, and some officers of quality, most of the rest we have prisoners, among which the Marquisse ...

The plunder from the house, one of the richest in the kingdom, was thought to amount to £200,000. Not long after Basing fell it caught alight – and burned for 20 hours until much of it was consumed. New Model Army Chaplain Hugh Peters revelled in the victory, marvelling not only at the fine furnishing and mounds of wheat and bacon which were seized, but the 'pride' of the idolatrous Catholic trappings and many 'Popish' books which now fell into Parliament's hands. He counted 74 bodies in the internal rooms of the stronghold.[23]

---

23 PRO WO 47/1 f 327. Cromwell and Peters quoted in Sprigge *Anglia Rediviva*, pp 137–142; also T. Hunt *The English Civil War at First Hand*, London, 2002, pp 149–150, and P. Young and W. Emberton *Sieges of the Great Civil War*, London, 1978, pp 88–98.

PONTEFRACT CASTLE: THE LAST ROYALIST STRONGHOLD

The medieval castle at Pontefract in West Yorkshire was secured for the King by Sir Richard Lowther in 1642, and served as a base from which Royalist forces struck out at Leeds and Bradford. Clarendon described its location as, 'very strong, no part whereof was commanded by any other ground'. Moreover, 'the house was very large, with all offices suitable to a Princely seat, and though built very near the top of a hill … yet it was plentifully supplied by water'. After the battle of Marston Moor, from August 1644 onwards, Pontefract became a key target, being almost continually besieged until the following summer. It was modified by its defenders both to resist artillery, and to fire guns from its ancient motte. Siegeworks have long since been identified at Harewood Park, whilst in the 1980s an excavation examined the castle interior. The significance of Pontefract as an example of how artillery was used rests principally upon the diary of Nathan Drake, composed during the first siege. This records in relentless detail virtually every shot of the bombardment over the festive season of 1644–1645. According to Drake no less than 1,406 artillery rounds were fired at Pontefract between Christmas and 28 January 1645, being shots from a 42 pound gun, a 36 pound, two 24 pound guns, and a 9 pound piece. The five days from 17 to 23 January were especially punishing, 400, 348, 282, 144 and 189 'great shot' being fired on each day respectively. This impressive cannonade would seem to prove that Civil War gunnery was slow only by modern standards, and that when circumstances demanded, and materials allowed, bombardments could be both intense and highly destructive.[24]

The diary also records that as result of gunfire on Christmas Day eleven men and boys of the garrison were left trapped in the church, afraid to make their escape lest they should be smashed to pulp by ordnance or shot by Parliamentarian musketeers. After five days of being marooned they were able to get away only by using a rope – even then one was killed, another wounded. On 19 January the Piper tower was systematically demolished by 78 shot. William Ingram, the garrison's gunner, replied to the enemy batteries, mixing case and solid ball in an attempt to clear bushes and other cover of troops. However shortage of shot was a problem for the Royalists, with the result that some of the besieged were forced to go out, 'every day into the graft [ditch] and fecht theire bullets for 4d a peece'. In this way Parliamentarian cannon balls were recycled back at those who fired them.[25]

---

[24] *Pontefract Castle: The Archaeology of the Civil War*, West Yorkshire Archaeological Service, Wakefield, 1988, passim; Harrington, *Archaeology of the English Civil War*, pp 18, 20, 24, 32–33, 52–53. Drake's diary is reprinted in R. Holmes *The Sieges of Pontefract Castle*, Pontefract, 1887, pp 1–146.

[25] Harrington *Archaeology of the English Civil War*, pp 32–33; D. Cooke *The Civil War in Yorkshire*, Barnsley, 2004, pp 145–159.

The first battle for Pontefract was conducted underground as well as on the surface. From the outside the Parliamentarians attempted to dig under the walls, to collapse or blast them. From the inside the Royalists dug their 'counter mines' from which the enemy could be intercepted, or blown up by smaller charges. Where these tunnels passed through the solid rock on which the castle was built, their remains have been well preserved. In one of them was found a pickaxe, and other evidence of the struggle. The defenders were at last saved from the outside at the beginning of March, by the forces of Sir Marmaduke Langdale. This was but a temporary reprieve, for within a couple of weeks Parliamentarian forces were back again. During this second siege they dug far more comprehensive works encircling the castle, and slowly but surely the defenders were compressed within an iron grip which confined them to the castle and All Saints church. Physical archaeological evidence has been found in the form of a ditch or droveway linking All Saints church with the east gate of the castle. Here musket balls and a low stone breastwork were discovered. Starvation eventually forced the surrender of the garrison in June 1645.[26]

In the Second Civil War Pontefract was seized by a subterfuge and again held for the King, serving as a base from which Royalist raiding parties harried the countryside. Though Cromwell succeeded in seizing the town on 10 August 1648, the castle had to wait until after the main Royalist and Scottish field armies had been defeated. Thereafter the Parliamentarians were able to indulge in a somewhat leisurely siege – safe in the knowledge that no relief force was at hand. Cromwell called upon Parliament to supply his efforts with 'three complete regiments of foot, and two of horse', as well as six 'good battering guns' with 300 rounds per piece. In November London pamphlets recorded that heavy artillery was being moved up to Pontefract from a variety of locations including the huge 'pocket pistol' from York, and a culverin from Nottingham, and some guns were moved by sea to Hull. Almost unbelievably Pontefract held out until 22 March 1649, by which time all the King's field forces had long since been defeated, and Charles himself had been dead for almost two months.

It has been suggested that the Parliamentarian failures to take Pontefract quickly were due to the poor performance of the artillery. Another more probable reason was the almost irrational bravery of the garrison – which fought on long beyond the point where lenient terms might be expected of their opponents. In the bitter dregs of the Second Civil War both sides were well aware of the score – as Cromwell put it, those within, were 'resolved to the utmost extremity; expecting no mercy, as indeed they deserve none'. Cromwell's words are worth noting, in part because they were no mere bloodthirsty threat, but actually reflected the laws of war as they were generally understood. There were

[26] Drake's diary, op cit n. 24 above, and K. Wiggins *Siege Mines and Underground Warfare*, Princes Risborough, 2003, pp 31–34.

also good practical explanations for slow progress at Pontefract: as Cromwell further explained to Parliament, the castle was well provisioned, moreover

> The place is very well known to be one of the strongest inland Garrisons in the Kingdom; well watered; situated upon a rock in every part of it, and therefore difficult to mine. The walls very thick and high, with strong towers; and if battered, very difficult to access, by reason of the depth and steepness of the graft [ditch].[27]

Certainly the taking of Pontefract was no easy matter on either occasion, as is attested by the scale of destruction to both town and castle. In 1644 the defenders attempts to clear their fields of fire and strike out at their opponents are said to have led to the burning of 100 houses. Later the church, town hall, courthouse, bake house and a windmill were all ruined – the total number of structures being destroyed being computed at 200, at a total cost of £40,000. Sometimes the defenders clearly gave as good as they got. As the author of the *Bloody Fight at Pontefract Castle* recorded in 1648, the 'great ordnance' from the towers very much 'annoyed' the besiegers, 'doing execution on our men as they lye in their Forts and trenches.[28]

GLOUCESTER: PARLIAMENT STRONGHOLD

Gloucester was first fortified early in the Civil War, though not without some local resistance against its energetic young Parliamentarian governor, the 23-year-old Edward Massey. Despite skirmishes, and a summons from Prince Rupert, it was not actually until August 1643 that the town was seriously threatened by the King's army, and this delay proved of considerable use to the defenders. By now almost 20 artillery pieces were available to Massey, and two powder mills within the city were also hard at work, producing three barrels a week to add to the existing store of 40 barrels. If the works were 'not half perfect' a continuous line had at least been formed by earthworks, the city wall, and ditches. Upwards of 1,500 men were ready to man the defences. That Gloucester meant serious business was demonstrated by the Parliamentarian's treatment of their own suburbs. Here a church and 241 houses were cleared, thus an creating an excellent field of fire for the defenders guns. The cost of this destruction was subsequently assessed at over £28,000.[29]

---

[27] T. Carlyle (ed) *Oliver Cromwell's Letters and Speeches*, London, 1866, vol 1, pp 329–332; BL E 473 (1) *The Moderate Intelligencer*, 14–21 November, Sig T2v.

[28] S. Porter *Destruction in the English Civil Wars*, Stroud, 1994, pp 86–87; F.H. Sunderland *Marmaduke Lord Langdale*, London, 1926, pp 103, 137, 147; BL E 469 (4) *A Bloody Fight at Pontefract*, October 1648, pp 2–3.

[29] BL E 67(31) J. Dorney *Briefe and Exact Relations of the Most Materiall and Remarkable Passages … in the late … Siegelaid before the City of Gloucester*, September 1643, p 3. M. Atkin and W.

The besiegers were certainly numerous, and included Rupert's army, Welsh forces claimed by Lord Herbert to number almost 5,000, and others. The total size of the Royalist army cannot therefore have been less than 15,000 men – and some estimates range much higher – suggesting that the defenders were outnumbered by a factor of more than ten to one. A Parliamentarian rhyme stated that the Royalists also had 'seven score' cannon. Though this is obviously a gross exaggeration the army was as well equipped as any Royalist force in this department, with ten guns in the 15 pound to 25 pound range, and two mortars. Critically however the King seems to have been short of the largest siege pieces, and ammunition, cartridges, ladles and granadoes. Without a battery capable of cutting a hole through modern earthworks there would be no obvious way to get the superior number of troops to count, though this was not apparent to the defenders at the time.[30]

Remarkably some of the attackers' first advances met with the extremely disquieting experience that those within Gloucester were actually better equipped to fire out, than they were to fire in. Issolds house in Barton Street, which had not been cleared by the defender's scorched earth policy, was occupied by the Royalists. From here they played

> with musket shot against us, till we by 5 or 6 cannon shot likewise from the Pen upon the West Gate, discharged upon the body of horse in Walham, and doing some small execution there made them goe seek better quarters. Our women and maides wrought all this afternoone, on the little Meade out of our workes in the very face of those houses, in fetching Turfe for the repairing of our workes.

Truth be told for all its bravado the Royalist command was in a difficult quandary. Just a couple of weeks earlier Rupert had carried Bristol by storm, but it had caused his army appalling loss. Whether another such adventure could be accepted was dubious. On the other hand it was not clear if there was enough artillery to do the job of reducing Gloucester by bombardment. Lastly there was a significant danger that if the Royalists did not act promptly a relief force might be sent to the town's aid. The strategy that remained was an awkward compromise. So it was that the day following the incident at Issold's house the pipes were cut which conveyed water to Gloucester from Robinhood's Hill, and entrenchments began at Gaudy Green. Meanwhile Sir William Vavasor and Welsh troops advanced through the Vinyard, but, 'upon their drawing up on the side of the hill our demi-culverin discharged from the Pen fell amongst

---

Laughlin *Gloucester and the Civil War*, Stroud, 1993, p 85 give a figure of 'about 15' artillery pieces in the town. On the destruction of religious sites see 'Gloucester Sites and Remains of Religious Houses' in *A History of the County of Gloucester*, vol 4, *The City of Gloucester*, 1988, web published version at british-history.ac.uk.; see also Porter *Destruction in the English Civil Wars*, p 77.

[30] I. Roy (ed) *The Royalist Ordnance Papers*, Oxfordshire Record Society, 2 vols, 1964 and 1976, pp 255–284.

them and did good execution: we discovered them through our prospectives [telescopes] conveying away their dead and wounded'. Cannon firing from the East Gate similarly claimed hits on the enemy in Barton Street.[31]

Given the spirited battering that their troops were getting from Gloucester's cannon and the failure of uncoordinated action, the King's commanders made the sensible decision to set up their headquarters on a reverse slope, where it could not be seen from the town, and to link the various portions of the Royalist army by a bridge of boats across the Severn. Massey, who had served as an engineer in Holland, understood the significance of these moves and took appropriate steps to counter them. Sallies were now directed both at the trenches, and at an embryonic battery being formed at Kingsholm. This was not however enough to stay the King's engineers, for by the afternoon of 12 August 'two great culverins' of 15 or 16 pounds were set up and employed on the east side of town,

> out of Musket Shot point blanke with which they made some store of shot, intending to batter the Town-wall but did no harm, although many fell into the town. They then likewise began making a redoubt in a field neer Lanthony towards Severn, making a breast work from it to Lanthony wall crosse the Causey and we perceiving by their Canon Baskets they placed their square redoubt in Gaudy Green that they intended a battery there, began the lining of our Toune wall from the South to the East Gate which we shortly after perfected.[32]

Next the Royalists brought into play the one thing which earthworks could not stop: mortars. According to Dorney 'several great grenadoes' were shot into the town on the night of 12 August. Happily there were not very many: according to the *True Relation* only three fell on the first night, and six on a subsequent occasion, with some damage to property but no harm to the garrison, the shells tearing up the ground 'as if a beare had been rooting up the earth'. Dorney believed that the enemy's biggest mortar broke on its first shot, which is very possible since Lord Percy reported that a mortar had been broken at Gloucester on 14 August. Another was requested from Oxford. This also fits with the fact that mortars had been present at Bristol the previous month, and that another was assigned 'to his Majesties service' on 4 August, together with 20 granadoes. On 12 August Percy had also asked for a further 20 granadoes, fuses, tampions, ten 'elles' of canvas, fireworks and spare wheels for guns. On 14 August Edward Sherburne had managed to dispatch most of these requirements, including the mortar, 30 granadoes, and spare wheels accompanied by five conductors, a clerk, two gunners and a matross.[33]

---

[31] Dorney *Exact Relation*, pp 3–4; Corbet, p 43; Whiting, p 10; a number of useful tracts are reprinted in J. Washbourne *Bibliotheca Gloucesterensis*, Gloucester, 1825.

[32] Dorney *Exact Relation*, p 3, see also Corbet, p 47.

[33] *A True Relation of the Siege Before the City of Gloucester*, 10 August 1643, reprinted in B.H. Blacker (ed) *Gloucestershire Notes and Queries*, 1887, vol 3, pp 464–466; also BL E 69(15) *A*

The defenders were not going to let their resistance be worn down: damage to the walls from the battery at Gaudy Green was repaired with wool sacks and cannon baskets, and the townspeople were vigilant against the menace of the granadoe. On 17 August mortar shells were again fired from Gaudy Green, with four hitting houses: 'one fell into the street neer the south gate, but a woman coming by with a payle of water, threw the water thereon, and extinguished the phuse thereof, so that it did not break, but was taken up whole; it weighed 60 lb'. At Kingsholm the next day the garrison were more aggressive, directing a major sally of 400 men against the enemy batteries, screened by 50 men making diversionary attack elsewhere. When the raiders reached the Royalist guns they disabled them by 'nailing' – or driving spikes into the touch holes. The *True Relation* has it that, 'they killed divers with the butt end of their muskette, and so returned, having broken their ordinance in the end, and nailed a steele pike in the titch hole'. As usual the preoccupation of the defenders was that part of the enemy which most seriously threatened the security of the town: his artillery. The defenders also appear to have become hardened to the bombardment. Corbet would have us believe that the shot and shells were delivered by providence to land in harmless places, and that their effect became 'contemptible'. In the battery of 18 August the Royalist guns on Gaudy Green and Friar's Orchard poured perhaps 150 shot into the walls, which, being countermured, sustained this punishment reasonably well. The Parliamentarians even felt happy enough to jeer when one of the shot struck down a pig.[34]

Not all the defenders were confident of the outcome, and a few slipped away to the enemy, including, according to Dorney, a gunner called Hatton. Morale cannot but have been further impaired by a sally intended to spike Royalist guns which miscarried on 21 August. This failure allowed the bombardment to be resumed, and Friday 25 August was one of the least comfortable days for the garrison, as noted in *True Relation*:

> They shot 5 grenadoes, two lighted in Southgate Streete & killed a woman, and one towards Captayn Bacchus' house; both the other fell neare the Katheryne Wheel [public house], and tore the brick wall. There was 7 red hott bullets shott outt of the Enimies cannons; one went through the hay, and did not fyre it; and they discharged their ordinance 13 tymes.

According to Dorney's version of these same events, the Royalists also shot stones from their mortars. He counted 'above twenty' of the red hot shot,

> some 18 pound, others 22 pound weight, in the night wee perceived them flyinge in the ayre like a starre shooting, most of them fell into houses and

---

True Relation, 4 October 1643, sig 'B'. *Royalist Ordnance Papers*, pp 268–275; Gloucester RO TRS 146.

34 Dorney *Exact Relation*, pp 6–7; *True Relation*, pp 465–466; Corbet, pp 48–51; Whiting, pp 12–13.

> stables where hay was but by God's providence did not hurt at all. One came through three houses, and fell into a chamber of Mr Cornelius the Apothecary and being perceived, many payles of water were cast upon it to quench the same, but that little avayling, it was cast into a cowle of water, where after a good space it cooled.

The fact that it had rained heavily the previous night, reducing risk of fire, might also have been put down to divine intervention. Either way it seems that the garrison were active in tracking down and extinguishing these incendiary shot.[35]

By this time the Royalist army was well advanced in adding a new terror to the siege: attempts to undermine, or blow up, the City defences. As early as 13 August the King had ordered 40 Gloucestershire miners, via the good offices of Baynham Throckmorton, Sherriff of the County, 'to repair to our Traine of Artillery before Gloucester by tomorrow night at the farthest with such tools as they use there to be employed in our service'. Again the defenders had remedies. At first the King's miners made slow progress in the face of underground springs and countermining by the garrison. When at last they got within striking distance of the East Gate, the defenders struck back:

> a sergeant with five daring men were put forth at a port hole in the dungeon at the East gate, came close to the mouth of their mine, took off the board that covered it, and for a while viewed the miners. One of these cast in a hand-granado amongst them, whilst the foure musketeers played upon them as they ran forth and with the noise of our men from the walls gave the whole leager a strong alarm, and crept in at the port hole without harm.[36]

By the end of August the Royalists before Gloucester were reduced to some pretty desperate measures. As Sir Samuel Luke would later confirm the King's cannon were supplementing their roundshot with 'loggetts of wood'. Instead of digging forward and making a breach with artillery troops were pushed over ground behind 'imperfect and troublesome engines' designed by Dr Chillingworth. Some Parliamentarian observers were convinced that such ideas were lifted directly from the Ancients, as well they might have been – though the notion that one of these devices was the inspiration for 'Humpty Dumpty' is disputed. In Dorney's account we do however learn how the wide ditches of the defences effectively prevented these modern siege engines from doing their job. By 5 September the game was up: Essex's relief army was in sight of Gloucester at Prestbury Hill, and even though heavy rain made the way 'deepe for the artillery', it was clear that he would soon reach the town. Rather than be crushed between the still defiant town and the avenging Londoners the King's army admitted defeat and withdrew. Estimates of the casualties varied:

---

[35] *True Relation*, pp 465–466; Dorney, p 9.
[36] Corbet, p 51; Dorney *Exact Relation*, p 9–10; the order for miners is Gloucester RO D115/9.

Corbet claimed that 1,000 Royalists were dead. About 400 'great' shot had been fired at the town, as well as 20 granadoes.[37]

Gloucester's siege and bombardment has left many lasting impressions: both physical scars upon the town and additions to folklore. A graze on the north side of the East window of St Mary de Crypt, the town's main magazine, is put down to the impact of shot. Excavations have brought to light the foundations of the East Gate, from which six men sallied against Royalist miners, and a few feet away a modern mural commemorates the Royalist battery. Shoes and clay pipes have been dug from the seventeenth century infill of the old fortification ditches. Greyfriars was badly damaged, and remains a ruin, whilst St Nicholas church lost part of its steeple: this was never completely stable thereafter and partially dismantled in the eighteenth century. Some of the most interesting evidence is preserved in Gloucester folk museum: part of the South Gate, restored in 1644, iron roundshot, and a mass of short tubular castings, some still joined, which are thought to be a form of case or scatter shot. These artefacts might also explain the mysterious 'bolt shot' referred to in contemporary literature, although this may be another term for 'bar shot'.

What is crucial to our interpretation of what happened at Gloucester is that we now have to recognise that, with the ordnance at their disposal in the summer of 1643, the Royalists actually stood little chance of bringing Gloucester to its knees. The artifactual and manuscript evidence are in agreement that the guns and ammunition they had were insufficient to cope with the artillery and earthen walls of the defence. Time was also limited. The Royalists knew all to well what the problem was, and as late as 2 September there were attempts to remedy the deficiency. A new train of artillery detailed for Lord Percy from Oxford that day was to include ten more guns, 400 shot, 19 wagons and more trained gunners. Though these may have helped to hammer the Trained Bands at Newbury they would be too late to make any difference to the outcome at Gloucester.[38]

LATHOM: 'NORTHERN COURT'

Lathom House, the Lancashire seat of James Stanley, Royalist Seventh Earl of Derby, has all but vanished from the modern landscape – being battered, then replaced with a polite eighteenth century country house, which has itself largely

---

[37] Dorney *Exact Relation*, p 12.

[38] *Royalist Ordnance Papers*, pp 276, 284. Nine shot recovered and now held by the Gloucester Folk Museum include just one 15 pound ball, the remainder varying from 2 pounds to just over 5 pounds. On finds of ball elsewhere in the county see Gloucestershire RO D2210/10, and 18. The five extra gunners sent to Lord Percy were Robert Williams, William Barefoote, John Clemms, Thomas Edward and Owen Rice: they were accompanied by matrosses David Pierce, John William, Hammond Hall, John Poppingay, Thomas Dance, William Slye, William Reynolds and William Blee.

been expunged by later hands. Nevertheless, as with Basing, it is misleading to think of Lathom as a simple 'house'. Indeed so rich and cultured had Lathom become, that by the early modern period it was being referred to as a 'Northern Court'. The central structure was predominantly fifteenth century, with turrets and courtyards, an arrangement ill calculated to withstand artillery. Yet topography and later works, plus timely stocking of Lathom's arsenal with guns and munitions, served to make the place one of the most secure in England.

From an early medieval military perspective the location of Lathom, beneath the crest of a low hill, was all wrong – but surrounded with a wall, outer palisade, earth banks, deep ditch, and surrounding waterlogged ground the place became difficult to see, and almost impossible to bombard. As one account explained, nature had formed a stronghold:

> before the house, to the south and south west is a rising ground so near it, as to overlook the top of it, from which it falls so quick, that nothing planted against it on those sides can touch it further than the front wall; and on the north and east sides, there is another rising ground, even to the edge of the moat, and then falls away so quick, that you can scarce, at the distance of a carbine shot, see the house over that height; so that all the batteries placed there, are so far below it, as to be little service against it; and let us observe, by the way that the uncommon situation of it may be compared to the palm of a man's hand, flat in the middle, and covered by rising ground about it, and so near to it that the enemy, during the siege, were never able to raise a battery against it, so as to make a breach in the wall practicable by way of storm.[39]

What had long seemed a somewhat poetic, even fanciful, description of the location and defences of Lathom has in fact been largely confirmed by recent archaeology. When excavated the rock cut ditch was found to be approximately nine feet deep and 40 feet wide, surrounding an area which was more than 900 feet east to west, and slightly less north to south. Masonry and timbers that had been incorporated into the eighteenth century house showed evidence of having been reused from an earlier structure. A massive drain helped to explain why wet ground, so obvious in the mid seventeenth century, was no longer readily apparent. In addition to the ditch and banking the original perimeter wall was given a lining of 'earth and sods, two yards thick' by the garrison. Lathom may have been relatively compact, but its artillery defences were unexpectedly strong.

Attacked in February 1644 by a local Parliamentarian army – at first directed by Sir Thomas Fairfax – it appeared that the fall of Lathom would be something of a formality. With over 2,000 men the besiegers outnumbered the defenders by at least seven to one, and they took their time to encircle the house at a distance, and offer terms. The Parliament men had however not taken into account the determination of Lady Derby, who remained within Lathom to encourage her troops. She played for time, and it was not until early March

---

[39] Seacombe *House of Stanley*, p 90.

that serious business commenced. As the *Breefe Journall* of the siege remarked, works

> were begun about a musquett-shott from the house, in a stoopeing declining ground, that their pioneers by nature of the place might be secured from our ordnances on the towers, and soe in an orbe or ringe-worke cast up much earthe everye day by the multitude of the countrey people forced to the service.

On 12 March however it was the defenders who seized the initiative: a hundred infantry and 12 cavalry commanded by Captain Farmer and his Lieutenants sallied forth. They held their fire until they were upon the enemy, then set to with a vengeance, killing 'about 30' and capturing many arms. Thereafter the beating of drums, or other stratagems, would be enough to throw the Parliamentarians into consternation. Nevertheless the besiegers were able to sap their way forward, little by little, working behind baskets and hurdles which covered the progress of the workmen from accurate fire. On 19 March they finally managed to set up a demi cannon within range of the house, but made little impression on the outer wall, soon switching their fire to the more vulnerable turrets instead. A week later the first siege gun was joined by a culverin, and a lucky shot penetrated the main gate – damage which was quickly repaired by stuffing the gap in the defences with beds and debris.[40]

A few days later there was a more serious development, for the Parliamentarians had now succeeded in emplacing a mortar in a circular pit on rising ground, within 'halfe a musket shot' south west of the house. Its first three shots were not exploding 'grenadoes' but large stones 13 inches in diameter, weighing 80 pounds. There was every danger that shells would follow and, as the *Breefe Journall* put it, not even 'the stoutest souldiers' had heart for granadoes. The only recourse was repeated raids and sallies, some of which degenerated into fierce hand to hand fighting in the Parliamentarian lines as the Royalists desperately attempted to put as many of the enemy guns out of action as possible. On 12 April a roundshot whizzed right through the 'claye walls' and entered Lady Derby's bedroom, and four days later the mortar finally showed what it could do:

> about 11 o'clock they played their mortar piece with stone, and p'ceaving it struck within the body of the house, they cast a grenadoe at the same levell, which fell into an old court. strikeing about half a yard into the earth, yet rose again with such vyolence in the bursting, that though its strength was much lessened, and deaded with earth, it shooke down the glasse, clay and weaker buildings neere it leaving only the carcase of the walls standing about

---

[40] *A Briefe Journall of the Siege Against Lathom* (BL Harleian Ms 2074) is reprinted in L. Hutchinson *Memoirs of the Life of Colonel Hutchinson*, London, 1846, pp 487–518 (another version appears in Ormerod's *Civil War Tracts*). See also Guizot de Wit *The Lady of Latham*, London, 1869, p 5; and C. Pilkington *To Play the Man*, Preston, 1991, pp 19–35.

it, yet without hurt to any person, saveing that 2 woemen in a neere chamber had theire hands scorcht … The mortar piece was now more terrible than formerly.[41]

Within another four days the Parliamentarian gunners managed to focus their two heavy guns on part of a tower, but were answered by snipers who killed a gunner. On 23 April the fury was directed against the central Eagle Tower, causing an alarming hole to appear in the staircase and more shot to go through Lady Derby's quarters. Crucially however they did not appear able to create a breach in any outer wall – and therefore could not facilitate any storming of the garrison. Another summons sent in to what the Parliamentarians imagined would be a compliant Lady Derby was torn up.

Brave as this gesture may seem the fight was actually far less one sided than has generally been assumed: for the besiegers were not as strong as simple numbers might suggest. For one thing their command structure was weak, and the leadership was certainly confused if not actually divided. Fairfax, a commander nominated by Parliament, had long since departed, and de facto responsibility seems to have devolved upon Lancashire Colonel Alexander Rigby. Yet Lathom lay in West Lancashire, and so on Colonel Peter Egerton's home turf. Colonels Ashton and Moore were other senior Lancashire Parliamentarian leaders present in April – and the former was on very poor terms with Rigby. Though Ashton was arguably a front runner Lancashire had no overall Parliamentarian supremo, and to have four officers of equal rank – three of them Members of Parliament – in charge of a siege was a recipe for dissension. To make matters worse finances were already tight, and the Parliamentarian troops were not all available simultaneously. Instead they were called out according to the 'Hundred' of the County in which they lived, attempting to bring their supplies with them, and once they were present spent only one day in three actually in the siege lines. Attempting to rest the troops was understandable, but it meant that if the Royalists mounted surprise raids, in strength, they were unlikely to be outnumbered at all. The last, but by no means least, of Parliaments problems was its guns – two siege guns was totally inadequate and the vital mortar was woefully short of ammunition. The weapon itself had been borrowed from Cheshire, and it arrived with only a handful of rounds. Whilst his engineers cast around for suitable rocks Rigby was reduced to begging Sir William Brereton for help:

We have already presumed upon the confidence we have of your interest in you and your affections to the public, and now having your mortar, it cannot be so useful as you desire, unless you please to furnish us with half a dozen or more shells for granadoes for the mortar piece, which I earnestly entreat, from you to be delivered to this bearer for the more expedition in the work which now detains us from other services, and what satisfaction you desire for

---

[41] *Briefe Journall*, pp 504–506.

them you shall receive, if not from the rest of the Deputy Lieutenants then from me.[42]

This message was dated 18 April, and is therefore most unlikely to have been acted upon, if at all, until a few days later – 80 pound shells being difficult to transport even if available. By 26 April it would be too late for shells, for by that time the Parliamentarians no longer had a mortar. For about four o'clock that morning, under cover of darkness, the Royalists had mounted their most ambitious sally to date.

> Captain Chisnall with his eighty men and two Lieutenants issued at the eastern gate, and before he was discovered, got under their cannon, marching straight upon the sconce where they had planted their great guns. It cost him a slight skirmish to gain the fort: at last he entered: many slayne, some prisoners, and some escaping. Now, by having command of that battery, their retreat being assured, Captain Fox, according to orders, seconds him with much bravery, beating up their trenches from the eastern to the south-west point, till he came to the work which secured the mortar piece, which being guarded by fifty men, he found sharp service in forcing his way through musket and cannon, and in beating the enemy out of the sconce with stones, his muskets, by reason of the high work, being unserviceable. After a quarter of an hour's hard service, his men got the trench, scaled the rampart, whereupon many of the enemy fled, and the rest were slain. The sconce, thus won, was made good by a squadron of musketeers, who much annoyed the enemy, who were attempting to come up again. The two main works being thus obtained, the two captains walked the rest of the round with ease; whilst Mr Broome, with a company of her ladyship's servants and some fresh soldiers, took care to level the ditch, and by a present device lifting the mortar piece on with ropes to a low drag, by strength of men drew it into the house. Captain Ogle defending the passage against another company of the enemy which played upon their retreat. The like endeavour was used to gain their great guns; but they lying beyond the ditch, and being of such bulk and weight, all our strength could not bring them off before the whole army would have fallen upon us; however, our men took time to poison all the cannon round …[43]

Five Parliamentarians were also taken prisoner, the most important of whom was Browne, their engineer. The mortar now lay in the grounds of Lathom like 'a dead lion'.

Though Rigby's men maintained the formalities of a siege for a further month it was clear that the struggle was all but over. Rigby wrote back to the committee at Manchester talking of his 'anxiety and fatigue': money now ran out, and according to his own account Rigby was now having to fund some of the proceedings out of his own pocket. Rain began to fall heavily, soaking

---

42 *CSPD* vol DI, 18 April 1644, p 126. Another mention of shortages appears in vol DII, 5 June 1644.
43 *Briefe Journall*, p 509.

the already demoralised besiegers, filling the trenches and a mine. By 26 May the Royalists determined that the Parliamentarian grip had slackened. Prince Rupert and a large army was on the way to the relief of Lathom.

This happy respite would last only until Rupert was defeated at Marston Moor, and by August 1644 a besieging force was back before Lathom. On this occasion time was on the Parliamentarians' side. However, despite the absence of both Lord and Lady Derby, Colonel Rosthern put up a powerful resistance, at first mounting raids against the opposition, then sitting out the months with stoic determination. In April 1645 it appeared this patience might be rewarded when it was at last thought another relief might be on its way. By July 1645 fresh batteries were in place, and the defenders were now squeezed into a tight and hungry corner. Though the King's army never materialised the Lancashire Parliamentarians were also running short of money and strength, and later had to call in their neighbours from Cheshire to prosecute the siege. Lathom finally threw in the towel in early December 1645 – after sieges that had totalled about a year and eight months. Final surrender was made to the Cheshire men, and almost resulted in a fight with the Lancashire Parliamentarians who felt robbed of both the honour and the plunder.

SEA POWER AND SIEGES

As we have noted, Parliamentarian control of the navy proved extremely useful in assisting the safe importation of stores from continental Europe – and made it more difficult for the King to bring men or munitions from thence, or from Ireland, but it also has to be recognised that sea power was tactically projected onto the land, at least so far as coastal sieges were concerned. Ships well handled could either bring succour to the besieged, or deny it to an enemy. Blockade, shore bombardment, and landing parties were all used with varying degrees of success. At Hull the navy was a lifeline, and at Liverpool Parliamentarian ships acted both to help the town, when occupied by Parliament, and hindered its resupply after it had been taken by Prince Rupert in 1644. Barnstaple recieved guns landed from merchant ships, but did not last long against determined attack. However Pembroke probably was saved more than once by the intervention of sea power. In Februrary 1644 for example the fleet assisted in the capture of Pill fort, Milford Haven, where combined bombardment from sea and land discomforted the occupants and a lucky shot from the Swallow took 'off the head' of one man, and the 'posteriors' of another.[44]

At Lyme Regis the fleet was a crucial factor in supporting the defenders

[44] J.R. Powell and E.K. Timings (eds) *Documents Relating to the Civil War*, Navy Records Society, vol 105, London, 1963, pp 128–135, 146–155; BL E 50 (25) *A Letter from the Right Honorable Robert Earle of Warwick*, 1644, pp 7–9; R.W. Cotton *Barnstaple and the Northern Part of Devonshire During the Great Civil War*, London, 1889, pp 119–120.

against Royalist besiegers. Supplies including meat, cheese, beer, and ammunition were landed from the Earl of Warwick's squadron, which put new life into the outnumbered 'tired soldiers' of Lyme. Dismounting cannon from the Mary Rose and Mayflower, and landing 46 barrels of powder put real punch into the defence, and must have made it difficult indeed for the attackers to mount their siege. Moreover the ships bombarded Prince Maurice's troops, 'firing divers great shot' in land, and forcing the Royalists to 'cast up a breastwork by the sea side for their own defence'. Despite repeated assaults and desperate attempts to fire the town with red hot shot, pieces of metal, and even fire arrows the townsmen were able to hold out.

According to the account of Captain Davies the fort near the Cobb had just four roundshot for each of its sakers when the storm began, but came under such concentrated fire that its gunners were able to pick up so much shot that they had 14 rounds apiece when the action ended. Sailors from the ships provided extra manpower for sallies mounted by the garrison which succeeded in disabling some of the Royalist guns in their batteries. Nevertheless according to one account of the siege, 'There was such a continual peale of small shot and great shot, that the toune semed to be all on a flame.' There was indeed 'scarce a house in the town that is not battered, and scarce a room is not unto which a shot hath been made. At the last great fire, two maids, carrying betwixt them a vessel of water had three of their hands shot off.' The *Kingdom's Weekly Intelligencer* had it that this nasty incident was the work of a chain shot. When the town was finally relieved Secretary William Jessop thanked God, Essex and Warwick for their intervention, claiming somewhat improbably that failure at Lyme cost the King's party not only more men than Bristol but 105 officers and 25 gunners.[45]

Later in 1644, and with varying degrees of success, vessels commanded by the Earl of Warwick, offered similar services at Plymouth and Dartmouth. Perhaps the navy's most obvious failure was its lack of ability to help the Earl of Essex in his hour of need when his army was trapped in the south west peninsula and brought to surrender at Lostwithiel. Contrary winds prevented anything like a full scale rescue attempt, Essex himself only made a somewhat ignominious escape in a fishing boat. Valuable guns were lost from the train of artillery, but this perplexing episode may ultimately have tipped the scales in deciding Parliament that it had to dispense with Essex and 'New Model' its army. In 1645, amongst other operations, the navy would act along the coast of Ireland, intercept transports off Wales, and intervene again at Pembroke. In 1646 there may have been less real fighting for the Parliament's ships, but

45 BL E (51) 15, W. Jessop *A Most Exact and Full Relation of Many Admirable Passages, Which Happened During the Whole Siege of Lime*, 1644, pp 2–3; E 50 (23) *An Exact and True Relation in the Relieving the Resolute Garrison of Lyme in Dorset-shire*, 1644, p 4; also E 42 (14); E 50 (26).

a blockade of the Cornish coast was successful in preventing relief reaching Pendennis Castle.

As the King enjoyed the loyalty of few warships in the first Civil War his use of them to project influence upon the land war was relatively limited, as we might expect. Nevertheless the Royalists were still able to make use of some of the guns that their ships carried, and in this it was doubtless very useful that sea type carriages were interchangeable with those used in many fortifications. Exeter in particular appears to have been heavily reinforced with naval ordnance, for whilst relatively few pieces were kept there by Parliament, after the Royalist occupation 55 iron and 20 bronze guns would be surrendered in 1646. Even Exmouth Fort gave up at least 16 or 18 guns, these being listed by Vicars as '13 great iron pieces', two drakes and three 'murderers'.[46]

Similar tactics were employed by the Royalists in defence of King's Lynn in 1643 when its new bastions were filled with guns taken from ships. At least initially the defence was far stiffer than was expected. As one Parliamentarian soldier reported:

> We resolved upon storming the toune Saturday morning, and to that purpose had called in many boats, with which we intended to attack it by water, and many cart loads of ladders, which we intended for the land side: during this hot service we lost about foure men, one a cannonier, who was shot through his side with a drake bullet, he was not dead when the town was taken, but it was no likelyhood but he would, he was a good cannoneer, and a man right to his party. We had one shot with a bullet through the shoulder, near the necke: and one Lieutenant had his arme shot off, on which he dies suddenly after, it was a cannon shot through a port hole, so skillfull were they, that they would shoot three times together into one port hole. In this violent playing with cannon and small shot we believe above eighty lost their lives on both sides ... it is true, storming and entering breaches usually wast men'[47]

As we can imagine the 1648 revolt of the navy would be serious and troublesome not merely because it threatened international communications and supply lines, but because of the potential of the navy to act in support of, or against, coastal targets – particularly in this instance in Kent and along the Channel coast. It was fortunate indeed that the revolt was relatively short-lived, and really failed to co-ordinate with any of the other forces ranged against the New Model Army in the Second Civil War. As it was 12 of the Summer Guard's 39 ships were at some point in rebel hands, and a further six were to some extent mutinous or disorderly.[48]

Our examples of sieges can only reinforce the impression that artillery was

---

[46] BL E 506(34) *Perfect Occurences*, April 1646, sig R3; J. Vicars *Parliamentary Chronicle*, 1646, part 2, p 72; Chadwyck Healey (ed) *Bellum Civile: Hopton's Narrative*, pp 26–28.

[47] BL E 67 (28) *A Briefe and True Relation of the Siege and Storming of Kings Lyne*, 1643, pp 1–2; A. Kingston *East Anglia and the Great Civil War*, London, 1877, p 131.

[48] On the Navy in 1648, see B. Capp *Cromwell's Navy*, Oxford, 1988, pp 15–41.

critical to the form and tactics of Civil War siege warfare – but they also help to demonstrate that without the correct train of battering guns and munitions great luck was required for success. Interestingly what the protracted instances of Basing, Lathom and Pontefract appear to have in common is that for all, or part, of their duration the besiegers failed, for one reason or another, to get the right guns to the right place with enough ammunition. Or alternatively that a defender, being determined and better supplied in this department, managed to frustrate attacks by counter battery action – as at Gloucester and Lyme. Whether Gloucester would have survived without the intervention of a relief force must remain debatable. Certainly when balance existed between defence and attack, with both sides using artillery, sieges could last weeks, months or even years. To this extent the maxim of Sir John Hale that gunpowder 'revolutionised the conduct but not the outcome of wars', holds good for the Civil War siege – if not the entire conflict.[49]

Eventually however every Royalist stronghold was reduced, and the war was won. Our examples could therefore be taken as atypical, for where the artillery train arrived promptly and well equipped, or defence was weak, many fortresses and towns succumbed far more quickly. Recording the exploits of the New Model Army in the last 16 months of the war, Joshua Sprigge states that Bridgwater took just 11 days to fall, Bristol 18 days, Launceston one hour, Berkeley Castle nine days, Winchester Castle nine days, and Dartmouth just seven. Really long sieges were certainly in the minority by the later stages of the First Civil War. Sprigge suggests that the New Model Army faced just three places that resisted them for more than two months, Exeter, Dunster Castle, and Wallingford Castle, though naturally we have the bear in mind that the New Model Army fought primarily in the south and therefore a number of significant sieges in the north, notably Pontefract and Lathom, are omitted from Sprigge's triumphal list. Nevertheless we are left with the impression that frequently, and compared to his enemy, the King found it difficult to put a modern siege train into the field with enough heavy guns. This failure certainly contributed to his losing the war. Both sides also found it difficult to maintain the very long sieges which led to victory by starvation or attrition – but again Parliament appears to have succeeded more often, despite many short term failures.[50]

The difference between Parliament's victory and Royal failure was however only a matter of degree. Dragging heavy expensive hardware around the country, destroying its towns, winning sieges, and storming fortifications brought almost as many problems as it solved. Garrisons were expensive, tied up troops, and populations disgruntled by what appeared to be occupation could be difficult

---

[49] J.R. Hale 'Gunpowder and the Renaissance, an essay in honour of Garret Mattingly', in *From the Renaissance to the Counter Reformation*, p 115.
[50] Sprigge *Anglia Rediviva*, pp 334–335.

to control. It is therefore significant that Parliament's policy in the latter stages of the conflict involved something of a calculated risk. Wherever it was deemed expedient Royalist strongholds were now no longer reoccupied by friendly troops – but 'slighted', or damaged in such a way as to make them impractical to defend. As Cromwell suggested to Parliament after the fall of Basing,

> I humbly offer to you, to have this place utterly slighted, for the following reasons: it will ask about 800 men to manage it; it is no frontier; the country is poor about it; the place exceedingly ruined by our batteries and mortar-pieces, and by a fire which fell upon the place since our taking it.[51]

'Slighting' did not necessarily equate to immediate and total destruction. Fortresses and mounds of earth were difficult and expensive to completely raze to the ground, and there were other cheaper ways to ensure that defences could not easily be put back into commission. Old castle keeps were therefore often deprived of their most vital wall, or explosives used to wreck batteries or towers. Thereafter local tradesmen might be granted rights to remove building materials: timbers, bricks, lead, and masonry. If middlemen could be induced to give something for what they took the castle could be made to pay for its own demise as ant-like scavengers stripped her stores, plumbing, roofs, floors, and even walls. Interestingly there were at least a few cases where the Royalists saved their enemies the bother of slighting – by damaging their own defences as they withdrew. In May 1644, for example, the Earl of Forth concluded that Reading, not long since fortified, was untenable. It was duly ordered that the place should be made 'unserviceable' and 'with all speed'.

Evidence of Parliament's precise thinking on the question of slighting does not appear to have survived – but we do know that Members had 'conferences' on the subject, and can deduce the sequence in which policy developed. One or two castles were destroyed after capture very early in the war, orders for the slighting of Sherborne being given from London as soon as November 1642: after which the Deputy Lieutenants of Dorset were empowered, 'to take down and sell away, all the lead, iron, boards, timber and other materials of the said castle, that will yield money; and convert the same for the defraying of the charge of the workmen and soldiers'. Some other places met with similar fates in 1643 and 1644. Slighting does not, however, appear to have become the common destiny of captured strongholds until 1645 – and even then could be controversial. When orders were issued for the destruction of a fort at Bedford, for example, local worthies petitioned Parliament that they would feel safer if it was preserved.

There was certainly strategic thought on the subject that year, for in October the Commons resolved that they would seek to establish 'a frontier' at Newbury. On the friendly side of this barrier the Parliamentary Committees of

---

51 Carlyle (ed) *Cromwell's Letters and Speeches*, p 192.

Sussex, Surrey, Hampshire, Oxfordshire, Buckinghamshire and Berkshire were to consider undertaking the besieging of remaining enemy fortresses, and 'the taking down and slighting such inland garrisons as shall be within this frontier'. Orders for the destruction of 'the fortifications at Farnham', followed soon afterwards. By 1646 slighting became a veritable epidemic, with Oxford, Newark, Tutbury, Barton House, and 'the garrisons' of Henley and Derby being just some of the places decommissioned. At Berkeley Castle the army detachment responsible was particularly enthusiastic in their task, 'pulling off the leads, pulling down the glass, and iron bars of the windows, the gates and doors both within and without the said castle, pulling up the boards and wainscots belonging to the same, and also breaking and burning trunks and chests'. Parliament was forced to admit that its soldiers had far exceeded their remit, and much too belatedly ordered the return of Lord Berkeley's looted personal goods. At this time it is interesting to note that Parliament was not only demolishing former Royalist strongholds, but actively engaged on a selective policy of dissolving its own garrisons.[52]

By March 1647 even the Eastern Association had been given instructions from the centre to consider which garrisons might be reduced, and a Parliamentary committee 'for the order for slighting garrisons' was in existence by the following month. Also in April 1647 orders were prepared for the destruction of castles in North Wales. Those towns 'disgarrisoned' in the current round were to have their keys returned from the military to civil officials, 'that the Government of those places may be as formerly it was before these unhappy troubles'. Ordnance was 'drawn off' London's defences at the end of 1646, and a rather badly timed order for the total abandonment of defensive lines was made in late 1647 – just in time to leave the capital vulnerable at the time of the outbreak of the Second Civil War. Yet the fighting in the Second and Third Civil Wars was merely a hiccup in the slighting and disgarrisoning process – for by late 1651 the Council of State was considering anew which 'inland garrisons' could be dispensed with. As late as 1660 indeed General Monck was given orders to destroy Chepstow castle. Interestingly the national pattern of outward facing fortifications and garrisons – so apparent in the 1630s – was therefore effectively revived by early 1660. Gunners and other small forces occupied forts on the Channel Islands, and along the south coast at Pendennis and St Mawes, Plymouth, Weymouth, Hurst, Portsmouth, Walmer, Deal, Dover and a few other locations. Defences were also manned in the Thames and at strategic points on the east coast such as Hull and Berwick. Though

---

52 *House of Lords Journal,*vol 5, 27 September 1642; vol 7, 8 July 1645; 31 October 1645; vol 8, 2 October 1646; 19 November 1646; 25 April 1646; vol 9, 14 May 1647; vol 10, 16 June 1648; *House of Commons Journal,* vol 2, 1 November 1642; vol 4, 3 June 1646; 15 June 1646; 6 August 1646; 18 October 1645; vol 5, 2 March 1647; 15 April 1647; 8 December 1646; vol 6, 25 July 1651; vol 8, 21 May 1660.

there were also a few small garrisons in Wales, manned inland garrisons were almost unheard of. Many were slighted, others simply abandoned. The few exceptions to this general rule included Shrewsbury and Windsor – both of which housed relatively minor detachments.[53]

---

[53] BL Harleian Ms 6844, 'An Establishment of the Forces', February 1660, passim.

6

Battle

A common body of tactics for the use of artillery on the battlefield existed long before 1642. During the decades leading up to the English Civil Wars, a number of key European texts containing tactical theory were translated and circulated, in either manuscript or book form. English and Scottish commentators also added their opinions, or reassessed artillery tactics in the light of their own experience. Unsurprisingly – given its recent dominant position and the military adventures of Spain at the end of the sixteenth century – many ideas came from the Iberian peninsula, or from soldiers who had fought in the service of the Hapsburgs. Different versions of Don Bernadino de Mendonca's *Theorica y Practica de Guerra*, originally published in Madrid in 1595, appear to have been especially influential in highlighting the importance of battlefield artillery. As he explained,

> Amongst other things (in my opinion) you are to consider, that the fury of gunpowder is such, with the artillery, muskets and arcabuses, that it not only breaks, as slings did the phalangs and legions, before they came to handy blowes, but it tears, breaks and opens the squadrons and battalions, and destroys them; and so the most part of the victoryes which have been gayned in these times, hath beene with artillery, or dispatch of the arcabusiers by their ready force disordering the squadrons of the enemy, soe that they putt them to rout, and ruine them, and you seldome see squadrons or bodyes of pykes to come to the push.[1]

Whilst Mendoca lumps together the effects of great guns and small arms in this passage his observation that gunpowder weapons were tending to reduce the numbers of hand to hand melees between opposing armies is an important one. Moreover, from the remarks which follow, it is obvious that he saw artillery proper, as opposed to firearms in general, as an important contributor to success in battle.

> For this reason, it is a matter much disputed, in what place the artillery is to bee in a day of battayle: some being of the opinion that it should march

---

[1] BL Harleian Ms 4138 (an English translation of Mendonca), 'The Theory and Practise of War', f 270.

before all the squadrons, for to offend the enemy afar off, by much shott, and to save the squadrons behind it from shott, who at closing are to open and pass by; the artillery being now noe futher usefull. Some are of the opinion, that it is a better place to devide the artillery in the voyd places betweene the squadrons, wherby they heed not when they goe to the shock, being a thing which begins disorder.

Either way guns were best deployed in such a position that they could be fired as soon as the enemy's squadrons were discovered. Even though it might happen that the artillery killed relatively few of the opposition its impact on morale was considerable, to the extent that it was seldom the case that cavalry could stand its ground if 'shott of great guns fall upon them'. In short artillery had the important battlefield effect of forcing units to attack prematurely, break up, or retire in the face of roundshot. This emphasis on the breaking of enemy formations was particularly significant: blocks of pikemen and musketeers were effective in resisting cavalry, or bringing useful fire to bear because they worked in unison. The cavalry charge was effective because a group of mounted men smashed home as a cohesive body. Breaking up the cohesion of the cavalry squadron or pike block was a first step to victory: taken far enough the enemy troops might become a mob. Pushed a little further still retirement or rout might be the result, and usually the majority of casualties in a battle would be caused when retreating troops could be struck from the rear or ridden down. Conversely the corollary of this vulnerability to disorder was that one's own troops should never be left standing in any position that left the enemy guns in a position to 'batter' them.[2]

In the years that followed 1600 the importance of gunpowder weapons on the battlefield increased steadily. Whilst 'shot' of all descriptions had usually formed a minority of an army's weapons in the late sixteenth century, a couple of decades into the seventeenth century firearms were as common as pikes and all other arms put together in Western European forces. Soon two firearms to every one pike would be a common proportion. Just as importantly there was a growing degree of standardisation amongst firearms, so that the infantry were now generally armed with muskets rather than a wide variety of gunpowder weapons. In England a standard size musket ball was decreed in 1630, and in 1640 the Ordnance Officers reported to the Privy Council that a barrel length of three and a half feet was most 'useful for field service'. Helmets for musketeers, though 'graceful for a parade', were declared inconvenient for general use. Uniformity was not achieved by 1642 however, and particularly in the provinces there would be many shortages.

There was also an increasingly noticeable tendency to field artillery which was sufficiently light to be moved to, and around the battlefield, rather than simply to attempt to drag siege guns – and all other types of ordnance – indis-

2   Ibid, ff 271–275. See also B.S. Hall *Weapons and Warfare in Renaissance Europe*, 1997, p 12.

criminately into action. So it is that we see that the large army raised to fight the Armada in 1588 was supposed to be accompanied by 28 pieces – and of these rather more than half were heavy guns of the size of demi culverins and above. The much smaller English army sent to France in 1627 had a train of artillery of at least the same number of guns, but the majority of them were light – heavier pieces having to be dismounted from the expedition's ships to make up satisfactory batteries to deal with enemy forts. Government stores of ordnance also seem to have reflected the change, holding increasing proportions of light artillery against the number of guns 'of battery'.[3]

By coincidence, or a continued use of the same old manuals of instruction, the train of artillery planned for war with Scotland in 1640 also featured 28 pieces of ordnance, being four mortars, four culverins and no less than 20 'drakes' of 3 pounds and 6 pounds. Orders were also prepared for the casting of more 3 pound guns, the King's Council of War concluding that, 'the more there be of this kind, the better'. Little wonder since the Scottish army that they were fighting was thought to have not only '12 great field pieces' but '40 drakes of Alexander Hamilton's invention which dischargeth 5 severall shott with one firing'. An additional advantage of small guns on the battlefield was that they could be loaded and discharged more quickly than heavy pieces. Light artillery might therefore be fired many more times during battle, and was not necessarily out of the action the first time friendly infantry marched past, obscuring observation.[4]

By 1639 the tactical role of the artillery had been further refined – along lines which Mendonca might well have approved. John Cruso's translation of Praissac's *Art of Warre* was a particularly significant addition to the tactical literature, not least because it was inspired by Phillip Skippon, a soldier of experience in the Low Countries and Germany, soon to play an important role in Parliament's army. As *Art of Warre* observed,

> the artillerie ought to be so placed that it hinder not the passage of the battalions, and that it may easily discover those of the enemie. For the most part the infanterie is within the body of the armie, in severall Battalions, disposed chequer wise: the cavallrie on their wings and reare in severall squadrons, and the Artillerie according to the convenience of the place, on the Front of the Armie, or on the Flanks of the Battallions.

[3] O.F.G. Hogg 'England's War Effort Against the Spanish Armada', in *Journal of the Society of Army Historical Research*,vol 44, number 177, March 1966, citing the Foljambe Ms; PRO SP 16/65, ff 35, 37; 16/66 ff 2, 6, 64; BL Add. Ms 26,051. On gradually increasing amounts of light artillery c. 1580–1600 see S.A. Walton 'The Art of Gunnery in Renaissance England', unpublished PhD thesis, Toronto, 1999, pp 258–260.

[4] *CSPD* CCCCXLI, 9 and 14 January 1640, pp 315, 334–335; CCCCXLII, 15 and 25 January 1640, pp 337, 375; CCCCXLIV, 3 February 1640, p 419; CCCCXLVI, 29 February 1640, p 499.

This plan would become almost the standard set piece template for an army fighting a major battle during the Civil Wars, infantry forming the main body in the centre, cavalry to the flanks, artillery to the front – unless a more convenient position for the guns could be found. With minor variations such deployment was employed at Edgehill, Marston Moor, and Naseby – as well as a number of lesser engagements. In all instances capturing the enemy's guns was regarded as a special mark of success. The artillery was to open fire as soon as formed bodies of the enemy were in range, 'making the batterie fitly and speedily, to disorder and scatter them [the enemy] before they come to give battle'. The obvious corollary was that standing under bombardment was acknowledged as a cardinal error, for

> As soon as you are within reach of the canon, you must go directly upon the enemie (unless you be sheltered from his Artillerie) by this means your soldiers are encouraged, you avoid the danger of the enemies canon, and you leave behind the place where your armie stood ranged.

Another antidote to decimation by gunfire was imaginative use of terrain. Hills were certainly used to mask artillery fire before the Civil Wars, though this is not mentioned with great frequency in the theoretical literature. One instance where this tactic is explicitly stated to have occurred is in the memoir of an English gunner facing the Irish rebellion. To his chagrin the rebels moved behind the brow of a hill, and in so doing, placed themselves 'in a naturall fort, that we had no other marke, but halfe head the colour and pike' – the guns were thus only able to be trained on the tops of the pike heads and colours. The English gun crew had to be satisfied with attempting to shatter the enemy's pikes.

One other – and potentially high risk – option in the face of artillery fire was to adapt the formation of the troops to their predicament. Some drill books noted that 'open orders' and 'double distances' were more viable under fire because the chances of any one individual being hit were reduced. Rupert is reported to have used just such a stratagem at Turnham Green, where the 'cunning' Prince 'opening, his rancks wide, the artillery did not so much execution upon them as was desired'. On the other side the Earl of Stamford adopted similar measures against the King's artillery in action as early as December 1642. The danger with such apparently elegant dispositions was that even thinly spread troops suffered some casualties – and diffused into open order or skirmish lines they were now vulnerable to infantry and cavalry. Nevertheless the period from 1600 to 1700 did see an increasing use of linear formations, and it may be argued coherently that the intention was not just to maximise the firepower of the formation, but to decrease the effect of incoming projectiles. Perhaps the most sensible thing that infantry caught in the open under artillery fire could do was lie down – and at least occasionally this is what they actually did. This was not an option readily available to cavalry; John Vernon's only advice was not to ride a white horse, so as not to make an easy mark for 'gunners and musketiers', and to get one's steed accustomed to the sound of guns.[5]

It was also possible for the infantry to fight fire with fire by having light field guns or drakes attached directly to their regiments. In the early days of the war the local armies of the south west and north had a few such guns sometimes without having separate 'trains' of artillery, and some of the lords who rallied to the King in 1642 brought field guns as well as men. In 1644 the London newsheet *Orders to be Observed* noted that it was intended that the Colonels of Parliamentarian foot regiments were to have their own drakes. Though this never appears to have become universal some were fielded in this way, and on the march it was found desirable to spread out light field guns amongst the columns, presumably allowing them to provide support wherever needed whilst being protected by the infantry around them. In later periods 'battalion guns' would become a feature of several European armies. How significant light battlefield guns became during the Civil Wars was underlined by Royalist soldier and theoretician William Throckmorton. Writing in 1649 he concluded that a full three quarters of a marching army's artillery should be guns not exceeding 'from 3 to 6 pound bullit ... denominated by the name of field pieces'. Given good guns well handled quality might prevail against quantity – as Sir Roger Dallington had put it in a witty maxim some years earlier, victory might well go hand in hand with 'great ordinance and good ordnance'.[6]

The guns were commonly drawn to the battlefield behind teams of horses. Larger guns might be dismounted from their field carriage and placed in four wheeled 'block' carriages, which spread the weight and were easier to manoeuvre over rutted tracks, and also spared wear and tear on the field carriage. However transferring a gun from one carriage to another often required a frame and pulley, and took significant time however well the task was performed. Smaller guns had the advantage of being moved in their field carriages, with the trail lifted off the ground by means of a small, wheeled, 'fore carriage'. A limber in all but name, this served to make the field gun of the mid seventeenth century almost as manageable as the field artillery of later eras. Some guns were provided with a 'chest' or box which rested on the trail of the gun during transport. This was handy to stow some of the gunnery equipment, and an immediate supply of cartridges and ball. The chest, moved with the gun itself,

---

5 BL E 137(15), *A True and Perfect Relation of the Chiefe Passages in Middlesex*, 16 November 1642, passim; BL E (83)10, *A True Relation of the Late Proceedings of Part of his Majesties Forces*, December 1642, p 5; BL E 89(17) *Speciall Passages*, 7–14 February 1643, pp 220–221; John Vernon *The Young Horseman*, 1644, pp 1, 10; BL E 145 (19) *A True and Perfect Diurnall ... by a Pointe Blanck Gunner*, 1643, p 5.

6 BL E 49(14), *Orders to be Observed*, May 1644, p 5; and BL E 49(21), *Newes of Prince Rupert*, May 1644, p 4; J. Cruso (trans) *The Art of Warre or Militarie Discourses By the Lord of Praissac*, Cambridge, 1639, pp 20–31; Sir Roger Dallington, *Aphorisms Civil and Militarie*, London, 1613, p 56.

ensured that it was unlikely that the piece would be separated from vital tools at the wrong moment, and that each gun had at least temporary independence from the general train of ammunition and spares wagons. Whilst there was little difference between the mobility of an early seventeenth century gun, and an early nineteenth century gun, once they were harnessed and moving, there were often lacunae in terms of draught and organisation – horses and wagons were usually hired or conscripted from civilian sources though they were usually directed by a military 'conductor'. The system of issuing 'warrants for carriages' to local Justices of the Peace would still be going strong in 1690 and change would only begin after the formation of the 'Royal Regiment' of artillery in 1716. Even then organisational separation between guns and regiments and their transport existed for a long time afterwards: certainly as late as 1914 the British Army would take with it to France some lorries still bearing a commercial civilian livery.[7]

In the Royalist instance the problems of draught were particularly acute. The Oxford army, acting on the authority of the King as vested in the Master of the Ordnance, Lord Percy, was empowered to impress horses, carts, and carters over a wide area of Gloucestershire, Warwickshire, Worcestershire and Oxfordshire. Some of the orders, delivered right down to parish level, survive – but Captain Henry Stevens 'Wagon Master General' often had an almost impossible task. Horses and their slower substitute, oxen, were quartered at Oxford and nearby Ifley, and at Kidlington during the winter. Yet with expenditure on the train running at two or three hundred pounds a week in late 1643 economies were inevitable. The oxen, being 'not so useful as horses', were sold off. Lack of means to move the King's guns soon became even more of a limiting factor than the number of pieces available. At the beginning of the 1644 campaign the train appears to have had only 260 horses on hand to pull its guns and wagons, and of 30 field guns on hand only a little over half were given teams and moved. The shortages were worse in early 1645, and though 20 pieces were fit for use just 14 set out on the road to Naseby. Of this very mixed train, which included two demi cannon and two mortars, 'not one carriage' would escape the King's defeat that June.

On the Parliament side there were similar problems, and the Earl of Stamford's artillery simply ground to a halt at one point in 1643 when, 'contrary to a general order, the carriages were dismissed as not able to serve longer' and no new supplies of horses came in. The Royalist propaganda organ *Mercurius Aulicus* attempted to dissuade civilian carters from working for Parliament by stating that those who turned up to drive the train would immediately be seized for use as front line soldiers. Nevertheless as they became more organised Parliament's resources proved more equal to the task. In April 1644 the Committee of Both Kingdoms determined that 800 'horses and mares' would be required for 'the train of artillery and carriage of victuals' gathering at St

---

7   M. Dalton *The Country Justice*, London, 1690, pp 47–48.

Albans. Each beast was alloted an 'average' price tag of £7, and Essex, Suffolk, Norfolk, Cambridge, Huntingdonshire and Hertfordshire were ordered to provide 500 of these between them. Middlesex, Buckinghamshire, Bedford-shire and Northamptonshire had a lighter burden with 150 to find, as did Kent, Sussex and Surrey whose quota was similarly 150 draught horses. Fortu-nately for Parliament East Anglia was not so badly devastated by the war as the King's Midland territories; even so £5,600 of quality horseflesh was a tall order to deliver in a short time frame. In March 1645 the New Model Army was voted the use of 1038 for its train under Lieutenant General Hammond, of which about 200 were devoted to pulling the guns.[8]

Contrary to popular belief there was no direct equivalent of 'horse artillery' in the Civil Wars, that is, field guns designed to be moved about the battle-field at the pace of the cavalry. No period illustration shows gunners being carried into battle aboard limbers or fore carriages, though some men did ride the draught horses. The few references to 'flying trains', 'marching trains', and even 'galloping' pieces have been found to relate to artillery which moved at the pace of the army in general, or as small independent trains which were detached to move to a specific location as rapidly as possible. The real distinc-tion in terms of speed of movement appears to be between groups of guns which were intended as battlefield assets, and thus included only the smaller types – and old fashioned 'trains of artillery' which also included siege guns and large mortars. In the event it was Parliament, later in the war, having access to a comprehensive range of modern gun types, that best succeeded in drawing the boundaries between trains of field guns, and general purpose trains. So it was that the New Model Army was sometimes able to take to the field with only 'field' guns, bringing up a slower 'battering' train, as and when required – such was certainly the method operated by Cromwell in south Wales in 1648. The King never seems to have achieved this same level of organisational luxury; nevertheless the Royalists still organised 'bye' trains or relief trains of artillery to deliver weapons and supplies to where they were needed most.

The part played by artillery varied from battle to battle, from none at all – to crucial. At the second battle of Newbury it was the Royalist artillery that formed the major obstacle. As the account of Sir A. Johnstone and John Crewe MP related:

> The King's forces were drawn up between Donnington and Newbury, near the castle, having no way to pass but by a wood and through lanes, we met with works and fortifications crossing those lanes, which the enemy had thrown up during the night and planted ordnance therein: they had also other ordnance, two bodies of horse, and two brigades of foot at a little distance. They played also from the castle upon our men with great shot. These [works] were very

8   M. Toynbee *The Papers of Captain Henry Stevens, Wagon Master General to King Charles I,* Oxford Record Society, 42, 1961, passim; R. Hutton *The Royalist War Effort,* London, 1982, pp 96–98; *Royalist Ordnance Papers,* pp 20–24, 55–57, 362–364.

hard to gain, yet it pleased God so to encourage the spirit, among whom the Lord General had a most special care, and so to bless their endeavour that about 5 o'clock, only half an hour of their falling to work, our men took it by storm and got four pieces of ordnance, afterwards beating the enemy off his ground, they got another five ordnance. The Lord General's foot took much contentment in regaining some of their ordnance. Our horse stood very gallantly under the view and danger of of the cannon playing directly upon them, when they were drawing themselves together to secure the foot, and by charging the enemy put them to a retreat, taking the Earl of Cleveland, who commanded that brigade. All the general officers performed very resolutely their parts, and the Earl of Manchester fell upon the other parts in seasonable time.

When eventually the Parliamentarian infantry overran the guns that so plagued them, they clapped their hats over the breeches of the cannon, to prevent them being fired upon their comrades – so stopping them suffering further 'terror and furie' of the ordnance. Long years later when the grave pits from the battle were reopened, curious bystanders noted the effects of ball, chain shot and case upon the victims.[9]

At Lansdown it was the Parliamentarian artillery under Waller that played a significant tactical role – first in influencing the Royalist retreat towards Marsh-field, and then in stoutly defending their hill top position. As Colonel Slingsby remembered, the enemy

> stood upon a ground almost inaccessible. In the brow of the hill, hee raised breastworkes in which his cannon and greate store of small shott was placed; on either flanke hee was strengthened with a thicke wood which stood upon the declining of the hill, in which hee put a store of musketieres; on his reare hee had a faire plaine where stood rang'd his reserves of horse and foote.

The Royalist troops attacked this formidable obstacle with the cry 'lett us fetch those cannon', but they suffered heavily toiling up the hill: according to Hopton just 600 of those that started out made it to the top. By evening the battle had deteriorated into a stand off, with the Parliamentarians pulled back to a range of about 'demi culverin shot', and 'within a stone wall'. Here they stood, and both sides 'played upon each other with their ordnance', but neither advanced being both soundly battered. It was only when the Parliament guns were drawn off during the night that the King's men knew that they had finally taken the field. According to one account the ordnance had fired 'plentifully' on both sides from three in the afternoon until eleven at night.[10]

---

[9]   *CSPD* DI, 13 April 1644, pp 114–115; BL E 100 (12) *A Most True Relation*, London, 1643, pp 2–3; BL E 16 (24) *Mercurius Aulicus*, 12–19 October 1644, p 1,203. *CSPD* DIII, 28 October, 1644, p 75; BL E 59(25), passim; W. Money *The First and Second Battles of Newbury*, 1884, p 161.

[10] Clarendon Ms, vol 23, number 1,738, and 'Hopton's Narrative' reprinted in C. Chadwick Healey (ed) *Somerset Record Society*, 18, 1902, pp 52–55, 94–96; BL E 59(25), *The Copie of*

The battle of Roundway Down, fought near Devizes in 1643, was effectively commenced by cannon signal. As Royalist Sir John Byron recorded, 'we shot off our ordnance from an high hill that overlooks the town, to let them know that we were there for their assistance; at the same time Waller appeared with his whole army upon an opposite hill within less than two miles of us'. This opening was acknowledged in like fashion by the Earl of Marlborough from 'the old castle where the trayne was'. As the King's troops advanced they came under effective fire from the Parliamentarian guns, playing at 'very near distance'. Though the Royalist army was extremely small, and composed mainly of cavalry, it nevertheless succeeded in defeating a larger force which comprised a balanced mixture of cavalry, infantry and artillery. Byron himself managed to capture two enemy guns and several ammunition wagons.[11]

At the crucial battle of Naseby in June 1645 the King's guns do not appear to have been able to show anything like their full potential, at least in part because Lord General Fairfax used the topography of the battlefield to hide the majority of his force from the fury of the ordnance. Much of the Royalist's effort in gathering a respectable array of 6 pound and larger guns was thus wasted. As Joshua Sprigge, chronicler of the New Model Army, related:

> ... seeing his [the King's] resolution to advance upon us, we took the best advantage we could of the ground, possessing the ledge of a hill, running east to west; upon which our army being drawn up, fronted towards the enemy. But considering it might be of advantage to us to draw up our army out of sight of the enemy; who marched upon a plain ground towards us: we retreated about an 100 paces from the ledge of the hill.

This modern sounding use of the slopes as cover is also represented in de Gomme's plan of the battlefield, though less apparent in the better known Streeter engraving.

Recent research certainly suggests that the Parliamentarians suffered but inconsequentially from the Royalist guns, since not only did they present little target but the King's foot obscured the fire of their comrades as they advanced. Parliament's own guns were in a better position to hit the Royalist formations as they came on, as finds of round shot would seem to confirm. A contemporary account suggests that just two of the New Model Army artillerists were badly wounded in the battle: matross Robert Guilbert who lost a hand, and a gunner named French who later died of his injuries. Despite Fairfaxes careful dispositions and advantage of numbers the battle proved extremely tough, with Prince Rupert breaking right through to the New Model Army baggage train and every unit in the Parliamentarian army taking some casualties. For the

a Letter sent from the Mayor of Bristol, 1643, p 2; and D. Underdown *Somerset in the Civil War and Interregnum*, Newton Abbott, 1973, pp 57–62.

11 *Sir John Byron's Relation*, York, 1643, passim; C.H. Chadwyck Healey (ed) Hopton's *Bellum Civile*, Somerset Record Society, 1902, pp 57, 98.

King the result was total disaster with barely a third of his 12,000 men, and none of his precious guns, escaping the battlefield.[12]

Given the difficult target artillery presented on the battlefield counter battery fire was problematic – but nevertheless it was attempted, sometimes successfully. At Langport in July 1645, for example, two Royalist guns were silenced by an overwhelming volume of fire. In what Sprigge described as the 'brave fight' the artillery of the New Model Army played its part in text book fashion. Once the troops had been deployed and the guns 'drawne downe to places of advantage', they

> began to play (a good while before the foot engaged) doing great execution upon the body of the enemies army, both horse and foot, who stood in good order upon the hill (about musquet shot from the passe) and forcing them to draw off their Ordnance, and their horse remove from the ground; Our foot advanced down the hill to the pass, and with admirable resolution charged the enemy from hedge to hedge.

It is difficult to avoid the conclusion that in this instance the guns did exactly what was demanded of them, shaking enemy formations and causing premature retirements – which were soon exploited by the Parliamentarian infantry. The Royalist guns had been comprehensively out shot.[13]

As we have noted, during the Civil War trains of field guns were commonly equipped with about 40 to 50 rounds of ammunition per gun, perhaps a little more on average for the Parliamentarians – a little less for the Royalists. Though the Royalist Ordnance Commissioners appear to have worked wonders with very little there were occasions when lack of munitions obviously did have a direct impact on the King's guns in battle. At the First Newbury in September 1643 the artillery fell silent very quickly, with Lord Digby complaining of lack of powder. In fact fresh supplies had been ordered that very day, with Secretary Nicholas demanding that the stores be sent 'away this night' – but they would arrive too late. Moreover this replenishment of the magazine stipulated only 20 round shot per gun, and would never have been enough for prolonged or repeated actions.[14]

Big set piece battles were relatively rare, and few battlefields were ideal isotropic planes; so there were many instances where guns were more imaginatively employed than is generally supposed. Occasionally it was possible to use small field guns as part of an ambush – or to conceal them amongst the ranks of other troops, only to reveal them once the enemy was close. Surprise could

---

[12] de Gomme in BL Add. Ms 16370; J. Sprigge *Anglia Rediviva*, London, 1647, pp 30–46; G. Foard *Naseby*, Whitstable, 1995, pp 219–300, 408–413.

[13] Sprigge *Anglia Rediviva*, pp 64–66; D. Underdown *Somerset in the Civil War and Interregnum*, Newton Abbot, 1973, p 103; *English Heritage Battlefield Report: Langport*, 1995, and since web published.

[14] *Royalist Ordnance Papers*, pp 55–56.

indeed be devastating to morale. In one incident in Cheshire it is recorded that Sir William Brereton's gunners opened fire on his Royalist enemies with drakes 'which wrought more terror than execution' in the rough terrain, but this was enough. The 'enemy cry'd, let us flie, for they have Great Ordnance'. In 1643 at Braddock Down in Cornwall the Royalist commander Hopton had only two small iron 'minion drakes', but used them to great advantage. At first he screened them from the enemy with 'little parties of horse' – unmasking them and letting fly at the vital moment before the far superior Parliamentarian ordnance could be deployed. Following a general advance of his entire force he caught the enemy completely off balance, capturing not only more than a thousand of the enemy and many of their colours, but all their ordnance which included two 12 pound guns, and a variety of smaller pieces.[15]

A back handed testament to the value of the artillery in battle was the way in which it became a magnet for attack. At Edgehill, Newbury, Lansdown and Cropredy both full scale charges and short rushes by infantry and cavalry were organised to nullify the threat presented by guns. Such counter tactics could prove costly, but there were quite a few commanders willing to sacrifice the troops required to put enemy ordnance out of action. At the battle of Cropredy Bridge, fought on 29 June 1644, field artillery was a significant component of both armies. The King's army was reported as having 12 light pieces with its 7,000 men, though it had left behind its heavy guns. Waller's Parliamentarian army comprised about 9,500 foot with at least 24 'pieces of ordnance great and small', including the famed 'leather guns' under Colonel James Weymss. When Waller crossed the Cherwell to take advantage of the strung out posture of the Royalist army, most of the guns were pushed across in the vanguard. Some of these were the agile leather guns, 'charged with case shot'. Opportunity however turned to disaster as the Royalists proved able to close up rapidly, effectively clamping the head of Waller's army in a trap. As Thomas Ellis reported the Parliament guns had 'unadvisedly' been drawn over the bridge 'before the foot were ready to march with them', and the King's army succeeded in capturing most of them, though the Tower Hamlets regiments managed to wrest three back. The loss of the guns was counted an 'extreme wounding' to Waller – as was the capture of Wemyss, whom it was later proposed to exchange for the Lancashire Royalist Colonel Sir Thomas Tyldesly. The popular Royalist press in the shape of *Mercurius Aulicus* would claim that the Parliament gunners at Cropredy had actually trained their pieces on the King himself, using 'perspective' glasses to improve their aim – but that they had been taught a just lesson about the perils of rebellion against their legitimate monarch. Richard Symonds had it that the enemy guns were poorly

---

[15] BL E(94)6, *Cheshire's Success*, March 1643, passim; *English Heritage Battlefield Report: Braddock Down*, 1995, and since web published; Chadwyck Healey (ed), *Hopton's Narrative*, p 30.

handled, and that Weymss had proved an ingrate – seeing that he had been much advanced in his fortunes by the King.[16]

Adwalton Moor near Bradford proved excellent artillery country, being an essentially open area pocked with flooded coal pits. The lack of trees and other cover allowed guns good targets, whilst the pits prevented the ready deployment of other arms. As the Parliamentarians under Fairfax quit the relative safety of enclosures at the edge of the moor they came first under artillery fire, which 'disordered them' and then cavalry and infantry attack. As the Royalist *Express Relation* explained,

> They lined several places with musketiers, and played so fiercely upon us … that we were forced to give ground. But when our cannon was well placed, and our foot once drawn up, within half an hour we put their foot on the right wing of battle to retire, and pursued them so hotly, that they were presently put into a disorderly retreat. Whereupon part of our horse fell upon that wing and the cannon playing upon the body of their horse killed many and routed them, together with our horse charging at that time, so we pursued them, killing and taking them to Bradford town end, which was more than two miles.[17]

At Hopton Heath artillery also played a significant role in the fight, and the Royalists succeeded in bringing a siege gun into action on the battlefield. It was said that its first round, hitting a dense enemy formation, killed or injured ten men. Another shot ploughed such a lane through the Parliamentarians that they were reluctant to close up their ranks. Thereafter charge and counter charge led to some of the ordnance changing hands anything up to three times during the course of the battle. Eventually the Royalists routed their enemies from the field, capturing their guns. Confirmation of the use of a 29 pound demi cannon at Hopton Heath was unearthed in 1940 when an ball of this weight was discovered during the construction of an airfield. At the debacle of Nantwich it was the Parliamentarian forces which managed to trap their enemy in an enclosed area around Acton Church, and in a spirited pincer movement captured all the Royalist artillery and baggage after 'two hours of hot fighting'. For Lord Byron this loss was catastrophic. As he recorded, 'I stayed above two houre after all the business of the foot was done, to try if anything could be done for the recovery of the cannon and carriages; but it was all in vain; so that I was forced to retreat to Chester, with what foot I could gather.'[18]

16 *An Exact and Full Relation of the Last Fight, Between the King's Forces and Sir William Waller*, London, 1644, passim; M. Toynbee and P. Young *Cropredy Bridge*, Kineton, 1970, pp 84–97, 118–133; R. Coe *An Exact Diary or a Briefe Relation of the Progresse of Sir William Waller's Army*, London, 1644, passim.

17 C.H. Firth (ed) *The Life of William Cavendish, Duke of Newcastle*, 2nd edn., London, 1907, pp 215–216.

18 *English Heritage Battlefield Report: Hopton Heath*, 1995, and since web published; BL E 94 (15); Byron's account printed in T. Carte *A Collection of Original Letters and Papers*, London, 1739, pp 36–40.

Whether gunners should stand and protect the ordnance in the teeth of infantry or cavalry attack – which was sometimes pressed home upon the guns irrespective of the casualties that might be inflicted upon it – was a moot point. Often it appears that, when charged, gun crews ran away to the protection of formed bodies of their own troops. In such circumstances the enemy might succeed in hauling off the guns, or disabling them, but this was by no means a foregone conclusion. On other occasions gunners certainly stood and fought. At Cropredy, where the Parliamentarian gun teams were set upon by cavalry, and had no obvious line of retreat, some at least put up stout resistance. Cornet Brooke of Sir William Boteler's horse waded into the fight with the staff of his cornet, or flag, reportedly killing a 'rebell cannoneer as he was giving fire to his peece of ordnance', but was 'sore hurt' for his pains. In return it is said that most of the artillery crews 'were slain', though it is likely that quite a few were captured.

Certainly many gunners, and their attendant infantry guards, were armed for the close defence of the guns. Using firearms, particularly those with smouldering matches in their locks, around the powder of the artillery was risky in the extreme. For this reason many armies included 'firelock' guards for their artillery trains – troops armed with weapons with striking flints rather than trailing matches. Gunners and matrosses also carried personal arms. Swords were probably common, but we do know that Royalist gunners were often armed with other edged weapons. A Royalist 'list of provisions' dated 28 May 1643 shows hatchets, 'long poleaxes', and brown bills, being carried in the spares carts which also carried ropes and ancillary equipment for the guns. In August of the same year three gunners who accompanied a small train of guns en route to Basing were issued with poleaxes. In the case of a 'bye' train prepared in March 1644 ten poleaxes were issued to the matrosses. A few hatchets were issued to the batteries defending Oxford at about the same time. Halberds saw fairly widespread use, with 108 being captured by the Royalists from the garrison of Dartmouth for example. Perhaps the most vicious arm used by any artillerist was the 'gunner's stiletto' – a nail like dagger with gun data engraved, by way of an *aide memoire*, onto its blade. As far as can be determined these were not issued, but a private purchase, and surviving examples are predominantly of Italian manufacture. In extremis the tools of the gunner's trade were sometimes brought into action. The wadhook, rammer, and handspike were undoubtedly intimidating, but at Teignmouth Castle it was reported that both pikes and 'gunner's ladles' were used to fend off the scaling ladders of the attackers.[19]

---

[19] PRO WO 55/459, ff 73–75, 186–192, 410–415; Rawlinson Ms. D 395, f 219. Royal Armouries collection, items X. 32, 249 and 250; BL E 458 (26), *Sir Arthur Hasilrige's Letter*, 15 August 1648, p 6.

EXAMPLES OF BATTLE: EDGEHILL

The popular picture of the artillery at Edgehill, the first major battle of the Civil Wars, fought on 23 October 1642, is of something ancillary to the main action – if not actually inconsequential. Moreover, whilst the Royalist artillerists are usually portrayed as having done better than expected, the Parliamentarian ordnance is thought of as slow and bungling. That this caricature has little basis in fact is clear from the way that the competing trains of ordnance were gathered and composed. As we have seen, the 20 Royalist pieces were roughly balanced by 23 Parliamentarian – though the King's guns were actually an ill matched hotch potch of various types, whilst 11 of the Parliament's pieces were modern 3 pound field guns. These accompanied armies of roughly equal strengths, perhaps 15,000 Parliamentarians, and 14,000 Royalists.[20]

Essex's army advanced first to Worcester, leaving in his wake a number of Midland garrisons. The Royalist Council of War decided on a swift advance from the north on London: as Clarendon later explained, it was sure the enemy would try and intercept them, and this would lead to a swift and hopefully victorious end to the matter. The King had no desire for a long campaign, especially since the longer battle was deferred, 'the stronger the Earl would grow by the supplies which were every day sent to him from London'. The order in which the Royalists deployed their artillery and train upon the march is known: pioneers and horse harness first, guns and cartridges next, followed by officers' wagons. A little behind came the spare powder, match and shot for the infantry and cavalry. The pace was measured, allowing the train and the rest of the army to maintain contact, for the overall speed of the King's movement made little odds: either the army would reach London, or Essex would have to give battle. The onus was squarely upon Essex to try to get between the enemy and their target, the capital.[21]

On the night of 22 October the Parliamentarian army was encamped in and around Kineton, but some detachments, including the train, were still many miles off. The King was now at Edgecote, but again it was only aggressive patrolling by Prince Rupert, the 22 year old General of Horse, that discovered that the main bodies of the two forces were only ten miles apart. The Roundheads' ignorance was if anything the greater, and the so called 'official' report makes interesting reading:

---

[20]   PRO WO 55/457; WO 55/387; see chapter three above; also S. Bull 'Artillery at Edgehill Re-Assessed', in *Journal of the Ordnance Society*, 4, 1992, pp 1–8; and P. Young, 'The Royalist Artillery at Edgehill', in *Journal of the Society of Army Historical Research*, 31, 1953, pp 127–131.

[21]   *An Exact and True Relation of the Dangerous and Bloody Fight*, 28 October 1642, passim; see also E.A. Walford, *Edgehill the Battle and the Battlefield*, Banbury 1886, p 11.

we marched from Worcester, Wednesday the 19th, upon intelligence that their army was removed from Shrewsbury and Bridgenorth and bending southward, our train of artillery was so unready by want of draught horses and through other omissions of Monsieur du Boyes, that we were forced to leave it behind to follow us, and with it the Regiments of Colonel Hambden and Colonel Grantham; and staying for it, we could advance no further than a little market town called Keynton in Warwickshire, 6 miles from Warwick; whither we came the Saturday night with 11 Regiments of Foot, 42 troops of Horse and about 700 dragoons, in all about 10,000 men; there we intended to rest the Sabbath day, and the rather, that our Artillery and forces left with it, might come up on us. In the morning when we were going to Church, we had news brought us that the enemy was 2 miles from us, upon a high hill, called Edge-hill; whereupon we presently marched forth.

We have to be careful about this evidence, for though it is the document promulgated by order of Parliament it was not composed by the Earl of Essex himself, but by a coterie of officers: Sir William Balfour, John Meldrum, Thomas Ballard, Denzil Holles, Sir Philip Stapleton and Charles Pym. Nevertheless the statement is worth examining in detail, for upon its veracity rests the main case for du Boyes ineptitude, later picked up by Godfrey Davies and Peter Young.[22]

Critically the 'official' account is just as important for what it leaves out as what is put in. The King had left Shrewsbury on 12 October. Essex took a week to determine this, and to react. The account blames du Boyes and the artillery for failure to keep up, but also says the army stopped to let it catch up – then action was joined with part of it absent. Maybe du Boyes had not managed the train well, and shortage of draught was a common problem, but if Essex was determined to confront the enemy, uphill, with only a portion of his forces, he had only himself to blame. Tellingly Essex left no account of his actions. Edgehill was a long way from London, and the King would be forced to take the initiative if he wanted to seize the capital. For senior Parliamentarian officers acting as apologists for the Earl of Essex du Boyes was the ideal scapegoat. Du Boyes was not an MP, mercenaries were never particularly popular, and as a Frenchman he was an easy target. No statement by du Boyes on the battle has yet come to light.

Whatever the case, by about half past eleven o' clock on the morning of 23 October the King's horse and foot had drawn up atop Edgehill, but the artillery was last to move into position. All was ready by about two in the afternoon, with the heavy guns deployed behind the Royalist right, guarded by 'firelocks' – soldiers armed with dog lock or English lock muskets, which had no smouldering match to endanger the powder. The lighter guns were grouped in twos and threes all along the front. Given the slope of the hill and the commanding position of the heavier ordnance the Royalists were in a position

---

[22] *An Account of the Battel*, reprinted in Young, 'Royalist Artillery at Edgehill', pp 306–307.

to fire at leisure upon their still under strength opponents on the plain below, or to resist attack from a position of strength.

Almost immediately however tactical advantage was thrown away. The whole army was ordered to advance down slope and reform their battle lines at the bottom. Not only did this mean that the enemy would no longer have to toil up the hill, but it also meant that the King's numbers and exact dispositions were obvious. It also entailed moving the guns, which had only reached their first positions with some effort. Perhaps worst of all, the Royalist commanders began to argue amongst themselves about the plan of battle. The Lord General, Robert Bertie, Earl of Lindsey, favoured a simple deep formation in an older 'Dutch' style; Patrick Ruthven Earl of Forth, supported by Prince Rupert, favoured drawing out the brigades into four smaller units each with a block of pikemen and four smaller units of muskets. According to the young Duke of York it was Ruthven who received the final order to deploy from the King, and Lindsey who, 'much displeased', flounced off to command his own regiment.[23]

This might have been the ideal cue for the Earl of Essex to attack a disordered enemy, but nothing happened, and soon afterwards the artillery on both sides began to fire. It is commonly accepted that Parliament's guns opened first, and if so it is likely to have been because the Royal ordnance took some time to descend the hill and redeploy. Ludlow states that the bombardment lasted an hour, others that it might not have been so long. Lord Bernard Stuart, commander of the King's Lifeguard, states that 'we gave fire with our cannon, then charged them with both wings of our horse ... upon our approach they gave fire with their cannon lined amongst their horse, dragoneers, carbines and pistols'. The Duke of York similarly suggests that the enemy opened fire as the King's troops advanced. An anonymous Royalist account actually suggests that the King's artillery was still a little way up slope, and that its fire was less effective than that of the enemy. 'The King had so great an advantage of the hill that it turned to his disadvantage, for being so much upon the descent his cannon either shot over, or if short it would not graze [bounce or skid] by reason of the ploughed land whereas their cannon did some hurt having a mark they could not miss.' Amongst the Royalist casualties were Lieutenant Francis Bowles of Fielding's regiment and Sir Richard Bulstrode on the right of the cavalry – a quartermaster in the Duke of York's troop.

The deaths and injuries occasioned to common soldiers were not so well recorded, but given the deaths of two officers, it would be surprising if the total killed and wounded were not several dozen. Similarly, even if we assume that only 15 Parliamentarian guns were able to fire for half an hour, it is unlikely that they would have shot off less than 150 rounds. Almost certainly the Royalist gunners fired fewer – for the six heavy pieces would have had

[23] T.S. Clarke (ed) *The Life of James II*, London, 1816, pp 9–18; *A Relation of the Battel Fought Between Keynton and Edgehill, Printed by his Majesty's Command at Oxford*, 1642, passim.

to shoot as an when they could, over their own army, and the lighter guns, dragged down the hill and redeployed would soon have been overtaken and obscured by their own infantry passing through them to attack. Whatever the real or imagined advantages achieved by Sir John Heydon's organisation, they were quickly thrown away. It may even have been the case that the decision to attack was actually prompted by enemy artillery fire, for to have left the King's army under effective bombardment would have done little for morale. In any case Rupert's horse soon managed to overrun some of the enemy artillery.[24]

The opening fire was not however the only part played by the artillery at Edgehill. Once the Royalist cavalry had routed Parliament's horse on the flanks and disappeared in the direction of Kineton, the two remaining Parliamentarian mounted units came into play. Sir Philip Stapleton and Sir William Balfour's regiments picked their way through openings in Meldrum's line of foot and charged the King's infantry. Breaking through Balfour now attacked the heavy guns behind the Royalist lines. According the Parliamentarian official account, Balfour broke

> … a regiment of foot which had green colours, beat them to their cannon, where they threw down their arms and ran away, he laid his hand upon the cannon and called for nails to nail them up [block the touch holes], especially the two biggest, which were demi cannon, but finding none, he cut the ropes belonging to them, and his troopers killed the cannoneers, then he pursued the fliers half a mile upon execution.

Royalist returns after the battle show that 16 rounds of heavy case shot were expended, so Balfour may not have had everything his own way. His failure to put the heavy guns out of action completely may also have meant that they were able to be brought back into use towards the end of the battle.[25]

On returning to their own lines Stapleton's regiment discovered that some of their own artillery was no longer manned or protected. The cause of this is unknown, though Young suggests that the gunners had simply run away. Whatever the reason Stapleton's men loaded and fired one of the guns with case shot in the direction of approaching cavalry. Luckily only one man was wounded, for it transpired that the other horse were Balfour's, returning from their successful engagement with the Royalist artillery. By the time the armies had fought to a standstill that evening the Parliamentarians had been reinforced by Colonel Hampden with two regiments of horse and one of foot, and the remainder of the train. The Parliamentarians withdrew toward Kineton, and the King's forces retired back up Edgehill, eventually taking with them seven of the enemy guns. How all these guns were captured is not entirely clear, but Sir Robert Walsh claimed two during a cavalry charge, and Sir John Smith

[24] BL, Harleian Ms 3783, ff 60 – 61, reprinted in G. Davies 'The Battle of Edgehill', in *English Historical Review*, 36, 1921, pp 30–40.
[25] *Exact and True Relation*, p 18.

recovered three from the field of battle the next day. As Smith removed his booty the enemy did not intervene, but the Royalists looked on with 'wonder and applause'. The Duke of York had it that in fact six pieces of the enemy ordnance and 'some' Royalist guns had to be left in the middle of field overnight. The pieces captured turned out to be two 12 pound, one six pound, and four three pound guns – valuable resources at a time when it was unclear how the King could procure more. On the field also lay about 1,500 dead – it was claimed that the largest number of these were Parliamentarians, but the disparity in losses is unlikely to have been great.[26]

So ended, inconclusively, one of the most important battles fought on British soil. On 25 October Essex withdrew towards Warwick. Artillery had played a significant part in the campaign, and, but for circumstances and the relatively unsophisticated tactics, its role might have been greater. Clearly, however, the artillery trains of Heydon and du Boyes were much more evenly matched than has hitherto been believed.

MARSTON MOOR

Having read modern accounts of the largest battle of the English Civil Wars, fought at Marston Moor on 2 July 1644, one could be forgiven for assuming that either no artillery was present – or that it had no impact on the action. Peter Newman's account deals with the ordnance in a single page, that of Peter Young contains a few scattered references. In fact Marston Moor was very probably the battle of the period where the most guns were deployed. The Royalist armies used at least 23 guns and two mortars – the largest train of artillery they had fielded for some time. Parliamentarian intelligence sources believed the enemy had many more: estimates before the Committee of Both Kingdoms in June 1644 suggested that Prince Rupert's forces had 58 guns with them. No exact documentary evidence has yet been presented for the strength of the artillery of the Allied armies, and it is probably this lack of a cut and dried figure which has led its role to be so casually dismissed. Yet this has not always been so. Mentent, in his eighteenth century history of the Civil Wars, was happy to accept that the guns at Marston Moor cannonaded all day.[27]

As the Allied army at Marston Moor were an amalgam of three forces – the Scots, the Earl of Manchester's and Lord Fairfax's – a precise statement of the numbers of guns on the side of Parliament is no easy matter. Even

26 PRO WO 457, f 62 'The Remaining State of his Majesty's Magazine'; also accounts reprinted in Young 'Royalist Artillery at Edgehill', pp 263, 270, 274, 282, 294, 299.

27 P. Young *Marston Moor*, Kineton, 1970, passim and P.R.Newman *Marston Moor*, Chichester, 1981, passim; R. Mentet *History of the Troubles of Great Britain*, London, 1735, p 165. Royalist strengths have been gathered primarily from accounts of pieces captured in BL E 2(14), Scoutmaster L. Watson *A More Exact Relation*, July 1644, pp 5–7; BL E 54 (20), *The Parliament Scout*, 4–11 July 1644, p 439; BL E 54(24), *The Weekly Account*, 4–11 July 1644, and *Mercurius Civicus*, 4–11 July 1644, p 570.

General Leven may not have been absolutely certain how many guns were at his disposal, either at the siege of York where his gunners had bounced 'Devillish Cannon Shot' around the Minster, or on the road to Tadcaster, whence Rupert's relieving force had suddenly sent them. Nevertheless it is perfectly possible to come to a viable and robust estimate. It is known that Alexander Leslie's Army of the Solemn League and Covenant began the campaign with 69 major pieces of ordnance and 88 light pieces, and even Young admits that 30 of the heavier pieces were present on the day of battle. Given that light pieces were far easier to transport it is hardly conceivable that less than 100 guns were available to the Scots, who fielded their own artillery general, Alexander Hamilton. According to John Spalding, writing in his *Memorials of the Trouble* the 'ordinary' Scottish field pieces used by the Covenanters were about 'three foot long' – firing what he inexactly described as 'an indifferent great ball'.

The Earl of Manchester was not as well equipped with guns as the Scots, but was at least moderately well provisioned. Before the city of York he was supplied with 18 pound shot, and enough powder that he had 100 barrels to pass on to his Scottish allies. At Lincoln, not long before Marston Moor, his army had enough guns and mortars to support a storm – and he had taken a further eight pieces from the garrison. The 'greatest ordnance' had to be left behind in the march north, though Wenham has assumed that during the siege of York the Eastern Association was supplied by sea from King's Lynn. Given an army of about 4,000 infantry and 4,000 cavalry Manchester would have been unlucky indeed not to be able to call upon half a dozen guns at least. He certainly had ordnance when he appeared before Sheffield House in August 1644. Much the same is true of Lord Fairfax with his army of 2,000 horse and 3,000 foot. To say that the Allied forces at Marston Moor had 110 guns under command at Marston Moor is therefore an extremely conservative estimate.[28]

A walk along the ridge line between Long Marston and a point directly to the south of Tockwith and comparison with modern maps confirms that the Allied front was something about two miles in length. Had the guns here been equally spaced there would have been one every thirty yards. Grouping them into small batteries of twos and threes would have allowed barely enough space for the units of infantry and cavalry to pass between them. With 25,000 troops deployed in two major lines the sheer firepower of the Allied force is readily apparent. As Newman observed the ridge line on which the Allied troops deployed was actually two ridges with a slight crease, known as 'the Glen', running along part of its length. A figure standing in this cleft, or behind the second ridge, was either partially, or entirely obscured from the plain below – as may still be confirmed by looking south from the area of the battle monu-

---

[28] T. Mace *Musick's Moments*, reprinted in P. Wenham *The Great and Close Siege of York*, Kineton, 1970, p 68; PRO WO 47/1 f 36; BL E 47(2), *A True Relation of the Taking of the City, Minster and Castle of Lincolne*, May 1644, pp 2–5; and BL E 47(3), *Perfect Occurences*, May 1644, sig A3.

ment. From here the feature known as 'Cromwell's Plump' appears perched on the skyline. This would be of great significance.

Major General Sir James Lumsden was riding away from the ridge, and had almost reached Tadcaster when the disturbing news arrived that Prince Rupert had sallied out from York,

> The alarme was sent us by our horss that Prince Rupert was with his wholl armie advancing which mad us presently march back to the bounds we had left, where we found him drawing up in one plain field 3 myles in length and in breidth. The fairest ground for such use we had seen in England. We finding him so their and no possibilitie to have our foot up in two hours, keepedt the advantage of ane Sleeke and the hills with our horss till the foot as they came up were put in order. In the meantime we advanced our canon and entred to play them on the left wing, which maid them a littel to move; which they persaving brocht up theirs and gave us the lyk. This continued not long when it was resolved we should advance down the hill throch ane great feild of corne.[29]

Royalist accounts agree both about the hill, and the artillery. Ogden reports that, 'The Prince discovered the enemy planted on a hill not above 3 or 4 miles from Yorke, where they had advantage of the ground, the winde, and a high corne field in which they had planted their ordnance.' Arthur Trevor similarly noted that Rupert's force was drawn up 'within play of the enemies cannon'. Sir Bernard de Gomme's plan, stylistic as it may be, depicted the initial deployment of the Scots and Parliamentarians behind a line of hills. This was critical since on the one hand the Allied generals and their gunners could see the Royalists army forming up on the plain below, and possibly even Newcastle's straggling force emerging to join the main army from the direction of York – but conversely it was impossible for Rupert to determine the strength of his opponents and any difficulties they had marshalling their forces. According to Captain William Stewart's account an opportunistic attempt was made early in the day to get a foothold in Bilton Bream:

> The enemy perceiving that our cavalry had possessed themselves of a cornhill, and having discovered neer unto that hill a place of great advantage, where they might have both sun and winde of us, advanced theither with a Regiment of Red Coats, and a party of horse; but we understanding well their intentions, and how prejudiciall it would be unto us, if they should keep that ground, we sent out a party that beat them off.

Some of the Royalist command was clearly uneasy about the disadvantageous position in which they now found themselves. Major General James King pointed out the situation and Rupert intended to draw back the army a little further out of harm's way, but it was already too late. Putting the forward

---

29 Lumsden's letter reprinted in Young *Marston Moor*, p 267.

elements into reverse, whilst more and more men were filing up from the rear, would have been an invitation to chaos. Lord Newcastle arrived at about this time, probably around two o'clock, and understanding that nothing was now going to happen that day retired to his coach.[30]

With the Royalists still gathering and no longer seeking a swift encounter the bombardment began. It has usually been accepted, on the authority of Sir Henry Slingsby, that this was but brief and ineffectual – but how Slingsby could have known what damage was inflicted is impossible to determine. He arrived with Newcastle at the rear of the army well after Rupert's main force, and was nowhere near the units affected. Other evidence suggests a far more ferocious battery with a duration of between two and five hours. Scoutmaster Watson, commonly a reliable witness, speaks of the guns being in action between 'two and five' o'clock; 'WH' a Parliamentarian officer stated that the artillery went on shooting from two until about half past seven. Even if we were to assume that half the Allied guns spoke for the minimum time – that is 50 guns for two hours – and that they fired at a slow deliberate rate – it is inconceivable that they could have fired less than 700 rounds. The ammunition for such a battery was certainly available: during June there were a number of orders for round shot for the armies, the largest of which was for 1,000 on 22 June, and prodigious amounts of powder was issued on 2 July 1644 to Robert Colquone, specifically for 'great and smale cannon'. In any case the main projectile used by the Scottish 'frame guns' that day was a species of case shot made up using musket balls.[31]

Quite how many Royalists fell as a result of the bombardment is more diffi-cult to determine than its magnitude. One definite casualty was Captain Roger Houghton, another was Thomas Danby, a gentleman volunteer, 'shot to death with a cannon bullet and cutt off by the midst of his body'. Many more humble soldiers would not have warranted such a detailed description of their demise. We do know however that the weight of the fire fell upon the Royalist front and right, mainly upon the cavalry of Molyneux and Byron, whose units were initially less than 3,000 strong, and to which even a fairly moderate loss might have had disproportionate effects. The Royalists attempted to reply in kind, but with 23 guns, and a target mainly concealed by a ridge, their success is likely to have been limited. Even so they managed to get at least one group of guns onto 'an advantageous piece of ground' – thought to have been 'Rye Hill' – within a reasonable range of the enemy's right flank. According to at least one account it was the annoyance caused by these Royalist guns that finally helped precipitate elements of the Allied army into the decision to attack. As

---

[30] Ogden and other accounts reprinted in Young, pp 113, 116–117, 217, 223–224, and de Gomme's plan, BL Add. Ms 16,370, f 64.

[31] WH *A Relation of the Good Success of the Parliament's Forces*, Cambridge, 10 July 1644, sig A3; P. Newman *Marston Moor, 2 July 1644: The Sources and the Site*, University of York Borthwick Papers, 53, 1978, pp 5–8.

Lumsden informs us when the Scots went forward the first objective of their brigades was to make themselves masters 'of the canon was nixt to them'.[32]

With the Royalist right wing now 'moving' a little, as Lumsden's euphemism for being shaken by gunfire put it, and the Allied armies now in good order, the time had come for Leven to act – or perhaps for Cromwell to take advantage of the situation. According to Simeon Ashe,

> towards six or seven of the clock we advanced about two hundred yards towards the enemy, our cannon (which had plaid one or two hourses before from the top of the hill) was drawne forward for our best advantage, our signal was a white paper, or handkerchiffe in our hats, our word was God with us.

From where 'WH' was standing, with the cavalry on the Allied left, things were somewhat more confused as the artillery duel raged more fiercely:

> we began about two of the clock in the afternoon with our great guns which continued till between 7 and 9 with equal success, then the main bodies joyning, made such a noise with shot and clamour of shouts that we lost our eares, and the smoke of powder was so thicke that we saw no light but what proceeded from the mouth of the gunnes.

Sir Thomas Stockdale was one eyewitness who saw the 'execution' wrought by the artillery on the nearest brigade of enemy cavalry, that

> forced the enemye to leave that ground and remove to a greater distance. And so both Armyes stood ranged in Battalynes viewing each other, and neither of them charging, till it was halfe an hour past 7 a clock at night, and then our Generals (seeing the enemy wold not advance) resolved to leave their ground of advantage & to engage upon the plaine ground, wch order being once given was most cheerfully undertaken.[33]

What happened between about seven and ten on the evening of 2 July is commonly regarded as 'the' battle of Marston Moor, yet by that time the scales had already tipped in favour of Parliament's forces. They had advantage of ground, advantage of numbers and had already shaken the Royalist right wing. The surprise therefore is not that Rupert's army was shattered, but that it put up such a fight. Even so the popular idea of a struggle which was characterised by a rapid cavalry charge on both flanks is probably erroneous – or at least oversimplified. In the case of Cromwell's brigade on the Allied left the picture we are left by Ludlow is one of a measured development in which infantry and artillery also played their part:

---

[32] Ibid, pp 20–21.
[33] Passages in: BL E 2(1), Simeon Ashe *A Continuation of True Intelligence*, July 1644, p 5; WH *Relation* sig A3; and Young *Marston Moor*, p 236.

the left wing of our army commanded by Colonel Cromwell … engaged the right wing of the enemy commanded by Prince Rupert who had gained an advantageous piece of ground upon Marston Moor, and caused a battery to be erected upon it, from which Captain Walton, Cromwell's sister's son, was wounded by a shot in the knee. Whereupon Col Cromwell commanded two field pieces to be brought in order to annoy the enemy, appointing two regiments of foot to guard them; who marching to that purpose was attacked by the foot of the enemy's right wing, that fired thick upon them from the ditches. Upon this both parties seconding their foot, were wholly engaged, who before stood only facing each other. The horse on both sides behaved themselves with the utmost bravery; for having discharged their pistols and flung them at each other's heads, they fell to it with their swords.

Whilst it may be argued that Ludlow was not himself an eye witness to these events the measured and timed nature of Cromwell's charge is agreed by others, as for example Colonel James Somerville. Rupert himself spoke of the 'improper' nature of Byron's charge.[34]

As Cromwell routed Rupert's right the opposite was happening on the other flank, where the Royalists were getting the upper hand, and the battle began to swing like a revolving door around a central pivot. This picture has been somewhat confirmed by recent research that shows that the main scatter of shot and debris from the battle followed a similar pattern across the field – roughly from north-north-west to south-south-west. Amongst this detritus was a quantity of cannon balls. With heavy casualties and several commanders on both sides quitting the field in the belief that the battle was lost, it looked for a while as though the Royalists might hold their protagonists to a draw, or even win the day. Nevertheless the nerve of the Allied forces held, and numbers and superior control began to tell against Prince Rupert. With most of the Royalist cavalry spent, or thrown into the centre to bolster Blakiston, the last reserves were hard pressed to hold the line. From about half past eight the battle deteriorated into an unequal grinding match with the foot of Manchester and the remaining Scots pushing their way to the north-east, over the bodies of the Royalist centre, and the infantry of Tillier, Eythin and Newcastle.[35]

As we can see, the artillery at Marston Moor was no token effort, nor simply a morale factor, but an important and integral part of both armies. It had a battle function to fulfil which was broadly understood by all the commanders – and remembered by Firth at the start of the twentieth century – but has since somehow become forgotten.[36] It annoyed the enemy at a distance, disordering

---

[34] See P.R. Newman *The Battle of Marston Moor*, Chichester, 1981, pp 68–75; T. Carlyle (ed) *Oliver Cromwell's Letters and Speeches*, London, 1866, vol 1, p 153.

[35] C.H. Firth, 'Marston Moor' in *Transactions of the Royal Historical Society*, vol 12, 1898, passim, and *Cromwell's Army*, London, 1902, pp 145–162.

[36] See also P.R. Newman and P.R. Roberts *Marston Moor 1644: The Battle of the Five Armies*, Pickering, 2003, pp 144–165, and *English Heritage Battlefield Report: Marston Moor*, London, 1995 and later web published, passim.

formations, causing casualties and forcing the decisions of the commanders, and confirmed the superior deployment of one side. Then at least a few guns were moved and the process began again – sparking the struggle which determined, ultimately, the fate of northern England. General Hamilton, Robert Colquoune, James Trotter, the gunners, and administrators behind the scenes, had all played their part in the Allied victory. The King's Master Gunner, Edward Errick, and 25 pieces of ordnance that the Royalists could ill afford to lose, fell into the hands of Parliament.[37]

---

[37] See also J. Barratt *Cavaliers*, Stroud, 2000, pp 121–132.

Conclusions

Without doubt ordnance was the arbitrating technology of the mid seventeenth century: it determined the design of the warship and fortification, and by extension was a significant factor in government expenditure – much of which was military. It was also crucial both to the outcomes of the Civil Wars, and the way they were fought. To ignore this is a fundamental misunderstanding of the period. The wars of the Low Countries had been struggles of sieges of artillery works punctuated by battles; the English Civil Wars would follow a similar trend, albeit that the protagonists sometimes had more space in which to manoeuvre, and took time to develop their capabilities. Writing in the 1670s of warfare in general Lord Orrery was of the opinion that sieges outnumbered battles by twenty to one. In Sprigge's account of the operations of the New Model Army from April 1645 to the end of the First Civil War, only 11 field actions are deemed worthy of particular notice against 50 sieges, stormings, and surrenders of towns, houses and castles. This imbalance may have been less obvious earlier in the war, and in the north of England, where the New Model Army did not operate at this period – nevertheless imbalance there was, and even the significant battles that did occur were often part of a campaign to secure, relieve, or storm a town. Cases in point include Edgehill, which interrupted the King's march on London, as did the non event at Turnham Green. The first battle at Newbury was a punctuation mark between the successful relief of Gloucester and the retirement of the Earl of Essex on London, whilst Marston Moor turned on the besieging of York. Less obviously several of the battles and skirmishes in the Midlands were part of efforts either to protect or threaten the Royalist capital of Oxford.[1]

Interestingly C.H. Firth had been very close to the mark when, early in the twentieth century, he offered the opinion that; 'artillery played a much more important part in the Civil War than is generally supposed, and its skilful handling exercised considerable influence in deciding the fortune of battles and campaigns'. He was also broadly correct in pointing out that at the start of the war Parliament, and the Earl of Essex in particular, were 'liberally supplied' with artillery, whilst the King was 'deficient'. That these nuggets of wisdom were so wilfully neglected by scholars of the succeeding generation is an excel-

---

[1] Joshua Sprigge *Anglia Redivia*, passim; J. Kenyon *The Civil Wars of England*, London, 1988, pp 48–53, 63–122; see also G. Parker *The Military Revolution*, Cambridge, 1988, pp 38–43.

lent proof that historical knowledge does not 'progress' sublimely, but can be strangely forgotten – or pushed into byways. For more than one Civil War commentator of the post 1945 era it seems that trench digging and round shot were simply not exciting, nor personalised enough, to be a significant part of the history of the 'romantic' Civil Wars. This is to forget that all wars are a dirty but often technical business in which the destruction of people and property usually bulks large. The victims of war are of course equally dead and bankrupted whenever and wherever such misfortune occurs. The Civil Wars certainly should not be regarded as light relief from the catastrophes of more recent times, being in Ranke's famous phrase 'equally close to God'. Moreover in a middle seventeenth century in which the air was the province of the birds and angels, and the tank was a brilliant but unrealised flight of Leonardo's fantasy, the metaphorical 'big guns' remained literally, the big guns. Ordnance was not only the 'last argument' of Princes, but recognised as symbolic of royal authority, and a thrilling spectacle for nobility and common people alike.[2]

The power of the ordnance was clearly recognised by soldiers of the period. This is demonstrated most clearly by the sheer effort, time, and expense which was put into the very real response to this threat. The majority of big towns, and a very large number of small – plus castles, manor houses and a variety of other sites, were reinforced with earth bastions and 'mud walls'. The combined length of these substantial defences comfortably exceeded that of Hadrian's famous wall, and the cost was hundreds of thousands of pounds in cash – and very probably a similar amount in lost production and revenues. Had contemporaries thought that the menace from cannon was negligible it would be unthinkable that they could have expended so much effort to combat it. Often, as in the case of London itself, those planning defences hoped for a long time that full scale entrenchment could be avoided – only to work frenetically when it appeared that an enemy force might be on its way and the construction of modern defence works could no longer be neglected.

It has been said that since some Civil War strongholds resisted successfully, or no breach was made in defences, artillery of the period must have been somehow poor or worthless. As we have seen this is not an adequate summation. Sieges failed for a number of reasons, most frequently because the attackers lacked the right types of ordnance, were short of ammunition or money, or were interrupted by relief armies; or simply because the defenders had the latest type of earthwork defence, and guns of their own – or were ready and prepared to fight to the death. None of this demonstrates that the guns of the Civil War were somehow inferior – on the contrary it suggests that siege warfare was itself geared around what the artillery might be expected to achieve. To say that cannon of the seventeenth century were less powerful or accurate than more modern weapons, and therefore pointless, is simply lazy

2   C.H. Firth *Cromwell's Army* (first published 1902), 4th edn, Oxford, 1962, p 149; J.S. Wheeler *The Making of a World Power*, Stroud, 1999, pp 94–215.

and anachronistic thinking. Moreover there is adequate evidence to suggest that the artillery of 1642 was, in point of fact, reasonably similar to that in use two hundred years later. A well made cannon of 1644 was not so different to one produced in 1800. More plausible, as both Parker and Wheeler have suggested, is the notion that technology and costs often outran organisation and finance. In any case, as many other conflicts have demonstrated, superior technology is not of itself any guarantee of success in war.[3]

The performance of artillery in battle has certainly been vastly underrated. It has been argued in the past that the prime function of ordnance in Civil War actions was to shake the morale of the enemy. It may be that it did, but artillery had been around for more than three centuries by 1642, and if it could not cause real damage this would have become common knowledge over the course of ten generations. As detailed studies of other periods have ascertained, soldiers fear what can harm them far more than the things they know cannot. The early seventeenth century development of lightweight battlefield artillery has long been acknowledged as part of the the legacy of Gustavus Adolphus of Sweden and his 'leather guns' – but similar developments were taking place elsewhere. The Scottish use of light 'frame' guns and leather guns was one example, but in England there were also determined and ultimately successful attempts to introduce small brass and iron battlefield pieces – 'drakes', and other 3 and 6 pound guns. Thereafter batteries of 'field' artillery would become a standard feature of European warfare. Light guns existed in quantity, and were deployed on the battlefield in similar proportions to the numbers of other troops from 1630 to 1660 as they would be from 1700 to 1815. Large amounts of money were expended on manufacturing field guns, equipping them, getting them to the battlefield and using them. Even in times of chronic shortage of funds ready cash would be found for artillery.

During battle guns were moderately accurate, and quite swift to discharge. The field artillery of 1642 was also efficient in a comparative sense, for whilst the artillery of the Civil War was technologically very similar to that of 1800, the matchlock musket and pike were demonstrably less efficient than the flintlock and bayonet of the latter period. Civil War artillery bombardments disrupted units, caused casualties, and on occasion changed the course of actions by forcing premature attacks, or retreats. Close range 'case shot' firing was a staple of battlefield artillery action, and ammunition supply ratios suggest that about a fifth to a quarter of all battlefield firing was done at close quarters, and is likely to have caused significant damage. Guns were also a priority target for

---

3 Just a few of the many examples of the 'inferior or ineffective artillery' school of thought may be found in A.W. Wilson *The Story of the Gun*, 4th edn, Woolwich, 1976, pp 16–21; C.V. Wedgwood *Civil War Battlefields*, undated, pp 4–5; C. Carlton *Going to the Wars*, London, 1992, p 140; P. Young and W. Emberton *The Cavalier Army*, London, 1974, pp 27–28; J. Kenyon *The Civil Wars of England*, London, 1988, p 86; P. Young *Civil War England*, London, 1981, pp 58–60.

the attacks of other arms. This significance was amply recorded in newsletters and books of the period for which the number of guns captured from the enemy was one of the key indicators of success in battle.

Artillery was not usually however the battle-winning weapon that it came to be, as for example in the early nineteenth century, and occasionally commanders chose the advantage of mobility over firepower – deliberately leaving their guns behind for forced marches and surprise actions. Cromwell at Preston in 1648 is the most dramatic example of this tactic. There appear to be a number of reasons why Civil War artillery was not as efficient as its Napoleonic successor. Relatively slender ammunition supply meant that gunners had to pick their targets carefully and could not afford to do much 'speculative' firing, long range work, or carry on bombarding a battlefield target for hours on end. Commonly a gun was supplied with 50 rounds or less, and given that some of these were case shot, this was adequate for, at most, about three hours of steady firing at medium range targets. Guns which were individual in their character-istics, and worry about overheating, barrel wear and flaws in metal also helped to encourage more frequent resting of pieces and pauses in fire. Transporting guns to where they were needed also remained a major headache, and only the lightest pieces could march alongside the army. If a siege battery was used it had to travel in its own convoy, or the whole army had to slow to its pace. Though guns were more mobile than many would imagine, 'horse artillery' in the nineteenth century sense of guns that charged about the battlefield with the cavalry did not exist – and this was not merely because civilian draught and heavy horses and oxen were not suitable to the task. The artillery was usually organised as part of the 'train', operated under a general of artillery or the army commander, or was occasionally attached directly to an infantry unit. It did not have the organisation or chain of command to operate as part of the cavalry, and did not have the means of rapid ammunition resupply that would have made such a deployment practical or potent.

The fact that artillery in its various forms was far more important in the England of the 1640s than has generally been acknowledged is obviously of great significance to students of the military history of the English Civil Wars. Yet it has to be asked whether this apparently arcane detail has any wider polit-ical or historical significance. The answer has to be that it does, though much more work is required to determine the precise relationship between the ways in which the war was fought, its costs, and the changing nature of industry, trade, taxation and government during the period. It is however possible to point to some substantive conclusions, and to highlight matters likely to be fruitful in terms of future research.

Something very significant that can plainly be seen in the logistical history of 1641–1642 is that if there were zealous individuals, either in Pym's coterie or amongst the King's advisors, keen to promote a move from verbal polit-ical and religious strife to force of arms prior to the fateful summer of 1642, they did not manage to lay the military foundations for war – nor plan any campaign ahead of time. Some of the much vaunted plots of the period may have been genuine, but in hindsight we may divine they had no serious military substance. Even when the King started to issue his Commissions of Array at the end of May, and through into June and early July, no 'master plan' is readily apparent. Moreover most of the key stores of guns, ammunition, and other military supplies were yet to be firmly secured by one side or the other. Amazingly there was still some doubt about the Ordnance Office and vital stocks at the Tower of London as late as August. All of this argues strongly that neither King nor Parliament had much by way of malice aforethought – and that war was blundered into rather than cynically planned. If King or Parliament actually wanted war as early as the beginning of 1642 the way they went about achieving it was slow, extremely inefficient, and poorly managed. The actual first months of the conflict were all about securing the wherewithal to fight – not any pre-emptive masterstroke. Once the leadership on both sides had come to the conclusion that a shooting war was unavoidable there appears to have been dismay upon the realisation that England was so badly prepared for any sort of fight. This underlines Anthony Fletcher's observation that 'few wars can have broken out so untidily as the English Civil War': Royalist recruiting did not begin in earnest until July 1642 – nor was there systematic collection of funds until this time. In fact a continuation of the short term approach was apparent for some months afterwards. Ongoing supplies of powder capable of sustaining a long war do not seem to have been fully organised until the beginning of 1643; the production and delivery of heavy ordnance would remain problematic for some time, and almost everywhere required new fortifications. It would be almost another year later before Parliament had mustered the financial muscle that would be required to bring the war to a successful conclusion.[4]

Moreover the evidence that we have demonstrates quite convincingly that what dictated the form of the conflict in its early stages – even what got the fighting started in earnest – was the perceived need of both sides to hold the machinery of war in its own hands. To turn the dictum of Marx upon its head, the leaders of both sides were racing to harness the 'means of destruction'. The crisis at Hull was very much about grabbing a valuable arsenal, as was the collision in Lancashire, though here it was muskets and powder rather than artillery which were at stake. The opening moves along the south coast were essentially about control of arsenals and supplies. In London control of the Parliament building itself, then the Tower and the Ordnance Office were critical factors. Until late August 1642 the strategy of both sides was directed essentially at seizing the means to make war – and very little about any future campaign, planned, or actual. Local forces were called up first, the central field armies of the Earl of Essex and the King came second. Artillery trains were

---

[4]   A. Fletcher *The Outbreak of the English Civil War*, London, 1981, pp 322–368.

still being set up even later. It is a moot point whether there could have been a protracted 'shooting war' if one side or the other could have succeeded in its early objective of effectively denying weaponry to the opposition. Gaining control of artillery – along with small arms and fortifications – was a crucial part of the process.

Parliament slowly overcame many of its difficulties – especially after a reorganisation of its finances from the latter part of 1643, and a reorganisation of its field armies from the latter part of 1644 – and throughout the war took advantage of the assistance that the navy could impart to operations on land. The supply of guns and powder was adequate and reasonably certain by the time the New Model Army came upon the scene. The King failed to capitalise on the advantages that he did have in 1642 and 1643, and at least some of the crucial failings of the Royalist armies were to do with ordnance. Bristol was more of a bloodbath than it needed to be because the King lacked the wherewithal for full scale bombardments, and Gloucester did not fall at all for much the same reason.

It is also apparent that the war of sieges and slighting, the fortifying and subsequent reduction and removal of garrisons – in which artillery was crucial – must have had some impact on the relationship between the provinces and the centre. When the country was divided up into what were effectively tiny artillery fort strongholds, financed mainly by county or town, the war certainly had the propensity to become diffuse, and bogged down in local factors. Men and money devoted to protecting Newark, King's Lynn, Lyme, or Lancaster, were resources unavailable to the central armies of the King or Parliament. Even with only partial statistics it is obvious that in 1643 far more men and guns were tied up in static fortifications than were part of mobile field forces. Parliament's calculated gamble to 'disgarrison', to 'slight' or abandon fortifications was an interesting one for several reasons. Fairly obviously Parliamentarian leaders must have come to a conclusion that generally speaking the existence of forts and garrisons – especially inland ones – was of more benefit to the enemy than to themselves. Doing without garrisons reduced the number of places that diehard Royalists could hold out, and freed up resources for more strategic objectives. The initiative did indeed shift to the centre, and it seems that 'slighting' became an integral part of the more obvious military successes of the New Model Army. Yet whilst the withering of local forces and the removal of garrisons may have given Parliament more control in the short term a more powerful central army was in political terms undoubtedly a double edged sword.

That Charles I realised the logistic disadvantages under which the Royalist forces laboured was exposed more candidly than he might have wished when he addressed his Cornish troops after the death of Sir Bevil Grenville, who had died in the teeth of cannon on the brow of Lansdown hill in July 1643. He frankly acknowledged that they fought a 'potent' enemy 'backed with so strong, rich and populous cities, and so plentifully supplied with men, arms, money and ammunition and provision of all kinds'. It was perhaps as close as he ever came to admitting that victory was unlikely.[5]

It is well known that Leonard Digges applied the term 'science' to gunnery as early as 1571. Nevertheless, and significant as the role of ordnance was, it is difficult to demonstrate the contention that the gunners of the sixteenth and seventeenth centuries in England, or anywhere else, were the 'first scientists'; or that they thought about their subject in what we might recognise as the modern scientific manner. Indeed most gunner authors of the period refer to their subject as 'an art'. Even so gunnery experts were beginning to do something highly significant. Most were thoroughly conversant with the idea of experiment – to determine ranges and strength of gunpowder for example. Equally they were familiar with the notions of constants and variables. If one could accurately replicate the materials and circumstances under which one cannon shot was made, it was much more likely that the piece would perform in delivering the next round to the same place. Both siege and battle demonstrated how valuable a skill it was to be able to replicate one shot with the next. Experienced gunners recognised that if the elevation, powder, shot, or other factors differed, the result would be a miss. This was the point made at great length, for example, in Thomas Smith's *Art of Gunnery* where he explains how the difference in a single variable is enough to alter the fall of shot. It is therefore perfectly valid to argue that the observation and experiment of gunners was hugely important, and a significant step towards like experiment in other fields. The knowledgeable gunner often became, to quote the early eighteenth century authority Edward Ward, 'a little King in his own conceit'.[6]

It is certainly true that mathematicians and practitioners of geometry frequently used gunnery examples to furnish material for their study; sometimes the models they used were correct by modern lights, sometimes hopelessly wrong. In some instances the authors were simply looking for an example to make a mathematical problem more interesting – in others they were genuinely concerned with the behaviour of real spheres of iron as they shot through the air onto castles and troops. Intriguingly however the word 'ballistics' does not seem to have entered common English usage until after the Civil Wars, and A.R. Hall has claimed that it first appeared in the work of Robert Boyle in 1671. Whether contemporaries were 'right' in their deductions is probably less important in the context of their times than that they so often chose artillery – over falling apples, bath water, the behaviour of animals, abstract numbers, or trains running from one point to another, all things beloved for mathematical problems in other periods. Gunnery was an important subject; Kings and Princes were going to be interested in any breakthrough in this field, and the

5 From a declaration given at Sudely Castle, 10 September 1643, and now painted on the armoury stairs.
6 T. Smith *Art of Gunnery*, London, 1643, pp 63–65; B. Capp *Cromwell's Navy*, Oxford, 1988, p 204; A.R. Hall *Ballistics in the Seventeenth Century*, Cambridge, 1952, pp 5–6, 34.

literate classes were often more fascinated by this than most other subjects – particularly under threat of real war. By 1600 gunnery had become, as Digges put it, a subject suitable for 'gentlemen'. To this very genuine extent therefore gunner authors, both practical and theoretical, catered to a literary demand, even expectation, of their times.[7]

Famously J.F.C. Fuller once claimed that 'in the beginning industry and war were one' – and in the archaeological record spears and arrow heads as well as blades lend this apparently extravagant claim some credence. Francis Bacon, writing as early as 1620, thought the compass, printing press and gunpowder had already changed the 'appearance and state of the whole world'. Quite a few modern historians have agreed that the combination of guns and sails, or military technology in general, did change the world during the seventeenth century. Less ambitiously, given that artillery, and the ships and forts on which much of it was mounted, was highly significant in middle seventeenth century England – and bulked so large in the making of war and the finances of government – it is reasonable to ask why the large scale manufacture of guns did not lead to an 'industrial revolution' in mid seventeenth century England.[8]

Leaving aside the fact that many commentators accept the notion of a 'pre' industrial revolution during the seventeenth century, there appear to be several reasons, some technical, others financial, why ordnance manufacture, fort, and ship building did not have more immediate and dramatic economic impact. Perhaps the most obvious is that war perforce brings with it economic disadvantage and destruction. For every furnace stoked and every penny spent during the Civil Wars there seems to be some economic or human disaster we can point to that more than out balances the benefit. Productive workers ignored their agriculture and trades to build forts, trail pikes and fire cannon. Malnutrition, disease, property destruction and death were the corollaries of technological innovation. Whilst the ordnance manufacturers of Kent – and Parliamentarian merchants of armaments, uniforms and supplies in general – prospered, leading Royalist families were sequestered and towns were battered and burned.[9]

It is also worth observing that the gun manufacturing industry of 1600–1660 was geographically and technically rather unlike the steam driven mill 'revolution' of later centuries. As with the early manufacture of cloth, the production of domestic ironware was very much a matter of small scale enterprise, and often one which did not represent the entire economic activity of any one

---

7   Ibid p 78. S.A. Walton 'The Art of Gunnery in Renaissance England', PhD thesis, University of Toronto, 1999, p 201.

8   J.F.C. Fuller *Armament and Industry*, London, 1946, p 17; C. Cipolla *Guns, Sails and Empires*, New York, 1966, passim, and *The Sixteenth and Seventeenth Centuries*, The Fontana Economic History of Europe, vol 2, London, 1974, pp 177–272, 354–426; G. Parker *Europe in Crisis*, London, 1977, pp 66–75.

9   S. Porter *Destruction in the English Civil Wars*, Stroud, 1994, passim.

group or family. Founding was organised in 'campaigns' – the production of a number of castings over a given time – followed by slack periods in which the furnaces might lie idle. Guns were bigger and more expensive, more profitable in general, but outside of war-time production was never continuous. Against this background there was little ongoing incentive to keep ploughing profits back into the business, and certainly no good reason to build up stocks of unsold guns. Part-time workers, and production dispersed to take advantage of charcoal, ores, and waterpower made it unlikely that centralised full-time workshops would emerge, let alone anything approximating to the 'factory systems' of later centuries. The Wealden iron industry therefore operated very spasmodically under the impecunious early Stuarts prior to 1642, and took advantage of the 'merchant' and foreign trade whenever it could – but was held back by foreign policy as well as boosted by government orders. It used to be claimed that gun founding had no impact upon industrial development. Whilst this may no longer be tenable it is certainly true that the impact was not as sustained as other types of trade and industry which were continuously ongoing and with many types of customer. Many people all over Europe and some other parts would be pleased to have a new shirt at a modest price, or at least to get the cast-off from the man who did – but very few demanded a full battery of cannon, second hand or otherwise.

Perhaps less obviously the seventeenth century industries of war were essentially demand led, and princes and politicians were just as keen on the 'peace dividend' as any of their modern counterparts. When wars ended orders for guns or other munitions were simply cut off mid flow, and as we well appreciate from troops who sometimes went unpaid, or the dramatic and ill-fated attempts to dissolve the New Model Army before its arrears were met, paymasters were just as keen to see soldiers disappear as they had been to raise them in the first place. When we look at the ordnance, Parliament was equally happy to see the Ordnance Office and the procurement and distribution system disintegrate. Though the main field armies of Parliament were 'New Modelled' in the winter of 1644 to 1645, a remodelled Ordnance Office would remain a work in progress. Only in July 1648 were the positions of the key officers formally reconfirmed when the House of Commons read and agreed a petition from George Payler, John White and John Falkner, whose titles were then given as 'Surveyor General', 'Clerk' and 'Storekeeper' of the Ordnance. Everybody else, a total of 47 artificers, clerks, labourers and the like, would have to wait for a decision from the Committee of the Navy as to whether they could be taken onto the books, and indeed be paid their arrears. With units disbanding, attempts being made to reduce establishments and garrisons, and the very defences of London falling into neglect, it can hardly surprise us that Charles and the Scots thought that a heaven-sent opportunity to reverse the fortunes of war had occurred in the spring and summer of 1648.[10]

---

[10] See also B.A. Holderness *Pre-Industrial England*, London, 1976, pp 83–115.

Even following the salutary shock of the Second Civil War, full revision of the Ordnance Office and the artillery had to wait until the setting up of a commission of the 'Committee of Merchants' that looked into establishments again in January 1649. The 'modernising' reforms then introduced seem to have had as much to do with economy and combating disaffection on the part of specific individuals as with any genuinely operational criteria. An important part of the plan was the disestablishment of the post of Lieutenant of the Ordnance. Conveniently enough the incumbent Lieutenant of the Ordnance was Sir Walter Erle – an MP of Presbyterian leanings who had already been excluded from Parliament by Pride's Purge in December 1648. He was now formally disbarred from the office. Master Gunner James Wemyss who had deserted Parliament to serve the king during the Second Civil War was also disbarred, and the appointment of Nicholas Wollaston was retrospectively confirmed. Amongst the more junior positions the Messenger and some of the labourers were also dismissed; Nicholas Cox the Messenger went specifically because he had made utterances to the 'scandall of the Parliament'.

The commissioners also made swingeing recommendations for the general reduction of the Ordnance Office to a Clerk of the Ordnance, Keeper of the Stores, Master Gunner, a Deputy Storekeeper at Portsmouth, two furbishers and twenty labourers. The Master Gunner would henceforth double as Proofmaster whilst the standing allowances for travel and stationery would be abolished, and officers would pay for any ancillary staff or materials themselves. The recompense for this decimation of the Ordnance Office was that the remaining officers would receive an adequate salary. Arguably this was the best part of the plan, being intended to free the work of the department from the web of perquisites and fees which had hitherto rather badly oiled the bureaucratic wheels. In practice however it would appear that many were aware that in time of peace an adequate and regular salary was not a very likely prospect, and the Navy Committee was uneasy that the proposed establishment would prove inadequate to the task. The result was a power struggle between the Merchants' and the Navy committees, which saw first the reinstatement of a Surveyor of the Ordnance, and in 1650 a revocation of the powers of the Merchants' Committee. By 1653 the establishment of the office was smaller than that pertaining during the Civil Wars, but larger than the truncated office demanded by the Merchants' Committee – and even the antiquated positions of 'bowyer' and 'fletcher' were brought back.[11]

Caroline payment systems also left a lot to be desired as the basis of any industry that wished to thrive and prosper. As with troops, successive administrations wanted guns, but were not keen to pay for them. There was an aspiration for a flourishing domestic ordnance industry, but a fear that high levels

---

[11] The changes may be traced through the establishments given in PRO WO 54; see also W. Reid 'Commonwealth Supply Departments within the Tower and the Committee of London Merchants', in *Guildhall Miscellany*, vol 2, no 8, September 1966, pp 319–352.

of production would simply lead to ordnance being exported to undesirable third parties. The standard method of getting paid for producing guns for the Crown or Commonwealth was always slow, and sometimes uncertain. As we have seen, guns were proof tested before they reached the Tower, and when they did arrive the contractor was issued with a 'bill' by the Surveyor and Storekeeper. This bill was then delivered to the Clerk, who took it and entered it into a ledger – but no money was handed over, the Clerk issuing a 'debenture'. The contractor then had to exchange the debenture for funds at some future date. Commonly the whole process from delivery to actual payment could take a year, whilst the iron master had to obtain his raw materials and workmen some time, possibly months, before getting his wares to the point of sale. John Browne had the temerity to ask for ready money, and to threaten to cease delivery. One method which seemed to offer a part way round this issue for a King without a Parliament was to grant a monopoly, but monopolies were a part of the grievances against him – and may well have increased the price above that in a less controlled market. The only other palliatives were for the producers to band together as a form of cartel, and to diversify production. Furnaces certainly were used for domestic products – from fire backs and pots to grave slabs – but there was a limit to what the market could absorb in an England where the majority had little in the way of disposable income. Without a modern banking system there was no pool of ready capital other than that which the gunfounders, their families and friends were prepared to risk. Neither was there any guarantee of export, for not only were other countries, notably Sweden and the Netherlands, entering into the competitive markets, but legislation could at any time outlaw the transportation of guns overseas.[12]

Wheeler is undoubtedly correct when he suggests that seventeenth century England saw the revision of financial systems and the invention of a number of new institutions, and that much of this came about as a reaction to the demands of war and the requirements of the navy. Equally clearly, such far sighted and often expensive developments were not embraced wholeheartedly prior to the death of Charles I, nor were Englishmen ever particularly anxious to pay the taxes required for such edifices to be constructed. The excise was a necessary evil and, importantly for our story, was used specifically to support the activities of the Ordnance Office – but John Pym and the excise of 1643 were only the beginning. Revenues shot up during the early 1640s, being nearly four times as great as they had been on the eve of the Civil Wars, but later they dropped back before growing again, and it would be well after 1688 before

[12] G.E. Aylmer *The King's Servants*, London, 1974, pp 420–421, 464–469; G.E. Aylmer *The State's Servants*, London, 1973, pp 38–40, and D.E. Lewis, op cit, pp 85–90; *House of Commons Journal*, vol 5, July 1648, pp 640–642.

the heady days of the military spending of the Civil Wars and the Protectorate were equalled.[13]

Undoubtedly we still have much to learn about the Civil Wars, but it is undeniable that the relationship between the progress of the wars and the way they were fought is crucial. In this sense the military history of the Civil Wars is at the heart of the conflict – and cannot be ignored as though it were a mere technical curiosity. Cannon and powder were no mere decoration: they are integral to explaining how campaigns progressed – and more than once their capabilities influenced strategy. Improving technology is not the same thing as success in war, nor is military technology an 'absolute'. The will to win – even the will to fight, numbers, terrain, politics, luck, and a hundred other factors make it very difficult to disentangle the role of one particular technology or weapon. However even cursory perusal of primary sources shows that those who lived through the Civil Wars thought that artillery was important. The bravest trembled at 'the furie of the ordnance'.

---

[13] Wheeler, op cit, pp 1–66, 211–216.

Appendix I

Ordnance Types 1634–1665

Ordnance types mentioned in the Tower Inventory, 1634
PRO WO 55/1690

Cannon of 8
Cannon of 7
Cannon Perrier
Demi Cannon
Demi Cannon Drake
Bastard Demi Cannon
Culverin
Demi Culverin
Saker
Saker Drake
Drake

Minion
Bastard Minion
Falcon
Falconet
Robinet ['Rabonett']
Murderer ['of forged iron']
Fowler
Brass Piece 'shooting three bullets'
Brass Piece 'shooting seven bullets'
Mortar [13 inch]
Mortar [8 inch]

Ordnance types according to Robert Norton
in The Gunner, *1643*

Name	Calibre in inches	Length in calibres	Weight (lb)	Powder charge (lb)
Cannon of 8	8	15	8000	40
Cannon of 7	7	16	7000	25
Demi Cannon	6.5	18	6000	20
Culverin	5.5	28	4500	15
Demi Culverin	4.5	32	2500	9
Saker	3.5	36	1500	5.25
Minion	3.25	30	1200	3.25
Falcon	2.75	42	700	2.5
Falconet	2.25	48	500	1.25
Cannon Perrier	9, 10 or 12	8	3500	3, 3.5 or 4
Demi Cannon Drake	6.5	16	3000	9
Culverin Drake	5.5	16	2000	5
Demi Culverin Drake	4.5	16	1500	3.5
Saker Drake	3.5	18	1200	2

Ordnance types according to William Eldred
in *The Gunner's Glasse, 1646*

Name	Calibre in inches	Weight of gun (lb)	Length of piece (feet)	Shot weight (lb)
Cannon Royal	8	8000	8	63
Cannon	7	7000	10	47
Demi Cannon	6	6000	12	27
Culverin	5	4000	11	15
Demi Culverin	4.5	3600	10	9
Saker	3.5	2500	9.5	5.25
Minion	3	1500	8	4
Falcon	2.75	700	6	2.25
Falconet	2	210	4	1.25
Robinet	1.25	120	3	0.75

Ordnance types occurring in the Tower Inventory of 1665
PRO WO 55/1699

'Traditional' types	'Modern' types	Mortars
Cannon of 8	24 Pounder	18.5 inch
Cannon of 7	12 Pounder	16.75 inch
Demi Cannon	8 Pounder	13.5 inch
Culverin	6 Pounder	8.75 inch
Demi Culverin	3 Pounder	8 inch
Saker		6 inch
Minion		4.25 inch
Falcon		

Appendix II

Shot Finds

Many – probably thousands – of seventeenth century cannon shot have been found in the years since the Civil Wars. It is likely that the largest number were picked up and reused, or scrapped, within a relatively short period of the time they were fired or lost. Shot are recorded as having been removed from many of the major battlefields, notably Marston Moor and Naseby, over a very long period of time. More recently similar finds have been better recorded, and have added to our knowledge of artillery of the period. A 29 pound ball was recovered from the field of Hopton Heath, in 1940 helping to confirm contemporary accounts of a demi cannon being used during the battle. Similarly a 3 pound 7 ounce minion ball was found near Lansdown in 2002, and a saker ball at Cheriton at about the same time. Even more recently a 3.5 pound shot has been found at Taynton, Gloucestershire, probably indicating the site of a Civil War skirmish. Professionally organised archaeological excavation has also produced a sizeable crop of shot finds, notably at Longton Castle, Herefordshire; Sandal in West Yorkshire; Corfe; Dudley; Laugharne in Pembrokeshire; Banbury and Basing House.[1]

Most Civil War cannon balls have simply been picked up from farm land, or, in the last few decades, found with the aid of metal detectors – but others have been located in rather more extraordinary circumstances. In 1845, for example, an ancient yew tree at Crowborough in Sussex was struck by lightning. When the shattered limbs were examined a ball was found still lodged in the wood. Later in the nineteenth century Bronsil Castle in Herefordshire only yielded up its secrets when the moat was being dredged. In 1915 a small round shot was removed from the tower of St Philip's church in Bristol, a relic of one of the sieges of the town. At a house in Maiden Street on the Melcombe Regis side of Weymouth there is still a shot wedged in the wall high above street level, and shot are similarly embedded in the masonry of Rushall Hall, Staffordshire. For many years there was also a ball cemented into the town wall of Hereford.[2]

A newspaper story from 2001 describes the surprise of a couple at Bishop Auckland who found a cannon shot in their vegetable patch: this was later attributed to the nearby Civil War siege of Witton Castle. In a similar vein a small ball was recovered from a garden in Garstang, Lancashire, not far from Greenhalgh Castle which was besieged at the end of the First Civil War. Another odd find occured during building works at the Butcher's Arms, at Prior's Hardwick, Warwickshire,

[1] J. Wroughton, 'An Iron Cannon Ball', in South Gloucestershire Council *Archaeology News-letter*, 3, 2002.
[2] The shot from the walls of Hereford is now item 2003–48 in the Hereford Museum and Art Gallery collection.

in 1970: the ball is imagined to be linked with the battle of Edgehill. As in so many instances context has proved crucial since some varieties of iron shot were in use before or after the Civil Wars, as well as during the critical 1642 to 1651 period.[3]

In some instances cannon balls found long ago have remained associated with a particular building or location with Civil War significance. Broughton Castle, seat of the Parliamentarian Lord Saye and Sele, retains a small collection of balls which relate to its brief investment in October, 1642. Colchester Castle, which has since become a museum, similarly keeps relics fired during the siege of 1648. At Highworth, near Swindon, a seventeenth century shot has for many years been retained in the church. At Gloucester a number of shot have been brought together in the collections of the Folk Museum, not far from where they were found. Warrington Museum likewise holds cannon shot associated with the local area. The collections of both the Royal Armouries and Royal Artillery hold large numbers of shot of all descriptions, though specific Civil War associations are more difficult to determine.[4] On a less grand scale a single complete and unexploded 'granadoe' was long associated with a house called 'Little Pitchford' near Yalding in Kent. It has been assumed that this artefact is a relic of 1648, but it is also near to some of the sites where such munitions were produced. Two shot examined at Fleetwood in the 1970s have been associated with the wrecking of the Spanish vessel *Santa Anna*, at Preesall, in 1643.

Cannon shot are not always as easy to recognise as might be supposed, and difficulty of positive identification is not due merely to rust and damage. Iron spheres have been used in a number of post seventeenth century machines, as for example in 'ball mills' used to crush material for the extraction of pigments. Weight, dimensions, and archaeological context therefore all need to be taken into account. Since 1997 the national 'Portable Antiquities Scheme' has made more systematic attempts to record metal detector and other archaeological finds, that predate 1700, and have come up outside the ambit of organised excavations. Using local 'Finds Liaison Officers' these are listed on a data base accessible via the internet. Where possible these are noted with find spots. The number of pieces continues to increase, but at the time of writing 45 'cannon' related artefacts are registered, of which a few are worth noting:[5]

SUR–563F66	A small iron ball weighing almost one and a quarter pounds, found in a Surrey garden. This is one of two shot believed to be linked to a skirmish at Redhill Common in 1648.
WMID2875	An iron ball supposed to be that of a 'robinet' – found in the Parish of Norton, Herefordshire.

3   *Northern Echo*, 20 June 2001, and Butcher's Arms publicity.
4   Category or class 'xx' in the Royal Armouries collections, 'xxi' in the Royal Artillery collections; Gloucestershire Records Office D 2210/10,18 'Finds of Shot', 1950.
5   www.findsdatabase.org.uk

WAW–4E4F31	An iron ball weighing just under 4 pounds, found during gardening at Powick, and assumed to be associated with the Civil War actions of either 1642 or 1651.
WAW–45EDE1	An iron ball weighing just under 8 ounces, found in Warwickshire.
LANCUM–C8BA64	A 14.5 cm diameter iron ball found by a metal detectorist in his own garden in Cumbria, along with small arms projectiles, and thought to be associated with the siege of Carlisle.
LANCUM–177960	A small cannon ball discovered at Higher Wheelton, Lancashire, whilst the finder was gardening.
LANCUM-F3A9A7	A ball of 47 mm discovered with a metal detector near Walton-le-Dale, Lancashire.
LANCUM–F3CD10	A ball similar to the above, found within a mile of the first.

These last three Lancashire examples have been interpreted as confirming the presence of Scottish artillery on Walton hill during the 1648 battle of Preston. One further saker ball, recorded in Oxfordshire in 2007, has not been added to the database due to uncertainty surrounding the find spot and date of finding.[6]

6 Thanks are due to Finds Liaison Officers Charlotte Burrill (Berkshire and Oxfordshire), Dot Bruns (Lancashire and Cumbria) and Frances McIntosh (Cheshire, Greater Manchester and Merseyside) for assistance with this data.

Appendix III

The Parliamentarian Artillery Train of 1642 details extracted from PRO WO 528/131/2, PRO WO 55/387, and the 'Catalogue of the Names', BL E 83 (9)

'An Account of Divers Necessary Provisions Materials and Instruments of War Bought of Several Persons for the Traine of Artillerye Under the Command of his Excellency the Earle of Essex Lord Generall of the Armies Imployed for the Defence of the Protestant Religion the safetie of his Majesty's Person and of the Parliament the Preservation of the Laws Liberties & Peece of the Kingdom and Protection of his Majesty's subjects from Violence and Oppression.'

Ordnance

Quantity	Description		
11	'short drakes of 3 lb bullet'	1	'demi culverin drake'
4	'6 pound brass ordnance'	1	'whole culverin'
6	'12 lb'	6	mortars

Artillery ammunition

2400	3 lb shot.
1043	6 lb shot – 'bought of Thomas Fosson'
400	Culverin and demi culverin shot
600	Granadoes – at least part of which 'bought of John Browne'
unclear	Crossbar shot – 'bought of John Browne'
300	'Cases for Shot' [case shot – various sizes]

Canvas, paper and formers, for 'tents and cartridges'

667.5 ells	'Bought of Richard Thorowgood'
10 quire	'Paper Royal'
50	Cartridge formers, various sizes.
unclear	Scoops and funnels, various.

Other artillery accessories

44	Linstocks
44	Rammers

Two per gun	Sponges
36	Wad hooks
Two per gun	Ladles
200	Handspikes
30	Budge barrels
48	Powder horns 'with strings'

Other tools

227	Hatchets
88	Large axes, various
213	Pickaxes
3220	Spades and shovels
94	Hammers all sizes (including sledge, pointing etc)
53	Mallets
30	Crow bars
66	Saws (pit, two man, hand etc)
110	Baskets, various (for shot, carrying, etc)
40	Hand barrows

Wood and leather working equipment, including punches, set squares, vices, shears, chisels, gimlets, needles, thread, wedges, spoke shaves, gouges, adzes, rulers, compasses.

Lighting equipment, including cresset lights and lanterns.

Equipment to secure prisoners, including chains, 13 pairs of handcuffs, neck collars, a 'bond of mercy', shackles etc, all enclosed in a special chest.

Ropes – of various sizes and lengths.

Chalk rolls and lines.

Mobile forge, complete with bellows 'great' and 'small' a hearth, bolts, pincers, tonges, rivets, nails, armour plate, spare iron, files, vice, spare fittings for carriages and wagons, horse shoe equipment, three large and four small anvils etc.

Small arms ammunition

30 cwt	Musket shot (plus 12 rounds per musketeer?)

*Officers of the Train, time of Edgehill and
published December 1642*

General of the Ordnance	John Earl of Peterborough
Lieutenant General of Ordnance	Philibert Emanuel du Boyes
Assistant	Nicholas Cooke
Engineer (with six assistants)	John Lyon
Commissaries of Ordnance	George Vernon and John Phipps
Surveyor General	Captain Peter Cannon

Gentlemen of the Ordnance

Thomas Holyman	Joshua Sing
Robert Barbar	George Ramson
Patrick Strelley	Samuell Beny
Edward Wase	Daniell Barwick
Anthony Heyford	Thomas Rawson
Robert Bower	Thomas Sippence
Henry Edson	Thomas Grosse
James Franklin	Thomas Ayres
Richard Honey	William Hickson

Carriage Master for Artillery	John Fowke
Principal Conductor	William Crawley
Quarter Master	George Wentworth
Captains 'to the 600 Pioneers'	Edward Frodsham, Henry Roe, John Dungan
Lieutenants 'to the 600 Pioneers'	Gerard Wright, Benjamin Hodson, Thomas Williams
Master Gunner	Lancelot Honiburne
Provost Marshal	Christopher Troughton
Battery Master	Edward Okely
Fireworker, Petardier	Joachim Haine
Fireworker, Petardier	William Roberts
Bridge Master	Herman Browning
Assistant Bridge Master	John Herdine
Captain to '100' firelocks	Lieutenant General du Boyes
Lieutenant to Captain du Boyes	Richard Price

Appendix IV

The Establishment of the King's 'Trayne of Artillery' (Oxford Army), June 1643 extracted from Rawlinson Ms D 395 ff 208–9

General of Artillery	Henry Lord Percy
(Secretary to the General)	
Lieutenant General	Sir John Heydon
(Two Clerks to Heydon)	
Comptrollers	Captain Younger and Monsieur Montgarnier
(Two Clerks to the Comptrollers)	
Commissary for the Munition of the Train	Captain Marsh
(Two Clerks)	
Commissary for the Munition of the Army	Mr Sherburne
(Two Clerks)	
Assistant to the Commissaries	Mr Eastbrooke
(One Clerk)	
Engineer	Mr Fluery
(One Clerk)	
Two Conductors	
'Another' Engineer	Captain Shebis
(One Clerk)	
Two Conductors	
Comproller of the Bye Train	Captain Fossett [Samuel Fawcett ?]
Battery Master	Mr Betts
(One Assistant ?)	
Twelve Gentlemen of the Ordnance	
Chaplain	Mr Lloyd
Paymaster	Mr Stanforth
(One Clerk)	
Commissary for the Draught Horses	Mr Wynn
(One Assistant and One Clerk)	
Purveyor	Mr Cole
Messenger	Mr Flowerdue
Quartermaster General	Mr Audeley

Surgeon	Mr Franklyn
(Two Surgeon's Mates)	
Principal Conductor	Mr Ball
(44 Conductors)	
Tentmaker	Mr Pickford
(One Assistant)	
Tent Keeper	
(Two 'Servants')	
Nine Gunfounders	
Master Armourer	Mr Sherman
(Six Armourers)	
Master Gunner	Mr Smith
Master Gunner's Mate	Mr Busy
Petardier	Mr Hendrick
(69 Gunners)	
Conductor of the Matrosses	Mr Atkins
(88 Matrosses)	
Captain of the Pioneers	Mr Balis
Lieutenant of the Pioneers	
(200 Pioneers)	
Master Smith	Mr Bastien
(Two Farriers)	
(10 Smiths)	
Master Carpenter	Collins
(11 Carpenters)	
(12 Wheelwrights)	
(Two Collar makers)	
Master Cooper	
(Two Servants)	
Gunsmith	
Gunstock maker	
Turner	
Ladle maker	
Wagon Master	
(43 Carters)	
Provost Marshal	
(One servant, four Assistants)	

Appendix V

The Equipment and Personnel for One Gun and One Mortar, and Infantry Munitions, dispatched from Oxford in May 1643: PRO WO 55/458.65, ff 7–8

Oxford 16 May 1643

A Proportion of Powder, Match, Shott &c to attend one Peece of Ordnance and one Morter Peece assigned for his Majesty's service under the Comaund of Prince Maurice; by warrant from his Majesty; the 16th of May 1643, viz,

Brasse Ordnance
Mounted with their Equipage   12lb Peece – one

Morter Peece of brasse
with its Equipage   one

Cases of Tynne with Musket shott for 12 lb Peece	10
Round shott of Iron for 12 lb Peece	40
Granadoes for the Morter Peece	24
Powder	10 Cartouches
Match	10 Skeynes
Budge Barrell	one

Materiallls and other Utensills

Shovells	4
Spades	4
Pickaxes	2
Spare harneis	6
Spare Rope	
Hedging Bills	2
Axes	2
Hurdles	
Cloutes	13
Cloute Nailes	250
Lynch Pinns	16
Horse Shooe	
Hores Shooe Nailes	

Munition for the Foote

Powder	20 cwt (and 30 lb for the fire master)
Match	40 cwt
Muskett shott	20 cwt

Waggons 2. Carts 10. Horses 67.

Officers and Ministers

Mr Herrick with the Fireworks

Conductors 4:
William Adamson and James Benoist   – to attend the Morter Peece
Richard Parke   – for the Munition
Robert Dalton   – for the Draught

Gunners 3:
James Severett to assist Mr Herrick
George Woodcock
Robert Gower

Matrozes 6: to attend the Morter Peece
John Peirce
Thomas Arnold
John Benningfield
Humphrey Terry
William Pare
Walter Sherman

Matrozes 4: to attend the 12 lb Peece
Richard Broomfeild
James Powell
Thomas Douse
Thomas Ketch

Carpenter	Thomas Davyes
Wheelewright	Thomas Belger
Smyth	John Alleyne

Appendix VI

Guns captured by the King's army at Bristol, July 1643 as Listed in Rawlinson Ms D 395 ff 138–139, 'Survey' by Samuel Fawcett

Demi Culverins	4
Sakers	19
Minions	33
Falcons	7
Falconets	11
Robinets	19
Murderers	4
Mortar	1

Total 98 Pieces

Munitions captured by the New Model Army at Bristol September 1645 as noted by Joshua Sprigge in Anglia Rediviva, 1647

Guns	151 (about 140 of which 'mounted')
Powder	100 barrels
Muskets	2–3,000

Appendix VII

The Artillery and Officers of the New Model Army
Details extracted from PRO WO 47/1, ff 108–118;
CSPD DIII, 1644, pp 499, 500, 517;
House of Lords Journal, 10, p 71, and
J. Sprigge *Anglia Rediviva*, London, 1647, pp 329–330

Artillery ordered for the train 30 September 1644

2	demi culverins
4	Sakers
14	Drakes

The 14 drakes were ordered from John Browne on 3 October 1644: in the meantime on 4 October the House of Commons ordered that two brass demi culverins; four brass sakers and two 6 lb drakes be provided out of the guns presently at Tower wharf.

Officers of the Train, as listed by Joshua Sprigge, 1647

Lieutenant General Hammond, Lieutenant General of the Ordnance
Captain Deane, Comptroller of the Ordnance
Master Hugh Peter, Chaplain to the Train
Peter Manteau van Dalem, Engineer General
Captain Hooper, Engineer Extraordinary
Eval Tercene, Chief Engineer
Masters Lyon and Tomlinson, Engineers
Master Francis Furin, Master Gunner of the Field
Master Matthew Martin, Paymaster to the Train

Also,
Master Phips, Commissary of Ammunition
Master Thomas Robinson, Commissary of the Draught Horse
Captain-Lieutenants of the Firelocks, Desborow and Brent.
Captain of Pioneers, Captain Cheese

Listed separately under senior officers and staff,
Master Richardson, Wagon Master General
Commissary General of Horse Provisions, Captain Cooke (killed at Naseby – replaced by Commissary Jones)

Omitted by Sprigge,
Master Fireworker Joachim Haine

According to the *House of Lords Journal* the complements of the various sections were,

Gunners: One Master Gunner; four gunner's mates; 40 gunners; 120 Matrosses
Engineers: One Chief Engineer; one Clerk; Master Fireworker; one petardier; one assistant.
Firelocks: Two companies, each comprising a Captain, Lieutenant and Ensign; two sergeants, three corporals, and 100 men.

The daily pay of the Chief Engineer was 6s, with 4s each for the Master Gunner and Master Fireworker. Gunner's mates and gunners received 2s, Matrosses 1s.

Appendix VIII

The Ideal Artillery Train
according to BL Harleian Ms 6844, 'A Short Treatise
Concerning All Things Needfull in an Armye
According to Modern Use', c. 1660

2   48 lb 'Whole Cannon', drawn by 42 horses.
8   24 lb Demi Cannon, drawn by 104 horses.
10   Block Carriages for road transport.
3   Spare Carriages for battery guns, with 17 spare horses.
6   12 lb 'Field Pieces', with 48 horses and two spare field carriages.
24   6 lb 'short Drakes', with 52 horses and four spare carriages.
24   3 lb 'small Drakes', with 28 horses and four spare carriages.
2   Heavy mortars firing 100 lb shells, with 17 horses and three carts or carriages.
3   Medium mortars firing 50 lb shells, with 17 horses and three carts or carriages.
3   Small mortars firing 25 lb shells, with 7 horses and four carts or carriages.

Each piece of ordnance to have 'its ladle sponge and rammers ... two wedges', touch holes to be covered with 'sheepes skinne', also a provison of spares and ropes, and 'cords' to allow man hauling of the pieces.

Ammunition

	Round shot	Cartridges
Cannon	600	100
Demi Cannon	400	400
12 lb	3000	300
6 lb	6000	3000
3 lb	6000	3000

Granadoes   800 of various sizes
Fireballs   400 of various sizes
Stone shot   800 of various sizes

Appendix IX

The Masters and Officers of the Ordnance c. 1610–1660 extracted from Ordnance Quarter Books, *DNB* and State Papers

The letters 'R' or 'P' denote Royalist or Parliamentarian allegiance during the Civil Wars.

Masters and Masters General

George Carew, First Earl Totnes	1608–1629
Horace Vere, First Baron Vere of Tilbury	1629–1634
Mountjoy Blount, First Earl of Newport (R)	1634–1661

Lieutenants and Lieutenants General

Sir Roger Dallison	1608–1616
Sir Richard Moryson	1616–1625
Sir William Harrington	1625–1626
Sir William Heydon	1626–1627
Sir John Heydon (R)	1627–1642
John Pym (P)	1643
Sir Walter Erle (P)	1644–1650
Major General Thomas Harrison (P)	1650–1652
Vacant	
William Legge	1660–1670

Surveyors of the Ordnance

Sir John Kay	1608–1625
Sir Alexander Brett	1625–1628
Sir Paul Harris	1628–1631
Francis Conningsby (R)	1631–1642
George Payler (P)	1642–1657
Elia Palmer (P)	1657–1660

Clerk of the Ordnance

Francis Morice	1608–1632
Edward Sherburne (Senior)	1632–1642

Edward Sherburne (Junior) (R)	1642
John White (P)	1642–1658
Lewis Audley (P)	1658–1660
Edward Sherburne (Junior)	1660–

Keeper of the Store

Sir Roger Ainscough	1610–1612
Samuel Hales	1612–1616
Ned Tracy Smart	1616–1621
Thomas Powell	1621–1638
Richard Marsh (R)	1638–1642
John Falkner (P)	1642–1660
Richard Marsh	1660–

Clerk of Deliveries

Robert Johnson	1603–1633
George Clark (R)	1633–1642
Stephen Darnelly (P)	1642–1644
Thomas Haselrigg (P)	1644–1646
William Billers (P)	1646–1660
George Clark	1660–

Master Gunners of England (1600–1660)

Stephen Bull	–1607
William Bull	1607–1611
William Hammond	1611–1623
John Reynolds	1623–1638
James Weymss (P: Captured at Cropredy 1644)	1638–1647
Richard Wollaston (P) Acting later confirmed in post	1649–1660
James Weymss	1660–

Proof Masters (1600–1660)

Often two proof masters in post simultaneously.

Stephen Bull & William Hammond	–1607
William Hammond	–1623
John Reynolds	1611–1638
John Dwarris	1623–1642
John Lanyon (R)	1638–1642
William Franklin (P)	1643–1647
William Roberts (P)	1647–1660

Richard Bagnell	1660–
John Lanyon	1660–

The Ordnance Office establishment also included a Plumber; Smith; Carpenter; Wheeler; Fletcher; Bowyer; Keeper of small guns; Cooper; Furbishers; and Keeper of Rich Weapons. Engineers were officially on the books from 1627 to 1634, and a Store Keeper and Proofmaster of the Armoury replaced the Keeper of Rich Weapons in the 1650s. There were also junior clerks and clerks to Masters, and 'Labourers' – commonly about 20 at any given time.

Appendix X

Typical Firing Sequence for
a Small to Medium Sized Gun using a crew of three:
reconstructed from passages in various sections of
William Eldred's *Gunner's Glasse*, London, 1646, and
other manuals of the period 1620–1650

1. The gun is moved into position, pointing in roughly the direction of the target – using additional matrosses if required by weight of the piece and roughness of the terrain.
2. The gunner's two assistants take position to the left and right of the gun. The right-hand man ensures that the sponge (and ladle if used) is placed on the right of the gun, 'between the wheel and carriage'. He then stands with a ball of the right calibre at the ready. The left-hand assistant attends to the wads 'of Ocam, or hay, or straw', making sure that two are ready to hand – perhaps placed between the spokes of the gun carriage wheels to make sure they are not blown away. He then brings up the budge barrel (or the bagged charge), on the left side of the gun.
3. If this is the first round of a bombardment or engagement the bore of the gun is 'searched' to check that there are no obstructions – for example if the piece has already been left loaded, or is blocked by other detritus. The ladle is handy for this purpose, and having no iron parts is unlikely to cause any dangerous sparks if wielded swiftly. Wads or damp bagged charges etc, can be removed with a wad hook. All operations around the bore are done with the gunner standing to one side of the muzzle or the other – so as to avoid being killed by an accidental discharge.

   If this is not the first round the piece will require sponging with a damp sponge. This makes sure that there are no hot embers to cause a premature explosion, and reduces the amount of burnt powder etc. fouling the bore. As an additional safety precaution one of the crew might 'serve the vent', by placing his thumb or finger over the touch hole. This would both prevent drafts of air keeping embers alight, or premature ignition by a crewman who had misjudged the sequence.
4. Loading the powder. For ladle loading the left hand assistant holds the barrel whilst the gunner charges the ladle, and then puts the powder into the bore, turning the ladle over and gently tapping to make sure that all the powder is deposited into the gun. The charge is then 'put up' by means of the rammer, and followed down by a wad and again rammed. For cartridge loading the bagged charge is slid into the muzzle, and firmly seated using the rammer.

5. Loading the shot. The gunner 'regards' the shot that he is handed by his assistant, double checking it is the right calibre. He then places it into the barrel of the gun and gently 'puts it home' with the rammer. The shot is followed by the final wad which is rammed with 'three strokes'.

6. 'Gaging' or aiming. The gunner takes aim along the barrel: if the target is very close, or very large, correction by eye is adequate. If particular accuracy is needed, or a small or distant target is engaged the gunner may use a 'dispart' as a fore sight and his own peep sight, or a slotted device to make sure breech, muzzle, and target are all in perfect alignment. Beyond 'point blank' ranges it may be necessary to use some elevation of the barrel to fire 'at randon'. Firing at very long ranges may be assisted by the use of a quadrant to judge angle of elevation, and a table relating elevation to range. To aid the gunner the assistants use handspikes and quoins (wedges) to produce fine adjustments to aim – one concentrating on the traverse, or horizontal movement, the other on the vertical, or elevation.

7. Priming. The gunner pushes a reamer or pricker through the touch hole, thus cleaning it out and piercing any bagged charge. He then pours powder from his flask into the hole, leaving a little exposed at the top. The gun is now ready to fire.

8. Firing. All the crew except one assistant retire from the piece, and the gunner views the target. At a signal or the command to give fire a linstock is used to apply a smouldering match to the touch hole. As he does so the firer stands to one side as far as possible, and moves smartly to avoid the recoiling gun.

After each shot the gun is 'put back' i.e. moved back to its firing position after it has recoiled. Thereafter the firing sequence can be begun again. Eldred appears to have been particularly keen to perform all the loading functions himself. In some other authorities second gunners, matrosses or assistants are sometimes left do the ramming and other physical tasks – leaving the gunner to worry about aim, safety, and the logistics of getting everthing in the right place and sequence. A gun could be left loaded, which was particularly common on shipboard or when a gun position was suspected to be at risk from surprise attack, or left empty. In either instance a wooden muzzle bung or 'tampion' would help prevent powder being spoiled or foreign objects entering the muzzle. In emergency the gun could be fired with the bung still in place, blowing it out.

Glossary

Arquebus, Harquebus Early form of hand held powder and shot weapon, for cavalry or infantry use. Usually of small calibre.

Astragal A band on a gun barrel.

Axletree, Extree Wooden beam or block upon which wheels are mounted; axle.

Bace, Base (single or double) Small piece of artillery, usually sixteenth century, often of iron and sometimes breech loading.

Basilisco, Basilisk Exceptionally large piece of artillery, often of bronze, named after the mythical creature with death dealing eyes. The 'Great Basilisco' of Dover was a specific long barrelled gun also known as the 'Queen's Pocket Pistol' which was actually cast in the Low Countries for Henry VIII.

Bastard Illegitimate in a general sense: a weapon not fitting its expected place regarding the standard weights and proportions of a given category. Often an artillery piece shorter, or of thinner metal.

Battel Main body of an army. Can approximate to 'battalion' in the modern sense rather than 'battle'.

Battery Group of guns; gun position; or the act of firing guns upon a target.

Beat In the artillery sense, to 'batter upon', or to dislodge.

Bed Support for gun or mortar, often wood. Mortar beds are sometimes also referred to as 'stocks'.

Blind Screen of canvas, wood, or other material designed to hide men or ordnance especially during siege warfare.

Block carriage Long road travelling carriage for heavy ordnance commonly constructed from baulks of timber and having four wheels. Unlike the field or garrison carriage a piece of artillery could not usually be discharged from the block carriage.

Bombard Large calibre piece of artillery common in the medieval period and sometimes reused in the sixteenth or seventeenth centuries with various forms of shot.

Budge barrel Wooden barrel to carry propellant powder or charges.

Bye train A subsidiary or independent train. See 'Train'.

Bulwarkes, Bulwarks Rampart or bastion, especially artillery defence.

Button Knob at breech end of gun. See also 'Cascabel'.

Caliver Short hand held firearm discharged from the shoulder; short musket usually smooth bored. Occasionally a mound upon which to place artillery. See also 'Cavalier'.

Cannon (Royal; seven, eight etc.) General term for ordnance for ship or siege: 'Cannon Royal' is the largest category; 'Cannon of seven' and 'eight' are guns with these calibres in inches.

Cannon basket   For protection of guns, crews, or troops. Similar to 'Gabion'.

Cannon perrier   Piece of ordnance for firing stone shot. Common in sixteenth century, sometimes breech loading mounted on swivels. Reused in seventeenth century usually on castles and ships.

Capsquare, Capsquire   Iron plate fitting over trunnions of a gun to hold it in its carriage; commonly fastened with a 'Capsquare Pin'.

Carcass   Type of artillery projectile held in a frame, usually of a incendiary or scattering nature.

Carriage   Wheeled support or vehicle for a gun: may be subdivided into field, ship, garrison etc.

Carriage master   Officer or official in charge of carriages for ordnance and stores.

Cartouche, Cartridge   Case of canvas or paper holding the powder charge for a weapon. Occasionally also used to describe scatter shot in a case or bag.

Casamate   Casemate; place of defence; vaulted chamber.

Cascabel, Cascable   Knob or button at the breech end of a gun; sometimes used loosely to denote the entire breech.

Case shot   Bag, tube, case, or other container of small shot or fragments for ordnance to engage close range targets.

Cavalier   Gentleman on horseback; arrogant; gun platform raised or 'proud' of surrounding area.

Chamber   Part of gun in which the charge is placed. Early breech loaders often had a separate removable jug- shaped chamber.

Champion   Field; open ground; similar to French 'champs'.

Chase   Bore of a gun; concavity; space inside barrel.

Cheek   Side piece of gun carriage or other equipment.

Circumvallation   An encircling trench or fortification; enclosing element.

Clive shot   'Cleaved' or split shot; shot in parts or articulated.

Cock   Moving part of firearm lock; moving arm with jaws evocative of the bird.

Coin   See 'Quoin'.

Cole   Charcoal.

Conductor   Junior officer in charge of the movement of artillery, carriages or men. Overseer of carters, transport officer.

Cornet   A pennant, or cavalry flag; the junior officer charged with carrying a cavalry standard.

Corslet   Suit of armour, especially a 'half armour' for pikemen, or 'three quarter' armour for cavalry.

Counterscarp, Counter sharfe   Outer wall or slope of a ditch. Area of line swept by defensive fire.

Culverin (demi, whole etc)   Long barrelled artillery piece originally noted for its high charge to shot weight ratio. Bores commonly ranged from four to six inches, demi being literally 'half' culverins. Commonly ranked under cannons in siege trains.

Curtain, Curten   Defensive wall, especially one linking two strong points, bastions or towers.

Curtal, Curtow   Early gun name approximating to 'Cannon'. Obsolete by seventeenth century.

Cutt, Cutts   Gun or guns with short barrel, and sometimes thin barrels.

Dispart   Difference between the radius of a gun barrel at the muzzle and breech. A stick or sight placed on the gun muzzle used to equal out this difference and so provide a valid line of sight.

Dog lock - Gun lock, usually for small arms, with a 'dog' or safety catch.

Dolphins   Moulded lifting handles or lugs on top of a gun barrel about the centre of gravity, often in the shape of a dolphin or fish.

Dowledge, Duledge   Pieces of wood or metal joining together the parts of a wheel.

Drake   A piece of ordnance, often light, and with a taper bored chamber. Common type in use with field armies of Civil War period, often used in conjunction with 'Case' shot.

Drug, Drugge   Low sledge or carriage for moving heavy objects, such as gun barrels.

Eprouvette   Device for testing gunpowder.

Ensign, Ensigne   Colours, or colour bearing junior officer, of infantry. A signal or flag.

Falcon, Fawcon, Faucon   Long barrelled light gun, often between two and three inches calibre, named after the bird of prey.

Fearn   Type of jack; piece of machinery with notches for lifting heavy objects.

Fellies, Felloes, Fellows   Curved pieces of wood forming the rim of a wheel.

Firelock   Small arm which operated by striking fire, usually reference to early form of flint lock.

Firemaster   Officer in charge of pyrotechnics, mortars and fireworks; type of siege engineer.

Flanking piece   Gun firing down a flank or across a breach; gun covering ditch, fortification or body of troops from an angle.

Floukemouthed piece   Bell mouthed, or oblong mouthed, short gun.

Forecarriage   Wooden, usually two wheeled, carriage for pulling a piece of ordnance. See also 'Lymer'.

Forelock, Forelockey   Similar to 'Capsquare', flat or pin designed to join hinging metal plates.

Forlorne hope   Skirmishers; small advanced guard.

Forme, Former   Cylindrical piece of wood used to make cartridges.

Fortified   Protected or reinforced. In ordnance used to denote thicker metal than usual.

Fowler   Small gun, usually breech loading. Obsolete by Civil War.

Gabion   Large container, usually of wickerwork, packed with earth to protect guns or troops.

Gages   Any measuring device, though commonly applied to a ring or rings through which shot were passed to judge their size.

Geometrical pace   Measurement of length or distance approximating to five feet.

Ginn, Gynn   Device for lifting heavy gun barrels, usually incorporating a tripod and pulley but possibly ratchet .

Granadoe, Grenade, Grenadoe   Explosive spherical shell or bomb. 'Hand' grenades were of about two inches diameter, the largest mortar rounds 18.5 inches.

Graze   To hit ground or object without halting, as in 'shot graze' etc.

Gunner's rule   Ruler, usually folding, with tables of data such as shot tables and distances. Could be used at the breech of a piece to measure elevations. Some incorporated a slot or hole for sighting.

Hailshot   Multiple or scattering shot. 'Hailshot pieces' guns firing such shot, common in the sixteenth century.

Halfemoon   'Half moon', or 'demi lune' a term often applied to crescent or half circle shaped defensive works.

Hall, Halle   Archaic term applied to the concavity or bore of a weapon.

Handspike   Lever, usually of wood, used to assist in turning or moving ordnance.

Home bored   Straight bored: having a chamber of the same internal dimension as the barrel.

Honeycombed   Like a honeycomb, perforated with small holes, especially imperfections from casting or wear.

Ladle   Scoop on a wooden shaft used for powder: could also be applied to a metal spoonlike tool used in metal casting.

Lames   Overlapping or articulating plates.

Langrel   Expanding, opening, or scattering shot.

Leather gun   Lightweight piece of composite construction, commonly having an internal cylinder of metal with bindings of wire, or ropes, and leather covering.

Linstock   Shafted implement, usually having screwed jaws or a slot, to hold a slow match for firing ordnance.

Limber, Limours, Lymers   Pole like shaft, or shafts, to assist in towing ordnance or carriage. Later applied to the two wheeled carriage which supported the gun whilst under tow. See also 'Forecarriage'.

Matchlock   Gun, usually a shoulder arm, set off with a match; also the mechanism designed to achieve this ignition.

Matrose, Mattrosse   Junior gunner; gunner's mate; artillery labourer.

Minion   Small artillery piece, usually long barrelled and of about three and a quarter inches in bore.

Mortar   Short piece of ordnance, usually of large bore, for throwing shells or stones at high angle and low velocity. Frequently used in sieges, but could occasionally also be mounted horizontally for firing scatter shot.

Murderer, Murtherer   Short barrelled gun firing anti personnel scattering shot. Frequently obsolete ordnance so used to cover close range access to forts and castles.

Musket   Long barrelled infantry arm, usually smooth bored.

Muzzle   Open end of barrel; fore portion of ordnance.

Organ gun, Organos, Organys Multiple barrelled weapon; weapon like an organ in appearance.

Partridge Multiple shot. Term possibly derived from game shooting, and sometimes confused, even in original sources, with 'Cartridge'.

Peterero, Pederero Similar to 'Cannon Perrier'; piece for firing stone shot.

Petard Explosive device or bomb used for blowing in gates or other parts of fortifications. Often comprised a metal container fixed to a base board.

Platform Gun position for mounting ordnance; usually of wooden boards and/or stone.

Plumbline, Plumb bob Weighted line for finding verticals.

Point and blank, Point blank To fire a gun horizontally; to shoot without using elevation. To shoot at a close range, literally at the 'white' of a target.

Portfire Fuse or match held in a staff or stick used to ignite ordnance or literally to 'carry fire'. Similar to, but often simpler than, a 'Linstock'.

Portpiece Small gun, often breech loading, usually mounted in fortifications to cover a 'port' or entrance.

Potgun Gun with separate chamber.

Pounder, 'Pdr' Gun measured in terms of its weight of shot. Hence '3 pdr': gun firing three pound shot.

Primer, Priming powder Powder, usually of small grain, easily ignited, to set off propellant charge.

Priming iron Spike used to clear the vent of a piece.

Proof To ensure or 'prove' a piece fit for service; to fire by way of test.

Quadrant Instrument similar to a large protractor with a line to show angles of elevation. Variations used in both astral navigation and gun aiming.

Quoin, Coyne, Coin Wooden wedge used to elevate the breech of a piece.

Rabinet, Rabonet, Robinet Small piece, sometimes described as 'of culverin type', with a bore of about an inch.

Rammer Staff implement used to drive home charges or wads, sometimes combined with a sponge or ladle.

Reinforce To build up or make stronger; especially thick part of barrel or breech.

Roundshot Solid shot, usually of cast iron, but also lead or stone.

Run up Push up or bring forward a piece of artillery. Return a gun to its place in a battery.

Saker Medium sized piece of culverin type, firing a ball of about five to seven pounds. A versatile and common type.

Sconce, Skonce Small fort; independent or semi independent strong point.

Scraper Tool for cleaning bore of a weapon.

Searcher Staff or staves designed or modified to check for flaws in a gun barrel.

Serpentine Any snake like object as for example the match holder on a matchlock weapon.

Serpentine powder Smooth powder not granulated, or other powder intended for use under the serpentine of the matchlock.

Shell   Case of metal or other material containing powder; explosive projectile. Term derived from the animal shells found in the natural world.

Skidd   Bed, sledge or rest for ordnance or other heavy item.

Screwed, Skrewed   To be turned; to have rifling; to be bored out; to have a screw in place.

Small shot   Hand held firearms; projectile weapon of small size.

Snaphance   Snapping jaw or lock; early form of flintlock.

Spike   Point, pointed tool. Also used as verb, i.e. to spike guns, blocking the vent and hence rendering unserviceable.

Sponge   Staff implement with head of absorbent material, such as sheepskin, for cleaning and damping the bore of a piece.

Stock   Wooden part of gun: term can be applied to small arms, or to the wooden bed of a mortar.

Stonegun   Weapon for shooting stone projectiles. See also 'Cannon Perrier'.

Strake   Metal plate, especially those fitted to wheels.

Swivel   Device allowing object or equipment to turn: often applied to pivoting 'swivel guns'.

Tampion, Tompion   A wad or board between charge and shot, or, more commonly a plug or bung to close the muzzle of a gun against weather or debris.

Touch hole   Small hole to which a match, wire or other incendiary agent is applied to set off a gun. Also known as the 'vent'.

Train   Artillery, baggage, and supplies for a force. Often used in the sense of a convoy, or to refer to a group of wagons and other transport.

Transom   Transverse piece or horizontal block, as in the piece of wood joining the cheeks of a gun carriage.

Traverse   To turn, especially ordnance.

Truck   Small wooden wheel, or carriage having such wheels. General term for small sturdy trolley or mount for ordnance etc.

Trunnions   Projections from a gun barrel, normally at the centre of gravity. These could be used to mount a barrel in a carriage, and allowed the piece to pivot in a vertical plane for elevation.

Turned   Worked on a lathe, or alternately 'drilled out'.

Vanguard   Forward part, advanced guard of army etc.

Vawmure   A wall, defence or emplacement to the front.

Vent   See 'Touch hole'.

Wad   Straw, cloth, grass or other material used to keep powder and shot in place, or put between powder and projectile to separate them.

Wadhook   Staff implement with hook (or spiral element) for removing a wad or charge etc. See also 'Worm'.

Windage   Gap, especially the internal space between the projectile and the bore of the gun when loaded.

Worm   A spiral resembling a worm; name for spiral implement to remove obstructions from a gun barrel. See also 'Wadhook'.

Illustrations

The Parts of a Carriage

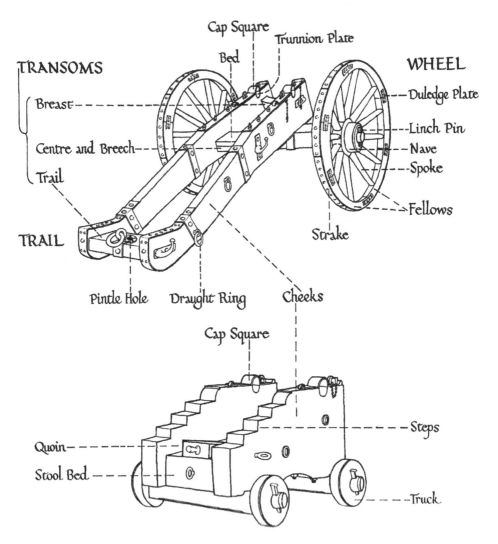

1. The parts of the gun carriage. Showing, top, a typical land carriage; bottom, a typical sea carriage, sometimes also used in fixed defences. (Howard Blackmore, 1976)

2. Bronze 'falcon' cast by the Owen brothers in 1549, on a reproduction carriage, on show at Carisbrooke Castle, Isle of Wight. Each parish on the island maintained its own field gun for local defence – and this one remained in situ from new until 1850. Many of the guns in the localities were already antiques by the time the Civil Wars commenced in 1642. (SB, 1985)

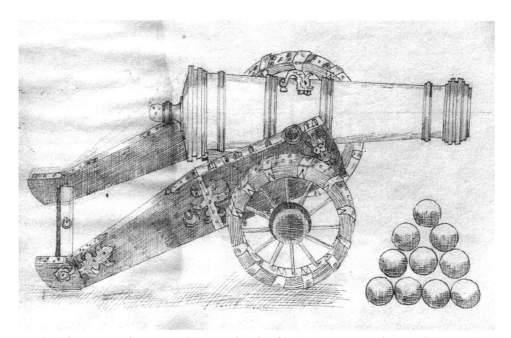

3. A mid seventeenth century German sketch of a siege cannon with typical iron work to the carriage and 'dolphin' type top lugs. Note the decorated 'cascable' at the rear of the barrel and the 'reinforce' rings which encircle the barrel at intervals. (Royal Artillery Institution, 1981)

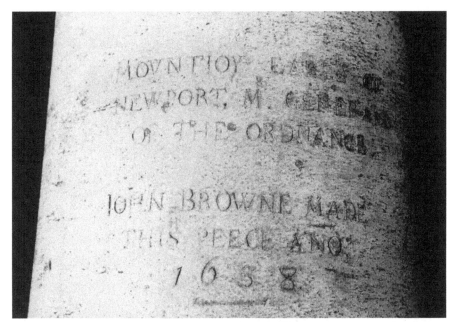

4. Inscription on a bronze 4 pound gun, which reads 'Mountjoy Earle of Newport Mr General of the Ordnance. John Browne Made This Peece Ano 1638'. It also bears the 'Rose and Crown' and 'CR' of King Charles I. A weight inscription reads '2–2–25', meaning 2 cwt 2 quarters and 25 pounds. Probably cast at Brenchley this gun is typical of modern bronze light ordnance in use during the Civil War period. (Royal Armouries Catalogue number XIX 170. SB, 1981)

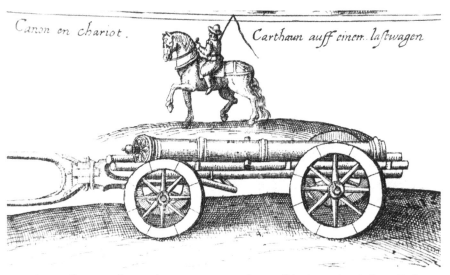

5. A heavy 'battering' piece being transported on a 'block carriage', from Robert Norton's *The Gunner*, 1628. Using four wheels smoothed the progress of barrels weighing thousands of pounds over the rutted roads of early modern Europe, but transferring the weapon back to its field carriage took time. Robert Norton (1575–1634) studied engineering and gunnery under Master Gunner of England John Reynolds, and was first granted a gunner's position in 1624. (SB, 1984)

Ætatis Suæ 83.

Ad Lectorem.

When Age, and Art, and Industry behold,
Doth all inure, Experience being guide e
Then who will fay, but furely this may bee,
A piece of Work exact from dotage free.

T. F.

6. Master Gunner William Eldred of Dover, pictured in 1646 aged 83. Eldred became known as author of *The Gunners Glasse*, a valuable compendium of knowledge published at the end of the First Civil War – though much of Eldred's experimentation actually predates the war by some years. (Royal Artillery Institution SB, 1981)

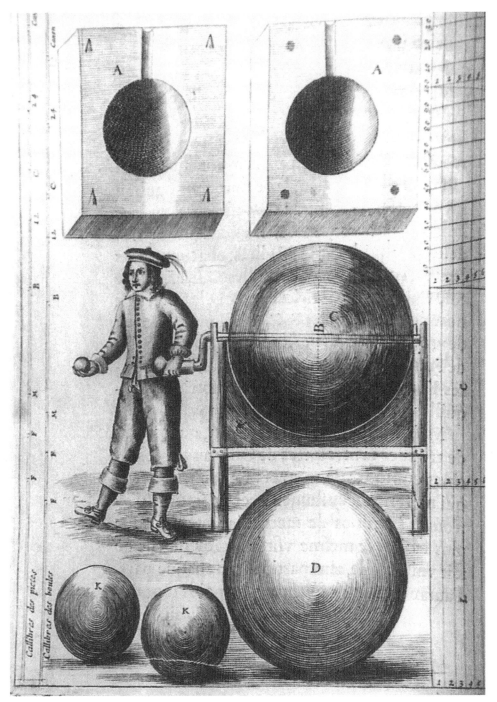

7. Shot and casting moulds from Malthus's *Pratique de la Guerre*, 1650. Basic iron roundshot were produced by casting in two part moulds which were keyed together, with the molten metal introduced through a narrow channel. (SB, 1986)

8. Making wooden fuses, from Malthus's *Pratique de la Guerre*, 1650. Effectively wooden tubes filled with slow burning powder fuses were used in mortar 'granadoes' and other pyrotechnics and explosive devices. (SB, 1986)

9. Shot used during the attack on Broughton Castle, Oxfordshire, seat of Lord Saye and Sele, in 1642, and kept at the same site ever since. (SB, 1985)

10. Shot at Lyme Regis Museum, used during the siege of Lyme, April – June 1644. (SB/Fowles, 1985)

11. An engineer or 'firemaster' lighting a mortar using two matches – one to ignite the fuse of the granadoe, the other to set off the propelling charge. From Malthus's *Pratique de la Guerre*, 1650. (SB, 1983)

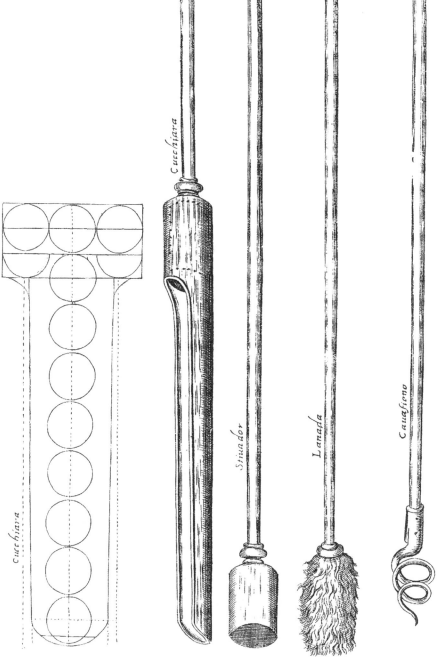

Cucchiara

Cucchiara

Striuador

Lanada

Cauafieno

12. Gunnery equipment: the ladle, rammer, sponge and worm or wadhook. From Pietro Sardi *L'Artiglieria*, Venice, 1621. (SB, 1981)

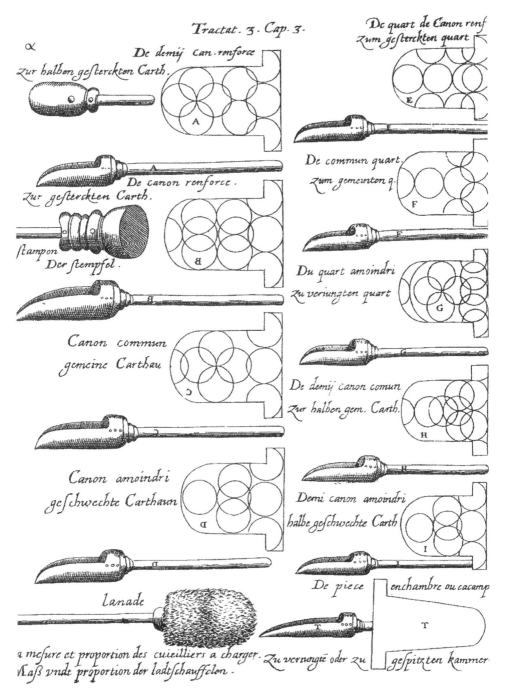

α

Tractat. 3. Cap. 3.

De demij can.renforce
Zur halben gesterckten Carth.

De quart de Canon renf
Zum gesterckten quart

De canon renforce.
Zur gesterckten Carth.

ftampon
Der ftempfel.

De commun quart.
Zum gemeinten q.

Du quart amoindri
Zu veriungten quart

Canon commun
gemeine Carthau

De demij canon comun
Zur halben gem. Carth.

Canon amoindri
geschwechte Carthaun

Demi canon amoindri
halbe geschwechte Carth

lanade

De piece enchambre ou cacamp

a mesure et proportion des cuieilliers a charger. Zu verrengte oder zu
Maß vndt proportion der ladtfchauffelen. gefpitzten kammer.

13. Ladles of different sizes, showing how they are produced in relation to the ball used
by the piece. Also shown are a sponge and rammer. From Robert Norton, *The Gunner*,
1628. (SB, 1981)

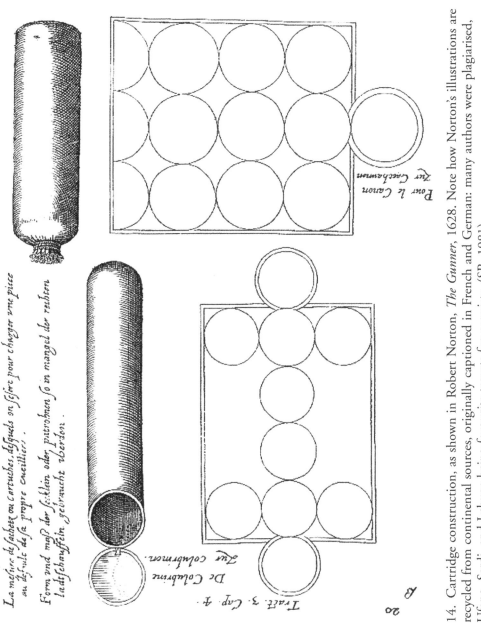

La mesure de sacher ou cartuches, desquels on se sert pour charger une pièce ou de suit de sa propre escuillières.

Form und maß der sacklein oder patronhen so in mangel der rechten ladtschauffein gebraucht werden.

De Colubrine
Zur colubrinen.

Pour le Canon
Zur Catthaunen

Tratt 3. Cap 4.

20
8

14. Cartridge construction, as shown in Robert Norton, *The Gunner*, 1628. Note how Norton's illustrations are recycled from continental sources, originally captioned in French and German: many authors were plagiarised, Ufano, Sardi, and Lehuga being favourite targets for copyists. (SB, 1981)

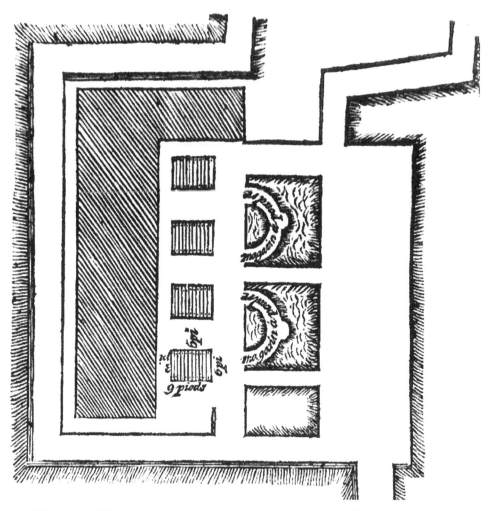

15. Plan of a well laid out siege battery position, with four wooden gun platforms fronted by a thick wall of earth and covered powder magazines to the rear. Trenches enable the gunners and matrosses to go about their business to and from the position unmolested by snipers. From St. Julien *La Forge de Vulcain*, 1606. (SB, 1986)

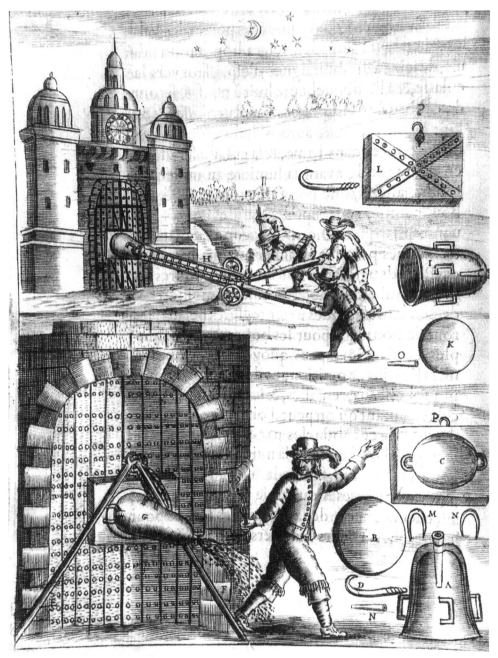

16. Petardiers at work, from the *Traité des feux Artificiels*. The petard was effectively a bomb on a wooden base plate which engineers would use to blow open the gates of fortresses. Engineer specialists or fireworkers with mortars and petards were usually included in the artillery trains of both sides. (SB, 1981)

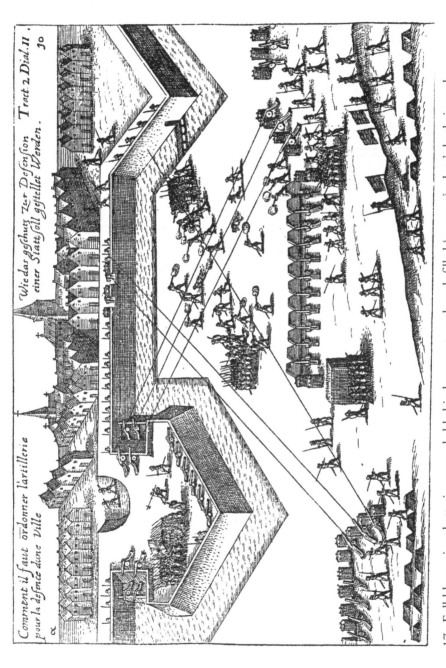

17. Full blown siege batteries concealed behind ramparts and earth filled 'cannon baskets' do their work against enemy bastions, from Robert Norton, *The Gunner*, 1628. The latest technique was to use several sorts of ordnance from different angles, lighter weapons being used to target enemy guns, whilst the biggest cannon smashed breaches in walls. (SB, 1992)

CHAP. XXXVI.

The manner of framing a Quadrangle Skonse.

His Foure-square Skonſe, is of greater ſtrength than your Triangle, and if it be favoured with a ſtrong Scituation, as great Rivers, or upon a Rocke, or where it may be flanckered from the Bulworks of a Fort, it will ſtand in great ſtead; otherwiſe it is not to be taken for a ſtrength of any moment: The Bulworkes and Curtines are to be made very high, thicke, and ſtrong, that it may endure the battering of the Enemies Ordnance.

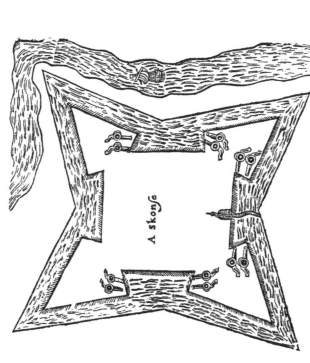

A Skonſe

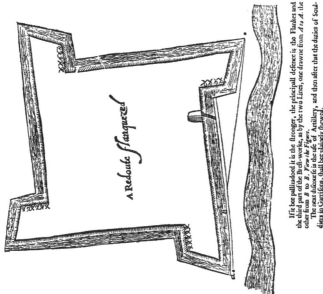

A Redoute Flanqured

If it bee palliſadoed it is the ſtronger, the principall defence is the Flankes and the third part of the Breſt-worke, as by the two Lines, one drawne from *A* to *A*, the other from *B* to *B*. *View the Figure.*
The next diſcourſe is the uſe of Artillery, and then after that the duties of Souldiers in Garriſon, ſhall bee plainely ſhewd.

18. Artillery sconces [skonces] from Ward's *Animadversions of Warre*, 1639. Note how rivers have been used in both instances to help cover one or more faces of the fortification, giving attacking troops another obstacle to scale if they are to storm the position. (SB, 1992)

THE QUEEN'S SCONCE, NEWARK

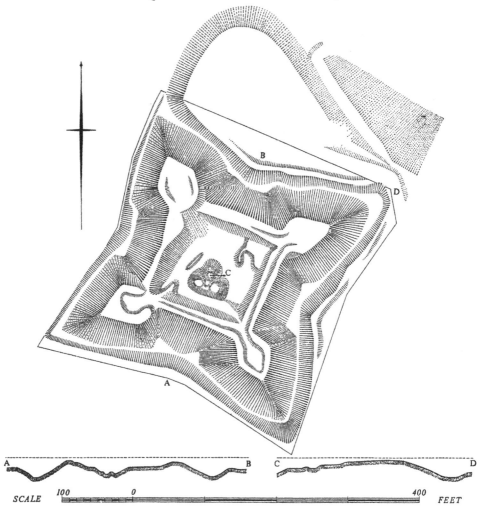

19. A twentieth century plan of the vast and impressive 'Queen's Sconce' at Newark. Contemporary confirmation of the scale of the Royalist defences may be found in the work of Robert Clampe, a Parliamentarian engineer who produced his own drawings at the time of the siege. Only masses of earth could hope to stop the shot of siege cannon. (Royal Artillery Institution)

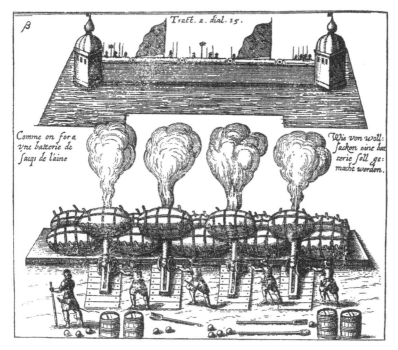

20. Detail of a four-gun siege battery position, with planked wooden gun platforms and wool sacks used as improptu cover to the front. Note the shot, powder barrels and ladles in the foreground. The gunners carry swords and use portfires or linstocks to fire the ordnance. The number of artillerists shown is far fewer than are mentioned in contemporary Civil War documents: 25 to 30 gunners and matrosses and a battery master would be much more likely to crew such a position. The battery itself would be constructed by pioneers and carpenters working under the direction of an engineer, and to the rear carters were needed to look after the wagons and horses required by the guns and ammunition. (SB, 1990)

21. A gunner 'gives fire' to his piece, standing, as contemporary instructions make clear, to the side of the gun, whilst other crew stand well back. Engraving by Jacque Picart, in Malthus's *Pratique de la Guerre*. (SB, 1983)

22. A dramatic moment during the siege of Prague, 1648. Many of the elements seen in this contemporary depiction were common to events in England. In the foreground is a communication trench covered with faggots which allows troops to advance unseen. Nearby a siege gun is being man hauled to its final battery position, on a platform partially defended by cannon baskets, whilst friendly troops attempt to engage the defenders' snipers. In the distance a mortar battery hurls granadoes at high trajectory over the defences into the City. With troops running up in numbers the storm is imminent. (SB, 2006)

23. A Swedish type 'leather gun' pictured at the Danish Royal Armoury or Tøjhusmuseet, Copenhagen. Though it is unlikely the leather covered thin metal barrels would have proved very durable, leather guns were extremely manoeuvrable and case shot could be very destructive at close range. Just how diminutive this piece is is shown by the arsenal catalogue in the foreground – a booklet just 22 cm high. (SB, 1982)

24. The gunner at work.

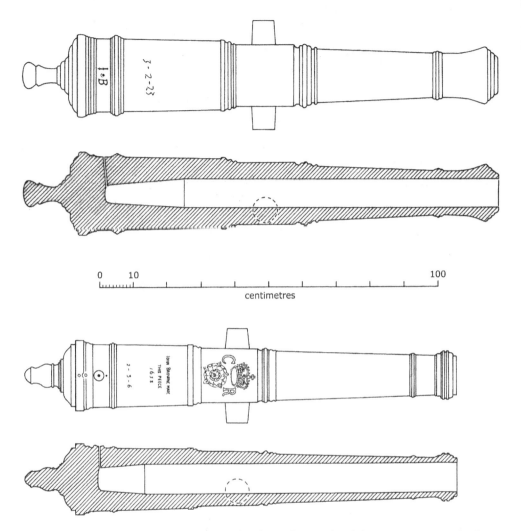

25. The John Browne iron 'Minion Drake' from the wreck of the pinnace *Swan*, built in 1641 and sunk in 1653 (top), and the similar bronze gun from Boston, Lincolnshire (bottom) dated 1638. Both guns fired four pound projectiles. The short length and taper bored chamber typical of Drakes are readily apparent in both examples. Note the weight and founders markings. (Drawings by Colin Martin; Boston depiction after an original by Rudi Roth)

26. The approved way to bring down walls: battering low and working upward in a concentrated pattern. From Thomas Smith *Art of Gunnery*, London, 1643 edition, page 45.

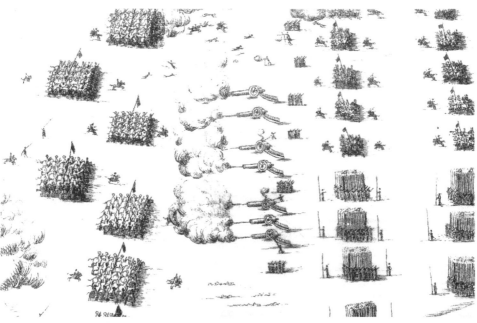

27. A typical battlefield deployment of the artillery, ahead of the main bodies of the infantry. Note that small groups of skirmishers are also seen about the gun line, and that the ordnance has opened fire on the enemy cavalry. From a continental drawing of the period.

Bibliography

MANUSCRIPT SOURCES

BRITISH LIBRARY

For BL E references, see 'Primary Sources, the Thomason Tracts', p. 232 below.

Additional Ms

5497   Notes on Gravesend 1642–1643.
5752   Documents relating to Naval and Military Affairs.
5754   'An Accompt of Dayes Expended by Bernard Johnson, Engineer'.
6703   'A True and Exact Journall', of the Isle de Rhe, 1627.
9298   'Proceedings' of the Isle de Rhe, 1627.
11,331   Letter Books of Sir William Brereton c. 1644–1646.
16,371   Plans of Sir Bernard de Gomme. (Naseby, Marston Moor etc)
23,224   Treatise on Military Tactics.
26,051   'Voyage of Rease' and the 'Order of March of … Prince Maurice'.
27,892   'Arte of Bombardry', 1728.
28,082   Army Establishments: Seventeenth and Eighteenth Century.
32,363   Illustrations of Kent, Including Fortifications.
34,325   Royalist Issues of Ordnance.

Birch Ms

4473   'A Table Werein You May Find the Names of Great Ordnance'.

Cotton Ms

Aug I Vol I   Plans of Dover Defences and Elizabeth Castle, Jersey.
Otho EIX   'A New Engine for Throwing Shot'.
Otho EXI   Papers Relating to Levies and Musters.

Egerton Ms
785–7   The Letter Books of Samuel Luke.
2584   Letters of Lord Zouch.
2642   Commuandre Collection 'Invention of that Horryble Intrument of Gonnes'.

Harleian Ms
304   John Sheriffe on Ordnance.
519   'The Instituition and Discipline of a Soldier'.
6851   'List of Officers' and 'Artillery in Carlisle', 1640–1641.
7364   Treatise on Tactics.

King's Ms
261   Treatise on Artillery.
265   Transcripts of Naval Papers, and the Army for the Palatinate, 1620.

Lansdowne Ms
213   William Georges. 'Survey of 26 Counties'.

Rawlinson Ms
395   Royalist Ordnance Correspondence.

Royal Ms
17A XXXI   John Linewray 'Survey of the Ordnaunce'.
17A LIII   George Carew 'New Forme of Great Artillerie', 1611.
17B XXXII   'The Siege of Julich', 1610.
17C XXII   John Shoote 'Remembrancer to a General', 1598.
17C XXXV   'A Description of Severall Fireworks', 1613.
18C XXIII   'Lord Wimbledon's Demonstration ... of War', c.1624.

Sloane Ms
562   Drawings and Notes of Prince Rupert.
629   'Militia New and Old'.
871   'The Coppie of Mr Linewray's Book'
2396   'Lyst of Provisions ... for the Trayne of 50 Pieces'.
3651   William Bourne, 'Book of Ordnance', c.1573.

DEVON AND EXETER RECORDS OFFICE

DD 391   Accounts of Pay and Fortification During Sieges and Civil War.
DD 34815   'List of Provisions', 1644.
DD 34816   'A Warrant for the Impressment of Pioneers'.
DD 34817   Horses, Provisions and the King's Defeat at Naseby.
DD 36995   Provisions for the Defence of Exeter, 1643.
48/26/7/1   Petition of Wlliam Venner, Sergeant at Lyme, 1644.
53/3/10/8   Commission to John Morgan, Captain of Matrosses, 1642.

GLOUCESTERSHIRE RECORDS OFFICE

D 115   Letters and Papers Concerning Gloucester, 1643.
D 2210/10, 18   Finds of Shot in Gloucester, 1950.

D 2510   Unpublished documents of Cheshire, Gloucester and Shropshire.
GBR F4/5   City Chamberlain's Accounts.
TRS 146   Artillery of the King at Gloucester, 1643.
TRS 168   Letter of Thomas Daunt Concerning Bombardments, 1646.
TRS 186, 199   Miners for the King at Gloucester.

KENT ARCHIVE OFFICE

Browne Ms
TR 1295/1–20   Property documents, bills and legal cases.
TR 1295/23   Will of George Browne, 1651.
TR 1295/24–27   Papers relating to Browne Servants, Wills and Expences.
TR 1285/47–96   Browne Business Papers, Lists of Cannon c. 1608–1665.
TR 1295/97   'The Pedigree of George Browne of Spelmonden', c.1650.
P45/1/1   Parish Register of Brenchley, 1539–1654.

LAMBETH PALACE LIBRARY

604, 615, 620   Letters to, and from, Lord Carew.
629   'A Perfect Note of all the Brasse and Iron Ordnance' (Ireland)
1611   Josias Bodlye on Irish Forts, Gunners and Artificers.

NATIONAL ARCHIVES (formerly Public Records Office)

State Papers Series (SP)
14/94   Ordnance Inventory, 1617.
16/58/89   Artillery Officers for the Isle de Rhe, 1627.
16/65   'Examination of Michael Donnivido, Gunfounder', 1627.
16/65/19   John Burgh, 'Complaints' 1627.
16/65/37   Warrant to Bernard Johnson to Appoint Deputies.
16/66/2,6   Sir William Heydon's Letters, 1627.
16/66/25   Warrant Regarding 'Water Engines', 1627.
16/80/45   Requirements of Carriages, 1627.
16/278   Regarding the Exchange of Brass Guns for Iron in Forts, 1634.
16/ 319, 350,371   Lists of Saltpetre Delivered 1632–1637.
19   Papers Relating to the Committee for the Advance of Money.
28/131/2   Essex Train of Artillery, 1642.

War Office Series (WO)
25/1   Commission Books, 1660–1684.
30/37   Contracts Register, 1654–1658.
47/1–4   Minutes of the Ordnance, 1644–1660
48/1   Treasuers Ledger, 1660–1664.
49/17–93   Debenture Books, 1592–1660.
49/110   Estimates, 1639.
51/1–3   Bill Books, 1630–1663.
54/1–20   Ordnance Office Quarter Books, 1594–1660.
55/386–387   Entry Book of Warrants, 1642–1643.
55/457–459   Warrants Relating to Stores, 1642–1644.

55/460–464   Various Warrants.
55/1625–1650   Issues to Parliamentarian and Royalist Forces.
55/1658   'Remain' of the Stores, 1634.
55/1659   Stores Issues from Oxford and London, Civil War.
55/1661   Royalist Stores at Oxford.
55/1672   'View and Survey' of the Ordnance, 1595.
55/1679–1680   Ordnance Inventories, 1620 – 1632.
55/1684   Distribution of Land Stores, 1627.
55/1685   La Rochelle Expedition 'Remain', 1628.
55/1689   'View and Survey', 1634.
55/1690   Inventories of the Tower, Navy, etc. 1634–1635.
55/1691–1695   Stores Distributions, King and Parliament.
55/1699   Ordnance Inventory, 1665.
55/1752   Master of the Ordnance, Papers on Stores and Arms 1578–1681.
55/1753   Indentures and Papers, 1578–1681.
55/1754   Warrants Relating to Stores, 1578–1681.
55/1937   Warrants Relating to Stores, 1642–1643.

NATIONAL ARMY MUSEUM

5903–142   Receipts for Ordnance Stores.
7405–13   Documents Concerning Arming and Tactics 1617–1643.
9010–31   Papers of Brigadier Peter Young

NATIONAL MARITIME MUSEUM

CAD C/1   Ordnance Office Survey, 1595.
CAD C/2   Remains of Stores after the Death of Thomas Bedwell.
PLA/P/11   'Wasted in the Primrose … 1573'.

ROYAL ARTILLERY INSTITUTION

MD 975   List of Payments by William Legge, 1667.
MD 976   Abstract of Orders and Commissions, 1414–1688.
MD 979   Inventory of Artillery for La Rochelle.
MD 997   Ledger of Prices of Stores and Equipment, c.1680.
MD 1438   Notes on Garrisons and Fortifications

Not numbered   The 'Feuerwerkers Buch' of A. Buchwitz von Breslau.
Not numbered   The Coates Manuscript, c. 1660.

PRIMARY SOURCES, PRINTED IN ENGLISH

Anon. *Chester's Triumph in Honour of Her Prince.* London, 1610.
Anon. *Englands Defense … in the Year 1588.* London, 1680.
Anon. *Englands Savety … in the Navie and Fortifications.* London, 1652.
Anon. *The Exercise of the English, in the Militia.* London, 1641.
Anon. *The Great and Famous Battle of Lutzen.* London, 1633.

Anon. *Instructions for the Musters*. London, 1623.

Anon. *The Invasions of Germany, with … all the Bloody Warres Therein 1618–1638*. London, 1638.

Anon. *Lawes and Ordinances … of Warre, for the Better Government of his Maiesties Army Royall*. London, 1639.

Anon. *The Mansion of Magnanimite … with a Briefe Table, Showing, what Munition Ought to be Kept by the Sorts of Her Maiesties Subjects*. London, 1599.

Anon. *The Military Discipline*. London, 1642.

Anon. *A Most True Relation of the Present State of His Majesties Army*. London, 1642.

Anon. *A New Invention of … Shooting Fireshafts in Longbows*. London, 1628.

Anon. *The Oppuguation and Fierce … Siege of Ostend*. London, 1601.

Anon. *Orders Established … And Agreed unto by the Societye of Armes*. London, 1616.

Anon. *An Ordinance of the Lords and Commons in Parliament for the Safety and Defence of the Kingdom of England*. London, 1641.

Anon. *The Overthrow of an Irish Rebell in a Late Battaile*. Dublin, 1608.

Anon. *Relation of the Battel Between Duke Bernard van Wimmern and John de Weerdt*. London, 1638.

Anon. *The Rudiments of Military Discipline*. Edinburgh, 1638.

Anon. *The Swedish Intelligencer*. London, 1632.

Anon. *A True Description of the Discipline of War*. London, 1642.

Anon. *A True Discourse of All the Sallyes Which the Soldiers of Grave Have Made*. London, 1602.

Anon. *A True Relation of the Victorie Atchieved by Count Maurise*. London, 1600.

Anon. *A Ture Report of the Great Overthrowe Lately Given Unto the Spaniards in Their Resolute Assault of Bergen Op Zoom*. London, 1605.

Achesone, James. *The Military Garden*. Edinburgh, 1629.

Adams, Thomas. *The Souldiers Honour*. London, 1617.

Anderson, Robert. *The Genuine Use and Effects of the Gunne*. London, 1674.

Babington, John. *Pyrotechnia*. London, 1635.

Barriffe, William. *Mars His Triumph*. London, 1638.

Barriffe, William. *Militarie Discipline or the Young Artillery Man*. London, 1635 (enlarged editions, 1643 and 1661, and reprinted 1988).

Barry, Gerat. *A Discourse of Military Discipline*. Brussels, 1634.

Barwick, Humphrey. *A Breefe Discourse, Concerning the Force and Effect of all Manuall Weapons of Fire*. London, 1594.

Bingham, John. *The Historie of Xenophon*. London, 1623.

Bingham, John. *The Tactiks of Aelian*. London, 1616.

Binning, Thomas. *A Light to the Art of Gunnery*. London, 1676.

Bourne, William. *The Art of Shooting in Great Ordnance*. London, 1578.

Boyle, Roger. *Treatise of the Art of War*. London, 1677.

Camden, William. *Remains Concerning Britain*. Edn. of 1614.

Carter, Matthew. *A True Relation of the Expedition of Kent, Essex and Colchester in 1648*. London, 1650.

Cavendish, Margaret. *The Life of William Cavendish*. London, 1667.

Cecil, Edward. *A Journall and Relation of the Action which E. Lord Cecil did Undertake Upon the Coast of Spaine*. London, 1630.

Churchyard, Thomas. *A Pleasant Discourse of Court and Wars*. London, 1596.

Clayton, Giles. *A Briefe Discourse of Martiall Discipline*. London, 1591.

Cooke, Edward. *The Character of Warre*. London, 1626.

Cooke, Edward. *The Prospective Glasse of Warre*. London, 1628.

Cruso, John. *Militarie Instructions for the Cavallerie.* Cambridge, 1632.

Cruso, John. *Don Praissac's Art of War.* Cambridge, 1639.

Cruso, John. *Castramentation, or the Measuring Out of Quarters.* Cambridge, 1640.

D, I. *Lawes and Ordnances Touching Military Discipline.* The Hague, 1631.

Dansie, John. *A Mathematical Manuel … and the Embattelling of Armies.* London, 1627.

Davenant, Charles. *Essays Upon Ways and Means of Supplying War.* London, 1695.

Davis, Edward. *Military Directions.* London, 1618.

Davis, Edward. *The Art of War, and England's Traynings.* London, 1619.

Dekker, Thomas. *The Artillery Garden.* London, 1616.

E, J. *A Letter from a Souldier of Good Place in Ireland.* London, 1602.

Eldred, William. *The Gunners Glasse.* London, 1646.

Fisher, Thomas. *Warlike Directions or the Souldiers Practice.* London, 1643.

Fludd, Robert. *Dr Fludds Answer … for Wiping Away of the Weapon Salve.* London, 1631.

G.A. *Pallas Armata.* London, 1639.

Gaya, Louis de. *A Treatise of the Arms and Engins of War.* London, 1678.

Gerbeir, B. *Interpreter of Fortification.* London, 1648.

Gheyn, Jacob de. *Exercise of Arms.* 1607.

Greaves, John. 'Experiments for Trying the Force of Great Guns', in *Philosophical Transactions*, 173, July 1685.

Grimestone, Edward. *A True Historie of the Memorable Siege of Ostend.* London, 1604.

Gumble, Thomas. *The Life of General Monck.* London, 1670.

Gunter, Edward. *The Description and Use of the Sector Crosse-Staffe and other Instruments.* London, 1636.

Heywood, Thomas. *A True Description of his Majesties Royal Ship Built 1637 at Woolwich in Kent.* London, 1637.

Hexam, Henry. *A Journal of the Taking of Venlo.* Delft, 1633.

Hexam, Henry. *The Principles of the Art Militarie.* The Hague, 1637–1643.

Hexam, Henry. *A True Relation of the Battel of Nieuport in Flanders.* London, 1641.

Hugo, Herman. *The Siege of Breda.* GHG trans, London, 1627.

Ive, Paul. *The Practise of Fortification.* London, 1589.

Kellie, Sir Thomas. *Pallas Armata, or Militarie Instructions.* Edinburgh, 1627.

L, A. *Speculum Belli Sacri: Or the Looking Glasse of the Holly War.* London, 1624.

Leslie, Alexander. *Exercising of Horse and Foot.* London, 1642.

Lithgow, William. *Present Surveigh of London.* London, 1643.

Lucar, Cyprian. *Tartaglia.* London, 1588.

Lucar, Cyprian. *A Treatise Named Lucar Solace.* London, 1590.

Lupton, Donald. *A Warre-Like Treatise of the Pike.* London, 1642.

Malthus, Francis. *A Treatise of Artificiall Fire-Works Both for Warre and Recreation.* London, 1629.

Marcelline, George. *The Triumphs of King James the First.* London, 1610.

Marcelline, George. *Vox Militis.* London, 1625.

Markham, Francis. *Five Decades of the Epistles of Warre.* London, 1622.

Markham, Gervase. *The Souldiers Accidence.* London, 1625.

Markham, Gervase. *The Souldiers Grammar.* London, 1626.

Markham, Gervase. *The Souldiers Exercise.* London, 1643.

Marlois, Samuel. *The Art of Fortification.* (H. Hexam trans) London, 1638.

Mernault, Peter. *The Last famous Siege of the City of Rochel.* London, 1680.

Monck, George. *Observations Upon Military and Political Affairs.* London, 1671.

Monro, Robert. *Monro his Expedition with the Scots Regiment.* London, 1637.

Moore, Jonas. *Elements of Modern Fortification.* London, 1673.

Neade, William. *The Double Armed Man*. London, 1625.

Niccols, Richard. *Londons Artillery*. London, 1616.

Nixon, Anthony. *The Wares of Swethland*. London, 1609.

Northumberland, Earl of. *Lawes and Ordinances of War*. London, 1640.

Norton, Robert. *Of the Art of Great Artillery*. London, 1624.

Norton, Robert. *The Gunner*. London, 1628.

Norton, Robert. *The Gunners Dialogue*. London, 1643.

Norwood, Richard. *Fortification, or Architecture Military*. London, 1639.

Nye, Nathaniel. *Art of Gunnery*. London, 1647.

Palmer, Thomas. *Bristolls Military Garden*. London, 1635.

Peacham, Henrie. *A Most True Relation of Cleve and Gulick*. London, 1615.

Peeke, Richard. *Three to One Being, An English Spanish Combat*. London, 1626.

Pelegromius, Simon. *A Description of S'Hertogenbosh … Together with the Principall Points … Concerning the Last Siege*. London, 1629.

Praissac, du. *The Art of War*. London, 1639.

Pricket, Robert. *A Souldiers Wish unto his Soveraigne*. London, 1603.

Prynne, William. *Eight Military Aphorisms*. London, 1658.

Rich, Barnaby. *The Fruites of Long Experience … A Looking Glass for Warre*. London, 1604.

Roberts, John. *The Compleat Cannoniere*. London, 1639.

Roberts, John. *Great Yarmouths Exercise*. London, 1638.

Rohan, Henri Duc de. *The Complete Captain*. London, 1640.

S, R. *A Briefe Treatise, to Prove the Necessitie and Excellence of the Use of Archerie*. London, 1596.

Scott, Thomas. *The Belgick Souldier*. Dort, 1624.

Segar, Sir William. *Honor, Military and Civill*. London, 1602.

Seller, J. *The Sea Gunner*. London, 1691.

Shute, William. *The Triumphs of Nassau*. London, 1613.

Simienowicz, Casimir. *Art of Artillery*. Trans J Shelrocke, London, 1729.

Silver, George. *Paradoxes of Defence*. London, 1599.

Smith, John. *A Seamans Grammar*. London, 1627.

Smith, Thomas. *The Art of Gunnery*. London, 1600 (new edn 1643).

Smith, Thomas. *Certain Additions to the Book of Gunnery*. London, 1627.

Smith, Thomas. *The Complete Soldier, Containing the Whole Art of Gunnery*. London, 1628.

Smythe, Sir John. *Certain Discourses Military*. London, 1590.

Smythe, Sir John. *Instructions, Observations & Orders Mylitaire*. London, 1595.

Sprat, Thomas. *History of the Royal Society*. London, 1667.

Sprigge, Joshua. *Anglia Rediviva*. London, 1647.

Stapleton, John. *History of the Low Country Wars*. London, 1650.

Stowe, John. *Survey of London*. London, 1598.

Stowe, John. *Annales*. London, 1630.

Strada, Faminius. *A History of the Lowe Country Warres*. London, 1650.

Styward, Thomas. *The Pathway to Martial Discipline*. London, 1591.

T., J. *The ABC of Armes*. London, 1616.

Trussell, Thomas. *The Souldier Stating His Own Cause*. London, 1619.

Turner, James. *Pallas Armata*. London, 1683.

Vicars, John. *Englands Parliamentary Chronicle*. London, 1646.

PRIMARY SOURCES, THE THOMASON TRACTS

Perhaps the single most important primary source for the English Civil War is the collection of 22,000 printed items brought together by London bookseller George Thomason (d. 1666), and now generally referred to as the *Thomason Tracts*. These are preserved in approximately 2,000 bound volumes in the collections of the British Library. A two volume catalgue to the collection by G.K. Fortescue entitled *Pamphlets, Books, Newspapers, and Manuscripts Relating to the Civil War, the Commonwealth, and Restoration, Collected by George Thomason*, was produced by the British Museum in 1908. The collection was later microfilmed, and a catalogue of the microfilmed edition was published in 1978. Rather than attempt to list here the many relevant items, that only feature once or twice each in the text, they are cited individually in the notes. Items from the *Thomason Tracts* series are readily identifiable by the British Library catalogue numbers which are prefixed 'E'.

SIGNIFICANT PRINTED WORKS IN FOREIGN LANGUAGES

Baudert, W. *Le Guerres de Nassau*. Amsterdam, 1616.

Belidor, Forest de. *Le Bombardier Francois*. Paris, 1731.

Bianco, Alessandro Capo. *Corona e Palma Militare dei Artiglieria*. Venice, 1602.

Biringuccio, V. *De la Pyrotechnia*. Venice, 1540.

Boyvin, Jean. *Le Siege de Dole*. Anvers, 1638.

Brechtel, Franz Joachim. *Buchsenmeistery*. Nuremburg, 1591.

Busca, Gabriello. *Instruttione de Bombardieri*. Turin, 1598.

Collado, Luigi. *Practica Manuale de Arteglieria*. Venice, 1586.

Davelourt, Daniel. *Trois Traictez sur le Faict de L'Artillerie*. Paris, 1617.

Freitag, Adam. *L'Architecture ou la Fortification Novelle*. Leiden, 1635.

Fronsperger, Leonhard. *Kriegs Ordnung und Regiment*. Frankfurt, 1564.

Furtenbach, Joseph. *Architectura Martiallis*. Ulm, 1630.

Furtenbach, Joseph. *Halintro-Pyrobolia*. Ulm, 1627.

Furtenbach, Joseph. *Buchsenmeisteren Schul*. Augsburg, 1643.

Lehuga, Christoval. *Discurso Del Capitan Christoval Lehuga*. Milan, 1611.

Malthus, Thomas. *Pratique de la Guerre*. Paris, 1650.

Rivault, David S. de Fleurance. *Les Elemens de L'Artillerie*. Paris, 1605.

Ryff, Walter. *Geometrischen Busenmeisterey*. Nuremburg, 1547.

Sardi, Pietro. *L'Artiglieria*. Venice, 1621.

von Schorndorf, J. Schmidlap. *Kunstliche und Rechtschaffene Feuerwerck*. Frankfurt, 1608.

St. Julien. *La Forge de Vulcain*. La Haye, 1606.

Ufano, Diego. *Trato De Artilleria*. Brussels, 1613.

von Wallhausen, J.J. *Archilery Kriegkunst*. Hanau, 1617.

Zubler, Leonard. *Newe Geometrische Buchsenmeisteren*. Zurich, 1619.

PRIMARY SOURCES: TRANSCRIBED OR EDITED WORKS

Adair, J. (ed). *They Saw it Happen. Contemporary Accounts of the Siege of Basing*. Hampshire County Council, 1981.

Atkinson, J.A. (ed). *Tracts Relating to the Civil War in Cheshire*. Manchester, 1909.

Bamford, F. (ed). *A Royalist's Notebook. The Commonplace Book of Sir John Oglander.* London, 1936.

Barlow, T.W. (ed). 'The Diary of Edward Burghall', in *Cheshire its Historical and Literary Associations.* Manchester, 1855, pp 150–189.

Bateson, M. (ed). *Records of the Borough of Leicester.* Three vols, Cambridge, 1899–1905.

Calendars of documents. *Calendar of the Acts of the Privy Council*

———. *Calendar of State Papers, Domestic.* London, 1856–1897.

———. *Calendar of State Papers.* Venetian. London, 1864–1897.

Carlyle, T. (ed). *Oliver Cromwell's Letters and Speeches.* Three vols, 1846.

Cary, H. (ed). *Memoirs of the Great Civil War.* London, 1842.

Coates, W.M. (ed). *The Journal of Sir Simonds d'Ewes.* Yale, 1842.

Copnall, H. (ed). *Nottinghamshire County Records ... of the Seventeenth Century.* Nottingham, 1915.

Cox, J.C. (ed). *Records of the Borough of Northampton*, vol 2. Northampton, 1898.

Dobson, A. (ed). *The Diary of John Evelyn.* London, 1908.

Dore, R.N. (ed). *The Letter Books of Sir William Brereton.* Records Society of Lancashire and Cheshire, cxxiii, two vols, 1984 and 1990.

Ellis, H. (ed). 'The Letters of Nehemiah Wharton', in *Archaeologia*, vol xxv, 1853, pp 310–334.

Evans, D.E. (ed). *Equipping a Seventeenth Century Army. An Estimate of the English Forces Required for War in the Palatinate.* Llanidloes, 1985.

Everitt, A. (ed). 'An Account Book of the Committee of Kent for 1647–1648', in *Seventeenth Century Miscellany*, Kent Records, vol 17, 1960.

Ferguson, J.F. (ed). *Papers Illustrating the History of the Scots Brigade in the Service of the United Netherlands.* Three vols, Edinburgh, 1899.

Firth, C.H. (ed). 'Sir Hugh Cholmley's Narrative of the Siege of Scarborough', in *English Historical Review*, 1917, pp 658–687.

Firth, C.H. (ed). *Ludlow's Memorials.* Two vols, Oxford, 1894.

Healey, C. (ed). *Sir Ralph Hopton's Narrative.* Somerset Record Society, vol 18, 1902.

Houghton, R.G. 'The Recovered Courthope Manuscripts: Transcriptions', in *Wealden Iron: Bulletin of the Wealden Iron Research Group*, Second Series, No 3, 1983, pp 12–17.

Houses of Parliament. 'Journals of the House of Lords'. www. british-history.ac.uk

Houses of Parliament. 'Journals of the House of Commons'. www. british-history.ac.uk

Jefferson, S. (ed). *Tullie's 'Narrative of the Siege of Carlisle'.* Carlisle, 1840.

Long, E.E. (ed). *The Diary of Richard Symonds.* Camden Soc. 1859.

Longstaffe, W.M.D. (ed). *Nathan Drake's 'A Journal of the Sieges ... of Pontefract Castle'.* Surtees Society, vol 37, 1861.

McCray, W.D. (ed). *Clarendon's 'History of the Rebellion'.* Oxford, 1888.

Messervy, J.A. (ed). *Journal de Jean Chevalier.* Société Jersaise, 1914.

Pafford, J.H.P. (ed). 'Accounts of the Parliamentary Garrisons of Great Chalfield and Malmesbury', in *Wiltshire Archaeological and Natural History Society*, vol 2, Devises, 1940.

Parsons, D. (ed). *The Diary of Henry Slingsby.* London, 1836.

Philip, I.G. (ed). *The Journal of Sir Samuel Luke.* Oxfordshire Record Society, vol 29, 1950.

Powell, J.R. and Timings, E.K. *Documents Relating to the English Civil War.* Navy Records Society, vol cv, 1983.

Raikes, G.A. (ed). *The Ancient Vellum Book of the Honorable Artillery Company.* London, 1890.

Roy, I. (ed). *The Royalist Ordnance Papers.* Oxfordshire Record Society, two vols, 1964 and 1976.

Rushworth, J. (ed). *Historical Collections*. London, 1680.

Searle, A. (ed). *Barrington Family Letters*. Camden Soc. fourth series, vol 28, 1983.

Terry, C.S. (ed). *Letters Relating to the Army of the Solemn League and Covenant*. Scottish Historical Society, 1917.

Thomson, G.S. (ed). *The Twysden Lieutenancy Papers 1583–1668*. Kent Record Soc., vol 10, Ashford, 1926.

Toynbee, M. (ed). *The Papers of Captain Henry Stevens, Wagon Master General to King Charles I*. Oxfordshire Record Soc., 1962.

Wake, J. (ed). *A Copy of Papers Relating to Musters, Beacons, Subsidies etc. in the County of Northampton*. Northamptonshire Record Soc. Kettering, 1926.

Warburton, E. (ed). *Memoirs of Prince Rupert and the Cavaliers*. Three vols, London, 1849.

Warner, G.J. (ed). *The Nicholas Papers*. Four vols, London, 1886.

Washbourne. J. (ed). *Bibliotechea Gloucesterensis*, Gloucester, 18.

Webb, T.W. (ed). *Memorials of the Civil War ... Hertfordshire and Adjacent Counties*. Two vols, London, 1879.

Wildridge, T.T. (ed). *The Hull Letters*. Hull, 1884.

Young, P. and Tucker, T. (eds) *Military Memoirs ... Richard Atkyns and John Gwyn*. London, 1967.

SECONDARY SOURCES, PUBLISHED

Abell, H.F. *Kent and the Great Civil War*. Ashford, 1901.

Adair, J. *Cheriton 1644: The Campaign and the Battle*. Kineton, 1973.

Anderson, M.S. *War and Society in Europe of the Old Regime*. London, 1988.

Andriette, E.A. *Devon and Exeter in the Great Civil War*. Exeter, 1971.

Anon. *The Danish Royal Arsenal Museum: Illustrated Guide to the Permanent Exhibition*. Copenhagen, 1979.

Anon. *The Church of St Margaret Horsmonden: A Short History and Guide*. Cranbrook, 1981.

Anon. *Records of the Board of Ordnance*. Public Record Office Leaflet, 50, December, 1980.

Arnold, T. and Ross, W.G. 'Notes on the Battle of Edgehill', in *English Historical Review*, 2, 1887, pp 137–142, 533–543.

Atkin, M. and Laughlin, W. *Gloucester and the Civil War*. Stroud, 1993.

Ashley, M. *The Battle of Naseby*. Stroud, 1992.

Aylmer, G.E. *The King's Servants*. London, 1961.

Aylmer, G.E. *The State's Servants*. London, 1973.

Aylmer, G.E. *Rebellion or Revolution?* Oxford, 1987.

Aylmer, G.E. and Morrill, J.S. *The Civil War and Interregnum: Sources For Local Historians*. London, 1979.

Bailey, S.B. 'John Browne and Prince Rupert's Guns', in R.D. Smith (ed) *British Naval Armaments*, Royal Armouries Conference Proceedings vol 1, London, 1989, pp 9–10.

Baldock, T.S. *Cromwell as a Soldier*. London, 1899.

Barnett, C. *Britain and Her Army 1509–1970*. London, 1970.

Barratt, J. *The Siege of Liverpool*. Bristol, 1993.

Barratt, J. *Cannon on the Mersey*. Birkenhead, 1996.

Barratt, J. *Cavaliers: The Royalist Army at War 1642–1646*. Stroud, 2000.

Barrett, C.R.B. *Battles and Battlefields in England.* London, 1896.

Baumber, M. *General at Sea: Robert Blake and the Seventeenth Century Revolution in Naval Warfare.* London, 1989.

Bayley, A.R. *The Great Civil War in Dorset.* Taunton, 1910.

Bedwin, O. 'The Excavation of a Late Sixteenth / Early Seventeenth Century Gun-Casting Furnace at Maynard's Gate, Crowborough, East Sussex, 1975–1976', in *Sussex Archaeological Collections,* vol 116, 1978, pp 163–178.

Beer, D. de. *The Art of Gunfounding.* Rotherfield, 1991.

Bijker, W.E. and Law, J. (eds). *Shaping Technology: Building Society.* Boston, 1992.

Blackmore, D. *Arms and Armour of the English Civil Wars.* Royal Armouries, London, 1990.

Blackmore, H.L. *British Military Firearms.* London, 1960.

Blackmore, H.L. *The Armouries of the Tower of London,* vol 1, *Ordnance.* London, 1976.

Blair, C. (ed). *Pollard's History of Firearms.* London, 1983.

Bond, W.G. *The Wanderings of Charles I and his Army in the Midlands.* Birmingham, 1927.

Boville, E.W. 'Queen Elizabeth's Gunpowder', in *Mariner's Mirror,* vol 33, London, 1947.

Boynton, L. *The Elizabethan Militia.* Newton Abbott, 1967.

Brett-James, N.G. 'The Fortification of London 1642–1643', in *London Topographical Records Society,* vol 14, 1928, pp 1–35.

Brown, G.I. *The Big Bang: A History of Explosives.* Stroud, 1998.

Brown, R.R. and Puype, J.P. 'A Great Gun Wherein a Man May Sit Upright: The King Acheen's Great Piece', in *Journal of the Arms and Armour Society,* vol XIV, number 3, 1993, pp 153–163.

Brown, R.R. 'Gunfounder to the Stuarts', part 1, in *Wealden Iron,* Second Series, number 25, 2005, pp 38–61: part 2 in number 26, 2006, pp 31–50.

Broxap, E. 'The Sieges of Hull', in *English Historical Review,* vol 20, London, 1905, pp 457–483.

Buchanan, B.J. (ed). *Gunpowder: The History of an International Technology.* Bath, 1996.

Buckley, J. 'The Siege of Cork, 1642', in *Journal of the Cork Historical and Archaeological Society,* Second Series, vol 22, 1916, pp 7–20.

Bull, S.B. 'Mortars at the Siege of Elizabeth Castle, Jersey', in *Fort, Journal of the Fortress Study Group,* vol 13, 1985, pp 61–68.

Bull, S.B. *Granadoe!* Leigh-on-Sea, 1986.

Bull, S.B. 'Evidence for the Use of Cartridges in Artillery 1560–1660', in R.D. Smith (ed) *British Naval Armaments,* Royal Armouries Conference Proceedings, vol 1, London, 1989, pp 3–8.

Bull, S.B. 'Pearls From the Dungheap: English Saltpetre Production 1590–1640', *Journal of the Ordnance Society,* vol 2, London, 1990, pp 5–10.

Bull, S.B. 'Artillery at Edgehill Reassessed: 1642–1992', in *Journal of the Ordnance Society,* vol 4, London, 1992, pp 1–8.

Bull, S.B. *Encyclopaedia of Military Technology and Innovation.* Westport, 2004.

Burke, J. 'The New Model Army and the Problems of Siege Warfare', in *Irish Historical Studies,* vol XXVII, Antrim, May 1990, pp 1–29.

Burne, A.H. *The Battlefields of England.* London, 1950.

Burne, A.H. *More Battlefields of England.* London, 1952.

Burne, A.H. and Young, P. *The Great Civil War: A Military History.* London, 1959.

Butler, R.M. 'The Civil War Defences of Nottingham', in *Thoroton Society Transactions,* 1949–50, vol 53, pp 26–33.

Capp, B. *Cromwell's Navy.* Oxford, 1988.

Carlton, C. *Going to the Wars*. London, 1992.

Carpenter, A.C. *The Cannon of Dartmouth Castle, Devon*. Plymouth, 1984.

Caruana, A.B. 'The Painting of Gun Carriages', in *Journal of the Ordnance Society*, vol 2, London, 1990, pp 78–81.

Caruana, A.B. *The History of English Sea Ordnance 1523–1875*, vol 1, *1523–1715, The Age of Evolution*. Rotherfield, 1994.

Charrier, P.A. *Cromwell: The Campaigns of Edgehill, Marston Moor, Naseby and of 1648 in the North of England*. London, 1906.

Childs, J. *Warfare in the Seventeenth Century*. London, 2001.

Cipolla, C. *Guns, Sails and Empires*. New York, 1966.

Clark, G.N. *War and Society in the Seventeenth Century*. Cambridge, 1958.

Cleere, H. and Crossley, D.W. *The Iron Industry of the Weald*. Leicester, 1985.

Cocroft, W.D. *Dangerous Energy: The Archaeology of Gunpowder and Military Explosives Manufacture*. Swindon, 2000.

Clode, C.M. *London During the Great Rebellion*. London, 1892.

Cockle, M.J.D. *A Bibliography of Military Books Up to 1642*. London, 1900.

Coleman, D.C. *Industry in Tudor and Stuart England*. London, 1975.

Colvin, H.M. (ed). *The History of the King's Works*. Four vols, London, 1963–1983.

Cooper, S.T. *Loyal Chester*. Chester City Record Office, booklet No 1, 1984.

Cotton, R.W. *Barnstaple and the Northern Part of Devonshire in the Great Civil War*. London, 1889.

Courtney, P. *Small Arms Accessories of the Mid Seventeenth Century*. Finds Research Group 700–1700, data sheet 11, Oxford, 1988.

Courtney, P. and Y. 'A Siege Examined: The Civil War Archaeology of Leicester', in *Post-Medieval Archaeology*, vol 26, 1992, pp 47–90.

Craze, J.M. 'Balls of Missive Ruin: Milton and the Gunpowder Revolution', in *Cambridge Quarterly*, 1997, vol xxvi, pp 325–343.

Crossley, D.W. 'A Gun Casting Furnace at Scarlets, Cowden, Kent', in *Post Medieval Archaeology*, 13, 1979, pp 239–249.

Davis, G. 'Edgehill', in *English Historical Review*, vol 36, 1921, pp 30–34.

Deane, J.B. *The Life of Richard Deane*. London, 1870.

DeVries, K. 'Catapults are not Atomic Bombs: Redefinition of Effectiveness in Pre-Modern Military Technology', in *War in History* 4.4, 1997, pp 454–470.

DeVries, K. *A Cumulative Bibliography of Medieval Military History and Technology* [to 1648]. Aylesbury, 2002, with updates, 2004.

Dore, R.N. *The Civil Wars in Cheshire*. Chester, 1966.

Douglas, W.S. *Cromwell's Scotch Campaigns*. London, 1899.

Duffy, C. *Siege Warfare: The Fortress in the Early Modern World*. London, 1979.

Duffy, M. *The Military Revolution and the State, 1500–1800*. Exeter Studies in History, No 1, Exeter, 1980.

Duncan, F. *The Royal Regiment of Artillery*. Two vols, 1872–1873.

Edwards, P. *Dealing in Death: The Arms Trade and the British Civil Wars*. Stroud, 2000.

Ellison, M. and Harbottle, B. 'The Excavation of a Seventeenth Century Bastion in the Castle of Newcastle Upon Tyne, 1976–1981', in *Archaeologia Aeliana*, fifth series, vol xi, Newcastle,1983.

Eltis, D. *The Military Revolution in Sixteenth Century Europe*. London, 1995.

Elvin, J.G.D. *British Gunfounders 1650–1850*. Greenwich, undated.

Farrow, G.W.E. 'Iron Gun Founding in the Mid Seventeenth Century: The Winter Blowings at Horsmonden, 1656–1659', in *Historical Metallurgy*, November 1984, pp 109–111.

Farrow, W.G. *The Great Civil War in Shropshire.* Shrewsbury, 1926.

Foulkes, C. *The Gunfounders of England.* Cambridge, 1937.

Firth, C.H. 'The Battle of Marston Moor'. *Transactions of the Royal Historical Society*, New Series, vol 12, 1898, pp 17–79.

Firth, C.H. *The Regimental History of Cromwell's Army.* Two vols, Oxford, 1940.

Firth, C.H. *Cromwell's Army.* Fourth Edn, 1962.

Fissel, M.C. *English Warfare 1511–1642.* London, 2001.

Fletcher, A. *The Outbreak of the English Civil War.* London, 1981.

Foard, G. *Naseby: The Decisive Campaign.* Whitstable, 1995.

Forbes, A. *A History of Army Ordnance Services.* London, 1929

Forshell, H. *Bronze Cannon Analysis.* Stockholm, 1984.

Fortesque, J.W. *A History of the British Army.* vol 1, London, 1899.

Gardiner, J.S. 'Iron Casting in the Weald', in *Archaeologia* 56, 1898, 133–144.

Gardiner, S.R. *History of the Great Civil War.* London, 1893.

Gaunt, P. *The Cromwellian Gazetteer.* Stroud, 1987.

Gaunt, P. *A Nation Under Siege: The Civil War in Wales 1642–1648.* London, 1991.

Gentles, I. *The New Model Army.* Oxford, 1992.

Gillingham, J. *Cromwell, Portrait of a Soldier.* London, 1976.

Glenie, J. *History of Gunnery.* Edinburgh, 1776.

Godwin, G.N. *The Civil War in Hampshire and the Siege of Basing House.* London, 1904.

Granville, R. *The King's War in the West: The Life of Sir Richard Granville.* London, 1908.

Guilmartin, J.F. *Gunpowder and Galleys.* Cambridge, 1974.

Guttery, D.R. *The Great Civil War in the Midland Parishes.* Birmingham, 1950.

Hale, J.R. 'Gunpowder and the Renaissance', in Carter, C.H. (ed) *Essays in Honour of Garret Mattingly.* London, 1965.

Hale, J.R. *Renaissance Fortification.* London, 1977.

Hale, J.R. *War and Society in Renaissance Europe.* London, 1985.

Hall, A.R. *Ballistics in the Seventeenth Century.* Cambridge, 1952.

Hall, B.S. and DeVries, K. Review of *The Military Revolution* (by G. Parker) in, *Technology and Culture*, 31, July 1990, pp 500–507.

Hall, B.S. *Weapons and Warfare in Renaissance Europe: Gunpowder, Technology and Tactics.* Johns Hopkins, Baltimore, 1997.

Harrington, P. *Archaeology of the English Civil War.* Princes Risborough, 1992.

Harrington, P. *English Civil War Fortifications 1642–1651.* Oxford, 2003.

Harrington, P. *English Civil War Archaeology.* London, 2004.

Hayes-McCoy, G.A. 'Strategy and Tactics in Irish Warfare, 1593–1601', in *Irish Historical Studies*, 2.7, 1941, pp 255–279.

Hayhurst, R. *The Use of the Cannon in the Civil War.* Derbyshire Archaeological and Local History Society, 1963.

Heath, E.G. (ed). *Bow Versus Gun.* London, 1973.

Heighway, C. *The East and North Gates of Gloucester and Associated Sites: Excavations 1974–1981.* Western Archaeological Trust Monograph 4, Gloucester, 1983.

Henry, C. *English Civil War Artillery.* Oxford, 2005.

Hime, H.W.L. 'The Field Artillery of the Great Rebellion: Its Nature and Use', in *Proceedings of the Royal Artillery Institution*, vol 6, 1870; reprinted as K Trotman *Military Monograph*, 76, Huntingdon, 2006.

Hime, H.W.L. *Gunpowder and Ammunition.* London, 1904.

Hime, H.W.L. *The Origin of Artillery.* London, 1915.

Hoeven, M. Van Der. *Exercise of Arms: Warfare in the Netherlands.* War in History, vol 1, Leiden, 1998.

Hogg, O.F.G. 'Woolwich Warren: The Royal Regiment's Nursery', in *Royal Artillery Journal*, vol 81, 1954, pp 164–179, 241–258.

Hogg, O.F.G. *The Royal Arsenal*. Two vols, New York, 1963.

Hogg, O.F.G. *English Artillery*. Woolwich, 1963.

Holderness, B.A. *Pre-Industrial England*. London, 1976.

Hollings, J.F. *Leicestershire During the Great Civil War*. Leicester, 1840.

Howard, M. *War in European History*. London, 1976.

Huddleston, F.S. *Catalogue of the War Office Library*. London, 1912.

Huggett, R. (et al) *Early Seventeenth Century Prices and Wages*. Bristol, 1992.

Hughes, B.P. *British Smooth Bore Artillery*. London, 1969.

Hughes, B.P. *Firepower: Weapons' Effectiveness on the Battlefield, 1630–1850*. London, 1974.

Hunt, T. *The English Civil War at First Hand*. London, 2002.

Hutchinson, L. *Memoirs of the Life of Colonel Hutchinson*. London, 1806.

Hutton, R. *The Royalist War Effort*. London, 1982.

Ingham, S. *Discovering the Civil War in Nottinghamshire*. Nottinghamshire County Council, Nottingham, 1992.

Kennard, A.N. *Gunfounding and Gunfounders: A Directory of Cannon Founders From Earliest Times to 1850*. London, 1986.

Jack, S. 'Sources in the Public Records Office For the History of the Wealden Iron Industry', in *Wealden Iron: Bulletin of the Wealden Iron Research Group*, West Sussex County Council, 1983.

Jackson, M.H. and de Beer, C. *Eighteenth Century Gunfounding*. Newton Abbott, 1973.

Johnson, B.L.C. 'The Foley Partnerships', in *Economic History Review*, vol 4, 1952, pp 322–337.

Kaestelin, J.P. *Catalogue of the Museum of Artillery in the Rotunda at Woolwich*. Part 1, London, 1963.

Kenyon, J. *The Civil Wars of England*. London, 1988.

Kenyon, J. and Ohlmeyer, J. *The Civil Wars of England, Scotland and Ireland 1638–1660*. Oxford, 1998.

Kingston, A. *Hertfordshire During the Great Civil War*. London, 1894.

Kingston, A. *East Anglia and the Great Civil War*. London, 1897.

Konstam, R.A. '16th Century Naval Tactics and Gunnery', in R.D. Smith and R.R. Brown (eds) *Guns From the Sea* (Conference Papers Reprinted from the International Journal of Nautical Archaeology), London, 1988, pp 17–34.

Lake, J.H. *Pendennis and St Mawes … the Part They Played in the Great Rebellion*. Falmouth, 1960.

Lattey, R.T. 'A Contemporary Map of the Defences of Oxford in 1644', in *Oxoniensia*, vol 1, 1936, pp 161–171.

Lavery, B. *The Arming and Fitting of English Ships of War 1600–1815*. London, 1987.

Lawley, R.N. *The Battle of Marston Moor*. London, 1865.

Leach, A.C. *The History of the Civil War in Pembrokeshire*. London, 1937.

Leadman, A.D.H. *Battles Fought in Yorkshire*. London, 1891.

Lefroy, J.H. *Official Catalogue of the Museum of Artillery in the Rotunda*. Woolwich, 1864.

Lewis, M. *Armada Guns*. London, 1960.

Lindsay, J. *Civil War in England*. London, 1954.

Lindsay-MacDougal, K.F. *A Guide to the Manuscripts at the National Maritime Museum*. Greenwich, 1960.

Litherland, T.L. *Battlefield Archaeology – A Guide to the Archaeology of Conflict*. Bradford, 2005.

Loeber, R. 'Biographical Dictionary of Engineers in Ireland', in *Irish Sword*, vol 13, 1979, pp 30–315.

Macksey, P.J. *The Southwold Guns*. Southwold Archaeological and Natural History Society, 1974.

Maland, D. *Europe at War 1600–1650*. London, 1980.

Manchester, K. 'The Paleopathology of a Royalist Garrison', in *Journal of the Osteological Laboratory*, Stockholm, 1979.

Manning, W.H. 'Excavations at Colonel Grey's Sconce, Near Newark', in *Thoroton Society Transactions*, vol 62, pp 36–42.

Markham, C.R. *A Life of the Great Lord Fairfax*. London, 1870.

Martin, C.J.M. 'A 16th Century Siege Train: the battery Ordnance of the 1588 Spanish Armada', in R.D. Smith and R.R. Brown (eds) *Guns From he Sea* (Conference Papers Reprinted from the *International Journal of Nautical Archaeology*), London, 1988, pp 57–73.

Martin, C.J.M. 'De-particularizing the Particular: Approaches to the Investigation of Well-Documented Post-Medieval Shipwrecks', in *World Archaeology*, vol 32, number 3, pp 383–399.

Martin, C.J.M. 'An Iron Bastard Minion Drake Extraordinary by John Browne from the Pinnace Swan 1641–1653', in *International Journal of Nautical Archaeology*, vol 33, No 1, pp 79–95, April 2004.

Mayo, C.H. *The Minute Books of the Dorset Standing Committee, 1646–1650*. Exeter, 1902.

McGrail, S. 'A Seventeenth Century Gunner's Tally Stick', in *International Journal of Nautical Archaeology*, 3.1, 1974.

Merton, R.K. *Science, Technology and Society in Seventeenth Century England*. London, 1938.

Money, W. *The First and Second Battles of Newbury and the Siege of Donnington Castle*. London, 1881.

Morrah, P. *Prince Rupert of the Rhine*. London, 1976.

Morrill, J.S. *Cheshire 1630–1660*. London, 1974.

Morrill, J.S. *Revolt of the Provinces*. London, 1976.

Morrill, J.S. 'Mutiny and Discontent in English Provincial Armies, 1645–1647', in *Past and Present*, vol 56, 1972, p 73.

Morris, R.H. and Lawson, P.H. *The Siege of Chester*. Chester, 1924.

Mungeam, G.I. 'Contracts for the Supply of Equipment to the New Model', in *Journal of the Arms and Armour Society*, vol vii, number 3, September 1968, pp 53–143.

Nef, J.U. 'War and Economic Progress', in *Economic History Review*, vol 12, 1942.

Newman, P.R. *Marston Moor … The Sources and the Site*. University of York, Borthwick Papers, No. 53, 1978.

Newman, P.R. *The Battle of Marston Moor*. Chichester, 1981.

Newman, P.R. *Royalist Officers in England and Wales*. New York, 1981.

Newman, P.R. *Companion to the English Civil Wars*. New York, 1990.

Newman, P.R. and Roberts, P.R. *Marston Moor, 1644*. Pickering, 2003.

Norris, J. *Gunpowder Artillery, 1600–1700*. Marlborough, 2005.

Nosworthy, B. *The Anatomy of Victory: Battle Tactics 1689–1763*. New York, 1990.

Oliver, S.P. *Pendennis and St. Mawes*. Truro, 1875.

Oman, C.W.C. *Castles*. London, 1926.

Oman, C.W.C. *The Art of War in the Sixteenth Century*. London, 1937.

O'Neil, B.H. St J. *Castle and Cannon*. Oxford, 1960.

Parker, G. *Europe in Crisis*. London, 1979.

Parker, G. *The Military Revolution: Military Innovation and the Rise of the West 1500–1800.* Cambridge, 1988.

Partington, J.R. *A History of Greek Fire and Gunpowder.* London, 1960.

Peachy, S. *The Battles of Launceston and Sourton Down 1643.* Bristol, 1993.

Peacock, E. (ed). *Army Lists of the Roundheads and Cavaliers.* London, 1863.

Pearl, V. *London at the Outbreak of the Puritan Revolution.* London, 1961.

Person, B.A. *Varberg Castle and Fortress.* Varberg, undated.

Peterson, H. *Roundshot and Rammers.* London, 1969.

Petrie, C. *King Charles, Prince Rupert, and the Civil War from Original Letters.* London, 1974.

Phillips, J.R. *Memorials of the Civil War in Wales and the Marches.* Two vols, London, 1874.

Pilkington, C. *To Play the Man: The Story of Lady Derby and the Siege of Lathom House.* Preston, 1991.

Pollard, T. and Oliver, N. 'The Battle of Edgehill 1642', in *Sanctuary*, MOD, Aldershot, No 32, 2003, pp 74 75.

Porter, S. *Destruction in the English Civil Wars.* Stroud, 1994.

Prest, J.M. 'The Campaign of Roundway Down', in *Wiltshire Archaeological and Natural History Society*, vol 53, 1950, pp 277–293, 426–429.

Puype, J.P. 'Guns and Their Handling at Sea in the Seventeenth Century: A Dutch Point of View', in *Journal of the Ordnance Society*, vol 2, London, 1990, pp 11–23.

Puype, J.P. (ed). *The Arsenal of the World: The Dutch Arms Trade in the Seventeenth Century.* Amsterdam, 1996.

Raines, G.A. *History of the Honorable Artillery Company.* Two vols, London, 1878 and 1879.

Reckitt, B.N. *Charles the First and Hull.* London, 1952.

Reid, W. 'Commonwealth Supply Departments Within the Tower and the Committee of London Merchants', in *The Guildhall Miscellany*, vol II, No 8, London, September 1966, pp 319–352.

Roberts, M. *Gustavus Adolphus.* Second Edn. Harlow, 1992.

Roberts, M. *Essays in Swedish History.* London, 1967.

Roberts-Jones, P. *Catalogue Inventaire De La Peinture Ancienne: Musées Royaux des Beaux-Arts de Belgique.* Brussels, 1984.

Robins, B. *New Principles of Gunnery.* London, 1742.

Robinson, R. *Sieges of Bristol During the Civil War.* Bristol, 1868.

Rogers, H.C.B. *Artillery Through the Ages.* London, 1971.

Rogers, H.C.B. *Battles and Generals of the Civil War.* London, 1969.

Ross, W.G. 'The Battle of Naseby', in *English Historical Review*, vol 3, 1888, pp 668–679.

Ross, W.G. *Military Engineering During The Great Civil War.* Professional Papers of the Corps of Engineers, Chatham, 1888.

Russell, C. *The Causes of the English Civil War.* Oxford, 1990.

Sandford, C.T. *Sussex in the Great Civil War and Interregnum.* London, 1910.

Saunders, A. *Fortress Britain: Artillery Fortifications in the British Isles and Ireland.* Liphook, 1989.

Schubert, H.R. 'The Superiority of English Cast Iron Cannon at the Close of the Sixteenth Century', in *Journal of the Iron and Steel Institute*, vol 161, 1949.

Schubert, H.R. *History of the British Iron and Steel Industry From c. 450 B.C. to A.D. 1775.* London, 1957.

Schwoerer, L.G. 'The Fittest Subject for a King's Quarrel: An Essay on the Militia Controversy 1641–1642', in *The Journal of British Studies*, Hartford, Connecticut, vol xi, November 1971, pp 45–76.

Seton, B.G. 'Notes on Scottish Artillery in the Sixteenth Century', in *Coast Artillery Journal*, vol 57, 1922, pp 243–248.

Simmons, W.H. *A Short History of the Royal Gunpowder Factory at Waltham Abbey*. London, 1963.

Simms, J.G. 'Cromwell's Siege of Waterford, 1649', in *Irish Sword*, vol 4, 1960, pp 171–179.

Simpkinson, C.H. *Thomas Harrison, Regicide and Major General*. London, 1905.

Skentlebury, N. *A History of the Ordnance Board*. London, 1975.

Smith, F.M. *Handbook of the Manufacture of Gunpowder*. London, 1871.

Smith, G. *Universal Military Dictionary*. London, 1779.

Smith, R.D. 'Iron Cannon of 7', in *Journal of the Ordnance Society*, vol 4, London, 1992, pp 9–20.

Smith, R.D. 'A 16th Century Bronze Cannon From London', in *Royal Armouries Yearbook*, vol 2, Leeds 1997–1998, pp 107–112.

Stern, W.M. 'Gunmaking in Seventeenth Century London', in *Journal of the Arms and Armour Society*, vol 1, part 5, March 1954, pp 55–100.

Stevenson, D. *The Scottish Revolution 1637–1644*. London, 1973.

Stevenson, D. and Caldwell, 'Leather Guns and other Light Artillery in Scotland', in *Proceedings of the Society of Antiquaries of Scotland*, 1976–1977, pp 300–317.

Stirland, A. (et al). 'Plucked in Her Prime: Mary Rose', in *British Archaeology*, September–October 2006, pp 17–25.

Stoyle, M. *Exeter City Defences Project Documentary Evidence for the Civil War Defences of Exeter 1642–1643*. Exeter Museums Archaeological Field Unit, Report No 88.12, December 1988.

Stoyle, M. *The Civil War Defences of Exeter and the Great Parliamentary Siege of 1645–1646*. Exeter Museums Archaeological Field Unit, Report No. 90.26, October 1990.

Stoyle, M. *From Deliverance to Destruction: Rebellion and Civil War in an English City*. University of Exeter, 1996.

Straker, E. *Wealden Iron*. London, 1931.

Taylor, T. 'Teignmouth Devon', in *Time Team: The Site Reports*. Channel 4, London, 1996, pp 22–27.

Teare, G.M. *Non Destructive Examination of a Leather Gun*. Quality Assurance Directorate, Ordnance Materials Branch, Woolwich, 1984.

Teesdale, E.B. *Gunfounding in the Weald in the Sixteenth Century*. Royal Armouries Monograph 2, London, 1991.

Terry, C.S. 'The Siege of Newcastle upon Tyne by the Scots in 1644', in *Archaeologia Aeliana*, Second Series, vol 21, 1899, pp 180–258.

Tibbut, H.G. *Bedfordshire During the Civil War*. Elstow, 1956.

Tibbut, H.G. *Colonel John Okey, 1606–1662*. Bedfordshire Historical Record Society, 1955.

Tomlinson, E.M. *A History of the Minories*. London, 1922.

Tomlinson, H.C. *Guns and Government: The Ordnance Office Under the Later Stuarts*. Royal Historical Society, 1979.

Tomlinson, H.C. 'Wealden Gunfounding: An Analysis of its Demise in the Eighteenth Century', in *Economic History Review*, second series, vol XXIX, number 3, 1976.

Torres, J.J.A. and Moral, F.S. *Burgos, Su Parque Y Maestranza de Artilleria*. Burgos, 1989.

Towes, R.M. and McCree, P. 'A Note on Drakes', in *Journal of the Ordnance Society*, vol 6, 1994, pp 39–47.

Towes, R.M. 'The Casting of Bronze Guns in the Weald in the Seventeenth Century', in *Wealden Iron*, first series, 11, 1977, pp 15–20.

Toynbee, M. and Young, P. *Cropredy Bridge, 1644*. Kineton, 1970.

Trenchard, C. *The Siege of Bridgwater*. Bridgwater, undated.

Underdown, D. *Somerset in the Civil War and Interregnum*. London, 1973.

Varley, F.J. *The Siege of Oxford*. London, 1932.

Walford, E.A. *Edgehill the battle and the Battlefields*. Banbury, 1886.

Wanklyn, M. *A Military History of the English Civil War: 1642–1649*. London, 2005.

Ward, S. *Excavations at Chester: The Civil War Siegeworks 1642–1646*. Chester City Council, Grosvenor Museum reports, No 4, 1987.

Webb, H.J. *Elizabethan Military Science*. Wisconsin, 1965.

Wedgwood, C.V. *Civil War Battlefields*. BBC, London, undated.

Wedgwood, C.V. *The King's Peace*. London, 1955.

Wedgwood, C.V. *The King's War*. London, 1958.

Wenham, P. *The Great and Close Siege of York, 1644*. Kineton, 1970.

Wheeler, J.S. *The Making of a World Power: War and the Military Revolution in Seventeenth Century England*. Stroud, 1999.

Williams, A. and Reuck, A. *The Royal Armoury at Greenwich 1515–1649*. Royal Armouries Monographs, vol 4, London, 1995.

Willis-Bund, J.W. *The Civil War in Worcestershire*. Birmingham, 1905.

Wilson, G.M. 'The Commonwealth Gun', in R.D. Smith and R.R. Brown (eds) *Guns From the Sea* (Conference Papers Reprinted from the International Journal of Nautical Archaeology), London, 1988, pp 87–99.

Wolf, A. *History of Science, Technology and Philosophy in the Sixteenth and Seventeenth Century*. London, 1935.

Wood, A.C. *Nottinghamshire in the Civil War*. Oxford, 1937.

Woolrych, A. *Battles of the English Civil War*. Second Edn. London, 1991.

Yonge, W.L. *Notes on the Early History of the Royal Artillery*. Woolwich, 1859.

Young, P. 'Rupert's Horse Artillery', in *The Gunner*, vol 27, part 12, March 1946, pp 184–185.

Young, P. *Edgehill*. Kineton, 1967.

Young, P. *Marston Moor*. Kineton, 1970.

Young, P. *Civil War England*. Harlow, 1981.

Young, P. *Naseby*. London, 1985.

Young, P. and Emberton, W. *Sieges of the Great Civil War*. London, 1978.

Young, P. and Holmes, R. *The English Civil War*. London, 1974.

SECONDARY SOURCES: WEB SITES, THESES, AND OTHER UNPUBLISHED MATERIAL

Anon. 'Seventeenth Century Military Treatises'. University of Illinois web published bibliography, www.history.uiuc.edn

Ashley, R. 'The Organisation and Administration of the Tudor Office of Ordnance'. B.Litt thesis, Oxford, 1973.

Aylmer, G.E. 'Studies in the Institutions and Personnel of the English Central Administration'. DPhil thesis, Oxford, 1954.

Brent, C.E. 'Employment, Land Tenure and Population in Eastern Sussex, 1540–1640'. PhD thesis, University of Sussex, 1974.

Bull, S.B. 'The Furie of the Ordnance: England's Guns and Gunners by Land 1600–1650'. PhD thesis University College Swansea, 1988.

English Heritage. 'English Heritage Battlefield Report: Marston Moor 1644'. www. English-Heritage.org.uk, 1995.

Farrow, G.W.E. Unpublished notes on 'Mortars'; 'Prince Rupert's Sketches'; 'Bomb Vessels', and 'the Brown Family', supplied in correspondence, Ledbury, 1992.

Harrison, G.A. 'Royalist Organisation in Wiltshire'. PhD thesis, University of London, 1964.

Hogg, O.F.G. 'Tudor Armament'. Notes for a publiaction, National Army Museum, London.

Hoskins, S.G. 'Sixteenth Century Cast Bronze Ordnance at the Museu de Angra Do Heroismo'. MA thesis, Texas A&M, 2003.

Illsley, J.S. 'Bibliography of Guns and Gunnery', University of Wales, 1997, www.cma. soton.ac.uk

Johnston, S. 'Making Mathematical Practice: Gentlemen, Practitioners and Artisans in Elizabethan England'. PhD thesis, Cambridge, 1994.

Johnston, S. 'A Revised Bibliography of William Bourne'. www.mhs.ox.ac.uk, c. 2005.

Johnston, S. 'History From Below: Mathematics, Instruments and Archaeology'. British Society for the History of Mathematics, November, 2005, www.Gresham.ac.uk.

Lewis, D.E. 'The Use of Ordnance in Early Modern Warfare'. MA thesis, Manchester, 1971.

Lewis, D.E. 'The Office of Ordnance and the Parliamentarian Land Forces'. PhD thesis, Loughborough, 1976.

Lopez-Martin, F.J. 'Historical and Technical Evolution of Artillery from its Earliest Widespread Use Until the Emergence of Mass Production Techniques'. PhD thesis, London Metropolitan University, 2007.

Newman, P.R. 'The Royalist Armies in Northern England 1642–1645'. PhD thesis, York, 1978.

Roy, I. 'The Royalist Army in the First Civil War'. DPhil thesis, Oxford, 1963.

Smith, V.T.C. 'The Civil War Fortifications of London'. Notes for a publication, National Army Museum, undated.

Thomlinson, H.C. 'The Organisation and Activities of the English Ordnance Office'. PhD thesis, Reading, 1974.

Walton, S.A. 'The Art of Gunnery in Renaissance England'. PhD thesis, University of Toronto, 1999.

Wanklyn, M.D.G. 'The King's Armies in the West of England'. MA thesis, Manchester, 1966.

Index

Lightning Source UK Ltd.
Milton Keynes UK
UKOW06n1213270616

277169UK00005B/38/P